"I think he's probably the greatest film actor ever. I wanted him for *Lawrence* [*of Arabia*] and *Ryan's Daughter.*"

—David Lean, director

"Within his being lurks the unregenerate soul of a Cro-Magnon."

—former wife Anna Kashfi

"It's like acting with God."

—Al Pacino

"If I had to say there was anybody I like, no matter what, it would be a guy like Brando."

—John Mellencamp

"He's a role model for everybody in the business. No matter who they think is their role model, that person probably had Brando as a role model. All roads lead to Brando."

—Matthew Broderick

"He has the reputation of being tough or cold, but in reality he is a very gentle, loving man."

—Rita Moreno

"He's a great actor and a great guy."

—Karl Malden

"I admire him for his conscience as an American. And his moral commitment when he believes in something. . . . He talks from the heart—and he means it."

—Johnny Carson

"Marlon Brando, one of the great acting geniuses of all time, could be called the king of lost causes."

—William Kuntsler

"Marlon is a combination of idealism and shrewdness. He knows exactly what he's doing. And he's all that a director could desire in an actor. Yes, Marlon's not only a great character but he's a great actor."

—Fred Zinnemann, director of *The Men*

MARLON BRANDO

LARGER THAN LIFE

NELLIE BLY

PINNACLE BOOKS
WINDSOR PUBLISHING CORP.

OTHER BOOKS BY NELLIE BLY

OPRAH! *Up Close and Down Home*
BARBRA STREISAND: The Untold Story

PINNACLE BOOKS are published by

Windsor Publishing Corp.
850 Third Avenue
New York, NY 10022

The P logo Reg U.S. Pat & TM off. Pinnacle is a trademark of Windsor Publishing Corp.

First Printing: November, 1994

Printed in the United States of America

*To All My Friends at
The Actors Studio*

Special thanks to Marc Cerasini for his invaluable research, to Debbie Cohen for her assistance, Tracy Bernstein for her editorial guidance, to Paul Dinas for his support, to Sophia Duffy for her cover design, and to Joyce Kaplan and Suzanne Henry for their endless patience.

"It is a simple fact that all of us use the techniques of acting to achieve whatever ends we seek. . . . Acting serves as the quintessential social lubricant and a device for protecting our interests and gaining advantage in every aspect of life."

Marlon Brando
(from his introduction to
"The Technique of Acting")

TABLE OF CONTENTS

Prologue

The old lion stirs. Aged and battle-scarred, he has retreated to his mountain lair. He has outlived the rivals of his youth: Montgomery Clift, James Dean. The generations of actors that came after him—Pacino, de Niro, Sean Penn, Keanu Reeves—regard him simply with awe. He is still the one.

And when he chooses to stir, it still makes world news. Today he is getting over three million dollars for a small role in his next movie, but money means little to a man who has seen his oldest son convicted of murder and his oldest daughter confined to a madhouse.

Now he is about to emerge from his retreat to share his version with the world—friend and foe alike. He has accepted $5.75 million for agreeing to tell his story. He has promised to tell it all, from his earliest memory of playing on his moonlit bed with his beloved nanny.

But there is another story—the one he will not tell—and this is it. BRANDO—The Untold Story.

One

The All American Boy

"Brando was irresponsible."
—His high school principal

Marlon Brando is such a perfect name for a matinee idol that it comes as a surprise to learn that the most controversial actor of modern times started out as Marlon Brando, Jr. and that for a good part of his life young Marlon was known to all as "Bud."

His parents were a picture-perfect couple, all-American, big, blond, the mother interested in the arts but not so much that it interfered with keeping a home and raising three baby Brandos. They lived in a series of important houses on a succession of good streets in Omaha, Evanston, and finally on a farm in Libertyville, Illinois. There were always servants to help with the housework and the children.

His father was Marlon Brando, Sr. The family name, originally Brandaus, descends from Dutch-Alsation ancestors who came to America in the early nineteenth century. His mother, the former Dorothy Pennebaker, known as "Dodie" was a sensitive, cultured woman who loved drink and drama equally. Their first child, Jocelyn, was born in 1920; another daughter, Frances, arrived in 1923, and Marlon came on April 3, 1924, at the Omaha Maternity Hospital. He was immediately dubbed "Bud." They lived in a three-story white clapboard house on Mason Street. A few years later, in 1926, the family moved to an even finer house on 1026 South Second Street.

Dodie's real love was the Omaha Community Playhouse which she helped found shortly before Bud was born. Working with director Gregory Foley, she had the charm and drive to raise funds and perform. She played leading roles in *Liliom* and *The Enchanted Cottage,* and *Anna Christie.* Marlon Sr. even joined her once as a pirate in *Captain Applejack.* But Dodie's devotion to theatre carried a price: it meant time away from her children. "I became mother to Fran and Bud," Jocelyn recalls.

In 1925, when Bud was just a year old, Dodie called her good friend Herberta Fonda. The playhouse needed a juvenile for Philip Barry's *You and I* and Dodie was convinced that Herberta's son Henry would be perfect for the role. Henry, who had just dropped out of the University of Minnesota and didn't have much in the way of plans, agreed to try out for the role. He got the part. The play only ran a week, but Henry liked the theatre and stuck around all summer as a volunteer. Later he co-starred with Dodie in Eugene O'Neill's *Beyond the*

Horizon. He had found his calling and he would remain grateful to Dodie for showing him the way.

Dodie also produced J.M. Barrie's *A Kiss for Cinderella* in which Dorothy McGuire, a member of the children's theatre, played opposite Fonda.

In 1930, Marlon Sr. went to work in Chicago, and moved the family to Evanston, Illinois. Dodie had to give up the thing that really mattered in her life: her theatre. Her drinking got worse.

"OF COURSE HE WAS A SPOILED BRAT!"

Bud established his rebellious nature at an early age.

"Of course he was a spoiled brat—he was the youngest and we doted on him," said Brando's sister Frances. "As a child he would charge into a living room filled with guests, leap onto the mantelpiece, topple to the floor and lie there like a corpse."

France recalled that as far back as kindergarten her little brother was playing hookey. But one day their older sister Jocelyn came up with an idea to make sure he went to school.

"She got hold of a good strong rope, tied it around Bud's neck—and dragged him to class."

But young Bud's bravado may have compensated for a sad family life. "He loved his mother very much," said school friend Bob Dunn. "But he was ashamed of her. When Bud was a teenager he would often be called to a town bar to take her home." She frequently went out to bars, leaving her son to roam wild.

The family soon moved to an apartment. And Bud at-

tended the Lincoln School where he met ten-year-old
Wally Cox. Cox's mother wrote mysteries and a novel,
Seedtime and Harvest. Bud was already a robust hellion,
Cox was sensitive and a frequent target of bullies until
Bud stepped in. "Bud came in one day filthy black from
top to bottom. Somebody had said something about
Wally and he had rolled Wally's critic around in the coal
shed. He looked like a Negro," a teacher recalls.

Another classmate remembers Bud's reaction to something else: "We were playing kickball or some such game
and the ball got slammed into Bud's face. I guess he
thought I was responsible. He pulled out his little dingus
and tried to pee on me."

But even Wally Cox came in for Brando roughhousing.
As Wally recalled years later: "One afternoon Buddy tied
me to a tree, then left me there overnight. My mother was
frantic. She called the police after I hadn't come home
for several hours. They searched the entire neighborhood
before they found me and cut me loose."

One of Bud's craziest stunts was dropping a stink
bomb into the school's ventilating system. "The smell
was so bad, everyone scrambled out of the classrooms."

TORN BETWEEN TWO PARENTS

By the time Bud was twelve, Dodie's alcoholism was
a family scandal. Dodie drank, her husband spent long
stretches of time on the road and like many men before
or since, he did not regard his casual liaisons away
from home as adultery. Dodie did, and drank more
when she found lipstick on Brando Sr.'s underwear. The

battles between Brando Sr. and Dodie would rage on into the night. "At least you could get your laundry done and I wouldn't have to see it," Dodie would scream. Brando Sr. would respond by beating her. Finally, at thirteen, Bud told his father that if it happened again, he would kill him.

There was already no love lost between father and son. "My father was indifferent to me," Brando recalls. "Nothing I could do interested him, or pleased him."

Dodie's drinking got worse, especially when his father was away. Sometimes Bud would get a call from some bar to come down and get his mother. Once he found her getting drunk with a marine, and when he tried to take her away, they told him to get lost.

Writer Maurice Zolotow observed Brando's relationship with his mother and commented: "She made it almost impossible for him to develop a sense of security about being a man. All his life Brando oscillated between the polar attractions of his parents and has had a difficult time finding out what he, himself, is."

In 1938, Marlon, Sr. moved his family to a farm near Libertyville, Illinois, and young Bud entered the tenth grade of Libertyville Township High School.

"He used to do a lot of farm work," a friend of the period recalls. "He loves to be on a farm. He's far from a city boy." He milked the cow every morning, and kept geese and hens and rabbits. He had his own horse, his Great Dane and twenty-eight cats.

He played snare drum in the band—a prelude to his beloved bongos. But he hated the discipline and restrictions of school. It has been said that he was in school plays, but Libertyville High magazine shows that he mainly worked backstage, as a member of the Curtain Raisers club.

"Brando was irresponsible," recalled his principal, H.E. Underbrink. "He wasn't interested in anything in particular. His record was poor. He rarely took part in any extracurricular activities because practically every afternoon he was in our 3:15 P.M. disciplinary period."

"HE WAS KIND OF A CHILD AT HEART"

He had also discovered his ability to charm women. His high school sweetheart was Carmelita Pope who would later go on to fame in television commercials. "I was the only all-American type he ever went out with," she recalled. "That period in his life has never been written about."

Carmelita grew up in Chicago, but spent summers in Wheeling and apprenticed at the Lake Zurich Playhouse, "making scenery, scraping gum off seats, and playing a role once in a while." There she met Jocelyn Brando who "was older by quite a bit and was already getting parts."

Young Bud would "drop over with a huge Great Dane dog," to see what his sister was doing. Carmelita was a pushover for animals and the Great Dane drew them together.

"Because the Brandos lived in what was country then, whenever he and I would have a date, he'd stay with us in Wheeling, sometimes for days," she says.

But young Bud was already a nonconformist. "I spent an entire date with him carrying an album on his head," she recalls. "He picked me up, we got on the bus, we got off the bus, we went into an ice cream parlor and had some ice cream, and all the while, he had the album of records on his head. I never asked him why he had an album of records on his head, which is probably why he liked me."

Even then, Carmelita recalled, he loved to fantasize. "He was kind of a child at heart," she explained. "One day he called me and told me he was in the hospital. He had broken his legs. Would I bring him some books? I said yes. The next day he called and asked if I'd gotten the books. I said yes and I would bring them to the hospital. He said no, he'd pick them up himself.

"He arrived, walking. His only explanation was that he'd wanted the books and didn't have the money to buy them himself."

BUD'S MOST DANGEROUS STUNT

Recalling Bud's most dangerous stunt at Libertyville, the Rev. Douglas Wright, a school friend, said: "One time Brando started a fire in English class. He had been sitting in back of the room playing around with pieces of paper. I didn't really see how it started. But before I knew it, smoke was belching from the back of the room and someone shouted 'Fire!' "

Frantically, the teacher rushed to Bud's desk and stamped out the blaze before it could spread. But Bud was not content with one hair-raising incident. A short time later he sent more shock waves through Libertyville high school.

"It happened when Bud and I were practicing in the

school band," said Rev. Wright. "We were marching poorly and the director jokingly blamed it on himself, saying, 'I'm sorry for fouling you up. I should get a swift kick for being so dumb.'

"Well, no sooner had the director turned his back on us than Bud put down his drum, broke ranks—and planted a swift kick in the seat of his pants. The director went sprawling. And grinning down at him was Brando who quipped, 'Well, you asked for a swift kick!' "

Brando was always daring his friends.

"Bud used to invite kids down to the river to see who would sink into the quicksand and stay longest without crying for help," said another friend, Bob Dunn.

To show his own enormous courage, Brando would leap in and let himself sink down into the mud—dangerously close to where he wouldn't be able to free himself. Then—and only then—would he call for a friend to pull him loose.

Brando remembers that he was a "rebellious" boy who really got his school principal hot under the collar when he set a fire in the classroom. "I took a bottle of hair tonic and traced some very crude words on a classroom wall. Then I touched a match to it," he recalls.

"A fascinating talk with the principal followed. When my dad arrived, we came to two conclusions: I'd repaint the wall and Dad would get me into a military academy to learn a new word: discipline."

Fed up with his shenanigans, Principal Henry E. Underbrink booted the seventeen-year-old Brando out of Libertyville High School in 1941.

His grades had been terrible, and he paid more attention to girls than books. "I was convinced he would end a deadbeat," said Betty Cuny, who dated him for eighteen months. Another ex-girlfriend, Betty Gossell, agreed: "He was always clowning around. He was certainly not the kind of person you'd expect to become a star."

BRANDO DISCOVERS HOLLYWOOD

After Bud was thrown out of school, his mother took him with her on a vacation to Hollywood—and what he saw there would change his life forever.

Mother and son visited Henry Fonda at his studio. While Dodie was talking to her old friend, Bud disappeared. They finally found him on the movie set. He was entranced . . . his eyes were glazed . . . and his attention was drawn to the powerful klieg lights like a moth to flame. "What's with Bud?" Fonda asked Dodie.

"I don't really know," she replied. "But I wouldn't be surprised if he wants to be an actor."

"HE WAS AN ACADEMIC DISASTER"

All the boy needed, Marlon, Sr. thought, was to be "whipped into shape." So in 1941 he shipped the seventeen-year-old off to Shattuck Military Academy in Faribault, Minnesota.

For a while he seemed to find himself in the regimen of military school. Surely the demands of order and rules must have been a far cry from Dodie's disorderly household. He played football until he damaged his knee. One of his teammates recalled "Bud was always horsing around. He could have been a terrific athlete. He was very fast on his feet and had a magnificent physique. But he didn't hold to his form."

He followed in his father's footsteps by joining the Crack Squad, a precision-drill team. He also joined the Shattuck Players. He was already demonstrating a love of Shakespeare but that didn't keep him from changing his lines.

And he loved his pranks and practical jokes: from emptying a chamber pot onto a superior officer's head, to setting off a bomb at a teacher's door. Finally, he landed on probation. When he broke probation to go into town it was the end. After two years at Shattuck he was expelled and sent home.

"He was an academic disaster," said the Rev. Joseph McKee, his English teacher. "He failed everything." Yet he did not fail at winning love. Nuba Fletcher, Shattuck's civilian headmaster, was met with a petition from other cadets asking for Bud's reinstatement. It didn't help.

For a time he was packed off to live with his grandmother in California—but he was booted out of school there, too. It was three strikes and he was out.

His irate father demanded that Bud look for work. He got a job as a ditchdigger. Soon after that, World War II broke out. Bud was turned down by the Army because of his damaged knee and poor eyesight. But he yearned to show he was as good as anybody else—if not better. He hit upon a daring scheme.

"Bud wanted to accompany a friend to his naval base in Milwaukee. He went to the Libertyville train depot, but he had no ticket—or any way of paying for one," recalled his sister Frances. "But he fooled everyone. He posed as a wounded veteran, and the GIs on board all chipped in to pay his fare." And amazingly, he continued his impersonation at the camp and was allowed to spend the night in the barracks.

Bud had given an incredible performance, and he realized what a terrific actor he could be.

He rushed home and announced to Marlon, Sr. that he wanted to become an actor.

Filled with rage, his father bellowed: "No one would want to see a yokel like you on stage." Time, of course, was to prove him wrong.

Two

Bright Lights, Big City

"Take acting seriously or go into business with your father."

—Dodie Brando's advice to her son

Barely nineteen, Brando arrived in New York at the end of May, 1943. "The first thing he did when he got off the train," Frances recalled, "was to have his shoes shined. And then he felt so sorry for the shoeshine man he gave him the five dollars in his pocket."

Unlike most new arrivals, he had family waiting for him. Both his doting sisters had established themselves in the city and welcomed their troubled younger brother. Jocelyn, who had just married actor Don Hamner, was on the road as understudy for Dorothy McGuire in *Claudia.* Frances, whose high school boyfriend had been killed in action, was studying painting at the Art Students League and living in a tiny apartment on Patchin Place in Greenwich Village. He moved in.

"Bud was thrilled at being free from all the restrictions

which he felt were a greater imposition than other people think they are," Frances said. "He just went head first into everything. He lived a typical Bohemian life, stayed up all night, went to parties. Everyone he met, he took very seriously. He believed they were what they said they were. Every odd, bizarre thing was marvelous. He was open to everything.

"He would bring almost anybody home to spend the night at the studio," Frances said. "Just because they didn't have any place to sleep."

Marlon sold lemonade, operated an elevator at the venerable Best & Co. department store on Fifth Avenue, and occasionally beat the bongo drums at the Cockatoo Club, while studying acting with the fabled Erwin Piscator at the New School. His faculty included Stella Adler and Lee Strasberg. Stella Adler, a legendary beauty, actress, and teacher, was to become a profound influence on Brando.

Of Stella Adler, Brando said: "Stella had the deepest influence upon me. She influenced my personal and my professional life. I am devoted to her. As a teacher, she has an infallible instinct for character and for knowing what people are. The spectrum of her talent is reflected in all she does."

On her part, Adler insisted: "I taught him nothing. I opened up possibilities of thinking, feeling, experience, and I opened the doors, he walked through. He never needed me after that. . . . He lives the life of an actor twenty-four hours a day. If he is talking to you, he will absorb everything about you, your smile, the way your teeth grow. His style is the perfect marriage of intuition and intelligence."

Under Piscator's direction, Brando first appeared on

the New York stage that April, playing two small parts
in Stanley Kauffmann's *Bobino* at the Adelphi theatre.
This was followed a few months later by *Hannele's Way
to Heaven* by Gerhart Hauptmann, again playing two
roles, that of a schoolteacher and then an angel in a
dream sequence. He also played the role of Sebastian in
Shakespeare's *Twelfth Night,* and appeared in adaptations
of two plays by Moliere.

Among those who came to see Marlon in performances at the Theatre Workshop were the agent Maynard
Morris of the Music Corporation of America (MCA) and
Meyer Mishkin from the talent department of 20th Century Fox. According to Mishkin: "Everybody else in the
cast of *Twelfth Night* looked pure 'drama school' until
this kid came on. His voice was unusual. He was strange,
different, a kind of renegade. When the show ended, I
turned to Maynard, who was sitting behind me, and said,
'That guy is interesting,' and he replied. 'He is. I just
took him on as a client.' "

"WOULD YOU GO TO BED WITH MY MOTHER?"

The summer of 1944, Marlon joined other members
of Piscator's workshop for a twelve-week engagement in
Sayville, a resort town on the south shore of Eastern
Long Island. The company included Elaine Stritch and
Carlo Fiore, who would later write an intimate memoir
of his friendship with Brando.

In those days, according to Fiore, Brando was still very
much the Midwest "preppy," dressed in button-down Ox-
ford shirts, cotton slacks and tennis shoes. Yet some
things would never change. His tastes ran to fast food:

hamburgers, french fries, and chocolate malteds, or that other staple of childhood: peanut butter and jelly sandwiches washed down with milk.

Dodie, on the wagon, visited him in Sayville. Fiore recalls Brando's surprise that his new friend's mother was "a true beauty," who asked him to dance, then behaved so seductively that he "couldn't help getting an erection."

But later that night, Brando asked him: "Would you go to bed with my mother?" Fiore assured him that he would never hurt his friend's feelings that way, but Fiore was never convinced Brando was joking.

After a disastrous performance of *Twelfth Night* in which Brando repeated the role of Sebastian, Dodie cut short her visit and left Sayville the next day. Her departing warning to her son: "Take acting seriously or go into business with your father."

It was probably a good thing that Dodie left when she did. A few weeks later, Marlon was expelled.

He had been found asleep, fully clothed on his bed with a girl. And although it was an innocent nap, it was a situation Piscator simply would not tolerate. He ordered Marlon to pack his bags and get out of town.

Back in the city, Brando and his current girlfriend, a dark-skinned former model, moved into the Park Savoy Hotel on 58th Street, near Seventh Avenue.

After yet another fight with Brando, Sr., Dodie left him and joined her children in New York, taking a ten-room apartment on West End Avenue and 77th Street. Her drinking got worse. For a time, Jocelyn and Don Hamner moved in to look after her, but they had their own careers to think about and were frequently on the road.

"HE COULD NOT FUNCTION SEXUALLY WITH LIGHT-SKINNED FEMALES"

One of the first things Marlon discovered when he came to New York was his love for black culture. He was strongly attracted to dark-skinned women and the night life of the black clubs in Harlem. He often sat in with the bands there, playing his bongo drums. He was already demonstrating a lifelong habit of entertaining several women in his life at the same time. And none of them were blond, midwestern types like his mother. They were black or Oriental or Spanish or Puerto Rican or Colombian. According to first wife Anna Kashfi, a self-described Indian, he once confided to her that "he could not function sexually with light-skinned females; darker women pose no Oedipal threat."

BROADWAY DEBUT: "WOMEN GASPED"

Maynard Morris's associate, Edith Van Cleve, was also impressed with the young Brando and she came up with just the play to showcase him: *I Remember Mama* by John Van Druten, based on the novel *Mama's Bank Account.* It was the story of a Norwegian immigrant family on Steiner Street in San Francisco, the family consisting of two daughters and a son Nels who is fifteen in the first act and twenty in the second. Van Cleve saw Marlon as perfect for the son. Brando showed the script to Stella Adler. She read it and approved.

By that time his Libertyville girlfriend, Carmelita Pope was also in New York. When he told her he was up for the part she warned him: "You've never read a line. You'll never make it."

Marlon read for Van Druten, who was also directing, and for the producers, Richard Rodgers and Oscar Hammerstein. Brando hated auditions and was never very good at them. The producers were not impressed and would have moved on, but Van Druten saw a special quality. He hired Brando for the role of Nels.

Oscar Homolka was Lars, the head of the family, and Mady Christians, as the mother, was its heart. For his biography in the playbill, Brando volunteered "Born in Calcutta, India, but left there at six months of age." It was the beginning of the Brando legend.

The play opened at the Music Box Theatre on October 19, 1944. His friends and sisters were there, but Dodie wasn't. She was said to be ill, which might have been a polite way of saying she was drinking again. Also in the audience, director Robert Lewis, who recalls "This boy came down the stairs, and I thought, 'It's an understudy they found on the street.' He had no technique—nothing, and then I realized he was something new in the theater—a completely fresh, real person, who made the rest of the cast seem theatrical." Yet the professional critics barely took notice. Only Robert Garland of the *Journal-American* had anything to say: "Marlon Brando is, if he doesn't mind my saying so, charming."

He was more than charming. As Fiore recalls, "When Marlon reappeared as the grown-up, handsome Nels, women in the audience gasped in audible admiration."

Even Carmelita relented. "Because he's a very sensitive person, the director was able to mold him," she said.

Maybe Brando had expected a quick flop. He was certainly surprised when the play settled into a long run and he faced the nightmare of repeating the same lines at performance after performance. Restless, he started to invent little bits of business and continued his lifelong practice of practical jokes. One night Oscar Homolka, whose role called for him to dump a whole sugar bowl into his coffee, discovered that he was drinking salt. Staying in character, Brando as Nels apologized for the prank. Homolka was not amused and stopped talking to Brando for months.

During the run, he joined Dodie on West End Avenue. As usual in all Brando homes, there was plenty of help, including a maid to serve dinner. Every night after the final curtain, Marlon's new friends would gather at the apartment.

Finally, Dodie was summoned back to Libertyville by Brando Sr.

It was a blow to Marlon. He asked her to stay, even tried to leverage the mutual attraction between her and Carlo Fiore, but her mind was made up. "I don't want her to go," he confided to Fiore. "I want her here. With me."

When *I Remember Mama* went on the road, Brando was the only member of the original cast who did not go along with it. Temporarily without his mother or a job, he moved into the Park Savoy Hotel with Celia Webb.

"THIS YOUNG PUPPY WILL BE BROADWAY'S BEST ACTOR WITHIN A YEAR"

The year 1946 would be a critical year for Brando. He would appear in a series of important but short-lived Broadway plays, drawing the attention of critics who marked him as a young man to watch. Even more significant, he would begin contact with Elia Kazan, who would direct him in his greatest roles.

Marlon's next role would be in *Truckline Cafe* a new play by Maxwell Anderson, co-produced and directed by Harold Clurman. He would play a World War II veteran who comes home to an unfaithful wife, kills her, and returns to the cafe to surrender. Clurman's co-producer was Elia Kazan who was unimpressed with young Brando's audition and pushed for Burgess Meredith for the part. Stella Adler, who was married to Clurman at the time, insisted that they cast Brando. "This young puppy will be Broadway's best actor within a year," she told them.

In time Kazan came to be one of Brando's greatest admirers and a major influence on his work.

The play opened at the Belasco Theatre, March 2, 1946. It would come to be regarded as a great playwright's worst play and closed March 9. The reviews were terrible, but Brando and Karl Malden were singled out for praise. George Jean Nathan, the influential theatre critic, wrote that "the acting company, except for Virginia Gilmore and Marlon Brando, was in major part second-rate." Later that year, in his *Theatre Book of the Year 1946,* Nathan would list Marlon's work as one of the "especially interesting performances of the season."

Although the play ran barely a week, Brando was once again seen by the right people. This time it was producer Guthrie McClintic, who saw the show with Mildred Natwick. "Marlon was wonderful," Natwick recalled. "Guthrie and I decided at once he would be perfect for the part of Marchbanks, the young poet in George Bernard Shaw's *Candida,* which Kit Cornell [Mrs. McClintic] was about to do for the third time, with me as the character Prossie."

Marlon, Sr. came to New York for opening night, April 3, at the Cort Theatre. Katherine Cornell was Candida, and Sir Cedric Hardwicke was her husband. Marlon, Sr. came backstage with Dodie. She had moved back to New York, but she was drinking again and disappearing for days at a time.

A FLAG IS BORN

Next, Brando appeared in Ben Hecht's *A Flag is Born,* with music by Kurt Weill, directed by Luther Adler.

To work with actors he admired, Brando took a cut from three-hundred dollars to forty-eight dollars a week. He even played on Hecht's celebrity baseball team, with Harpo Marx, Robert Sherwood, Marc Connelly and Charles MacArthur.

A Flag is Born opened at the Alvin Theatre on September 5. It was a political play with a message, strongly criticizing Britain's role in Palestine, and the world's general indifference to the plight of the Jews. Proceeds went to aid the American League for a Free Palestine.

Most of *Flag* was set in a graveyard by the side of a road leading to Palestine, along which two old refugees (Paul Muni and Celia Adler) make their way. They stop at the graveyard to rest and pray, and there meet a bitter, cynical, young Jew called David (Brando), who voices Hecht's concern for his race and his contempt for the rest of mankind. By the curtain, the old couple has persuaded David to join them on their trek and to become freedom fighters for the Palestinian underground.

Actress Rita Gam was also in the cast and recalls "I would watch Marlon from the wings, in awe of his strange explosive dynamism."

REUNITING WITH WALLY COX

Around this time Brando discovered an old friend: Wally Cox. They had lost touch while Marlon was at Shattuck. Wally and his ailing mother had moved to New York. He went to work as shoemaker, silversmith, and puppeteer to support her. He was drafted, but collapsed during basic training at Camp Walters in Texas and was discharged as 4F. He returned to New York to study jewelry design.

One day, Marlon and Frannie were fooling around on a Village street when they turned a corner and ran into— Wally Cox. They recognized each other immediately and resumed their friendship as if they had never been parted.

When Frannie married Richard Loving, they lived across the street from Wally's apartment on Tenth Avenue. Marlon was still living at the Park Savoy, but he would frequently bring girls to Wally's place, leading to the impression that he lived there. Among the girls he was seeing besides Celia: Faith Dane, a dancer, and Stella Adler's daughter Linda.

He studied yoga and it was said he could rotate his stomach muscles, danced with Katherine Dunham, even appearing in some of her exhibitions of experimental dancing. He played his bongo drums. He loved village nightclubs, jazz bistros, and even the last remnants of vaudeville in Times Square. He was a big fan of comic Willie Howard, formerly of the team of Eugene and Howard, who specialized in dialect humor and double-talk.

Things went into a lull after *Flag* closed. Van Cleve sent him to meet Alfred Lunt and Lynn Fontanne, who were casting *Oh Mistress Mine*. When he arrived at the theatre, he was told to go on the stage and read from the script. Always nervous under such circumstances, he just stood alone on stage, script in hand and said nothing. Lunt gently prodded him, saying he could recite whatever he wanted. Brando recited: "Hickory, dickory, dock," walked offstage and never looked back.

On another occasion, he was up for a new Noel Coward comedy, *Present Laughter*. He read the lines to himself, threw the script down and said to Coward, "Don't you know there are people in the world starving?"

Around this time, Tallulah Bankhead, a leading lady notorious for her excesses, was looking around for a leading man for her next vehicle, *The Eagle Has Two Heads* by Jean Cocteau. Van Cleve suggested Brando for the part, and Tallulah agreed to interview him at Windows, her country house, to decide if he was suitable. Nervous about meeting the voracious Tallulah, Brando sought the advice of veteran director Robert Lewis and arranged to stop first at Lewis's house in Pound Ridge, before heading for Windows in nearby Bedford Village.

Lewis recognized that Brando might have a problem with hard-drinking, hard-partying Tallulah, since both of them used such different methods of work and both had vivid personalities and what he described as "unshakable independence of spirit." He recommended that Brando get a two week notice clause in his contract. That way, if things became intolerable, he would have a way out.

Brando went on to Windows where he greeted Tallulah with: "Are you an alcoholic?" to which she replied, "No, darling, just a heavy drinker."

Later, on her sofa, her hand wandered up his leg.

"What did you do?" Lewis asked him.

"Well," he reported. "I was interested, from an engineering point of view, to see if it was possible for her to gain her objective through that difficult route. You know," he marveled, "it was."

In any case, Tallulah did cast him, but it was not a match made in heaven. According to Lewis, "Tallulah, for all her fiery talent, clung to the old tradition of certain stage stars, namely that when they are holding forth in a scene, everyone for miles around should be immobilized. They count any move or reaction from the other actors as distractions. Marlon on stage, is the kind of actor who has a continuous life going for him, a life which results in scenes rather than star arias surrounded by accompanying robots. Tallulah even placed spies out in the audience to report to her if Marlon was acting behind her back in sections where she could not keep an eye on him. Finally, his irrepressible sense of truth unnerved her and she had him fired. Marlon Brando was replaced by Helmut Dantine, who stood still."

This incident did not discourage Van Cleve from pushing him as a candidate for the season's next big play, Tennessee Williams's *A Streetcar Named Desire.* Elia Kazan, who was directing, was not as sure, but agreed to a reading after which he told producer Irene Selznick that "However risky and unreliable, Marlon will be a very interesting Stanley." He sent him to meet Tennessee on Cape Cod.

FIXING TENNESSEE'S PLUMBING

Williams had broken through in 1944 with the huge success of *The Glass Menagerie.* He was sharing a house with friends near Provincetown, and when Brando arrived, the plumbing was flooded and a light fuse had blown. According to Williams, he immediately set to work: "First he stuck his hand into the overflowing toilet bowl and unclogged the drain, then he tackled the fuses. Within an hour, everything worked. You'd think he had spent his entire antecedent life repairing drains. Then he read the script aloud, just as he played it. It was the most magnificent reading I ever heard, and he had the part immediately. He stayed the night, slept curled up with an old quilt in the center of the floor."

Williams was immediately impressed with Brando's appearance. He was at the height of his youthful beauty and must have been the embodiment of Stanley Kowalski as Williams had imagined him. But Williams, no matter his feelings, kept the relationship strictly business. "I have never played around with actors," he said in his memoirs. "It is a point of morality with me. And anyhow Brando was not the type to get a part that way."

Back in New York, Brando had a meeting with Irene Selznick, who agreed with Kazan and Williams, and signed him at a princely $550 a week. Jessica Tandy was to play Blanche Du Bois, Karl Malden, Mitch, and Kim Hunter, Stella.

While in rehearsals, Marlon became a member of the Actors Studio, with which his name would be forever identified. The Studio, founded in October 1947 by Kazan, Bobby Lewis, and producer Cheryl Crawford, was a workshop where talented actors could get together and work on their craft. Kazan and Lewis divided the "classes" in two. Brando was in Lewis's group, which also included Karl Malden, Montgomery Clift, Sydney Lumet, Maureen Stapleton, and others with whom he would work closely in the future. The class met three times a week.

These were not exactly classes, however, since most of the members were already established actors. Lewis encouraged them to stretch themselves by trying roles they would not usually be cast in. It was a chance to work on characterizations that might open up new areas of performing for them.

With this idea in mind, Lewis suggested Brando work on the role of Archduke Rudolf Maximilian Von Habsburg in Robert Sherwood's *Reunion in Vienna*.

"I want a complete physical characterization, Marlon," Lewis said. "The works—full uniform, including a sword, mustache, and monocle, long cigarette holder, accent, habsburg lip, and waltz music offstage."

Marlon was horrified, but reluctantly began to rehearse with Joan Chandler, his Elena, the woman whose love his character wanted to rekindle. "Each week, I would call for the scene to be performed," Lewis recalled, "but Marlon always had some excuse: he forgot the phonograph record for the waltz music, he didn't have some article of costume, or his monocle wouldn't stay screwed in his eye. Finally, convinced I was never going to give up, Marlon presented the scene. He came onstage and slowly circled his Elena. Then in that unpredictable way that was to become his trademark, Marlon suddenly slapped her, grabbed her, kissed her passionately, and then murmured, 'How long has it been since you were kissed like that?' "

"The roar of approval that this evoked from his fellow students (well known as the toughest audience in the world) spurred Marlon on to give a hilarious light comedy performance that is still remembered by all who were there that day."

Lewis and Brando did not always get along. Like many great teachers, Lewis liked to hold forth and could lose patience if he thought a student was not paying sufficient attention. David Garfield, author of *A Player's Place,* a history of The Actors Studio, reports that once, noticing that Brando was deep in a newspaper while he was talking, paused and asked: "Marlon, what was I saying?" Brando looked up and shot back, "You stepped in what?" silencing the director for the moment.

Lewis asked Brando to repeat the scene as part of a fundraiser for The Actors Studio and to get certain people interested in the organization. Brando declined, but offered instead to organize the event on his own. That spring, the Actors Studio held its first "benefit." He put together a unique evening which included Wally Cox performing stand-up, Brando himself playing bongos for some dancer friends from the Katherine Dunham group, and a selection of Charlie Chaplin movies.

The Actors Studio may have been responsible for Brando's first known dramatic appearance on television. On January 9, 1949, he starred in "I'm No Hero," an episode in *Actors Studio,* one of television's first dramatic anthology series. The half-hour drama aired on the ABC network and was regarded as a pioneering experiment in national broadcasting. It would be thirty years before Brando would act again on television.

"I WAS AFRAID OF ANALYSIS AT FIRST"

He also began seeing a psychiatrist recommended by Kazan, Dr. Bela Mittelman. "I was afraid of analysis at first," he has said. "Afraid it might destroy the impulses that made me creative, an artist. A sensitive person receives fifty impressions where someone else may only get seven. Sensitive people are so vulnerable; they're so easily brutalized and hurt just because they are so sensitive. The more sensitive you are, the more certain you are to be brutalized, develop scabs. Never evolve. Never allow yourself to feel anything, because you always feel too much. Analysis helps. It helped me."

Mittelman specialized in creative people. He treated composer Alan Jay Lerner, Burgess Meredith, and Kazan himself. Meredith recalls encountering all three men in Mittelman's waiting room: "We would pass each other with a shrug of the shoulders as we went, separately, to lie down on the couch, trying to find out what brought us here and where the hell we were going thereafter."

After the traditional out-of-town tryouts in New Haven, Boston, and Philadelphia, *Streetcar* arrived on Broadway, opening at the Barrymore theatre on December 3, 1947. By that time, Brando's idiosyncratic style had alienated his costars, but he became an instant sensation.

Irene Selznick managed to get Brando into a jacket and tie for the lavish opening night party at "21." Marlon, Sr., Dodie, Jocelyn and Don Hamner, Frannie and Dick Loving, and Wally Cox were all there.

Overnight, Marlon was a star, but for the rest of his life, at least for the twenty-five years until *The Godfather,* he would be identified with the role of Stanley Kowalski, a man Brando himself described as "so muscle-bound he could hardly talk." As Brando saw the character, "Stanley didn't give a damn how he said a thing. His purpose was to convey his idea. He had no awareness of himself at all."

His lifestyle hardly changed. He moved into a studio apartment on West 52nd Street, known for its jazz clubs, sharing a bathroom. He had a motorcycle.

"I HONESTLY THINK THAT BROKEN NOSE MADE HIS CAREER"

But he was bored and restless backstage, and took to boxing to keep occupied. According to columnist Cindy Adams, "Brando's people had asked stagehands to don boxing gloves and spar with him so, in the scene when he comes into the house after playing softball, he'd be properly sweaty and breathing hard." The stagehands refused, so a boxer turned building inspector named Byrnes, whose job was to check for fire hazards, did it. "Carried away, Byrnes began punching with force. Byrnes threw a right and broke Brando's nose. To Brando's credit, he went on that night."

"I honestly think that broken nose made his career—especially in movies," said Irene Selznick. "It gave him sex appeal. Previously, he was just too beautiful."

He was already demonstrating his indifference to the press and publicity. Sheila Graham, the popular gossip columnist who had once been the mistress of F. Scott Fitzgerald, visited her friend Jessica Tandy backstage to ask to be introduced to the new star. "He's so virile, so exciting, with that torn shirt," she gushed. Marlon's dressing room seemed to be as narrow and as long as eternity, as, guided by Jessica, Graham stumbled toward the stationary figure at the other end.

"Oh, Marlon," said Tandy, who was also flustered by his stern expression, "I want you to meet—"

He interrupted: "Your mother?"

Graham was completely deflated. "He was probably joking," she wrote later, "but I didn't stay long enough to find out. In fact this was the only close encounter I ever had with him."

Recalling her run with Brando, Tandy said, "I think he cared about Broadway but I don't think he really cared about acting." Yet, according to Tandy, he told her that he would *never* make a film.

THE ENDLESS WOMEN

During the run of *Streetcar* he dated a series of dancers, models and actresses.

He was also reunited—onstage only—with Carmelita Pope, who understudied Kim Hunter and later stepped into the role of Stella when Hunter left the show. What was it like to play opposite the great Brando?

"Hmmm!," she said, raising her eyes to heaven. "He was so good. You know the scene, after he beats his wife up and he's standing at the bottom of the stairs yelling 'Stella!'? I came down those stairs, and tears were rolling down his face. You didn't need to be an actress with him. I came down those stairs and melted in his arms."

Marlon Brando wanted to share his success with those he loved most, and that included Wally Cox who was making his living creating costume jewelry with Dick Loving. Brando encouraged Cox to try out his popular party monologue in a Greenwich Village club, the Village Vanguard, in December 1948, and a comedy career was born.

Jocelyn and Don Hamner were now the parents of a four-year-old son, David, and living in a cold-water flat on West 69th Street. Her big break came when she was cast in the only female role in *Mister Roberts,* which starred her mother's discovery, Henry Fonda. *Life* magazine ran a story on the young acting Brando clan.

FAYE EMERSON

Brando was as mischievous as ever. He was scheduled for his first television interview with Faye Emerson, who

was famous for her low-cut gowns. She was concerned
about Marlon's reputation for hating TV, and she asked
publicist Bob Condon to make sure Marlon showed up.
He got Marlon to the studio two minutes before air time.
Miss Emerson's gown was low, her endowments high,
and, according to Condon, "all through the interview,
Marlon never once took his eyes from that monumental
sight." Miss Emerson, noted for her poise, got frantic but
no matter how the camera moved there was Brando staring "like a laser beam at the cleft just inches in front of
him."

This pretty much guaranteed that Brando would not be
invited on other television shows, at least until Condon
himself became a writer for an interview show with his
friend Eve Hunter and prevailed on him to appear. Brando
agreed if he could include Wally Cox, who was starting
to make his mark in nightclubs. They agreed.

"I had arranged the spot so that sound and camera
would be on Wally and Marlon for thirty seconds before
Eve joined them—as though we had caught their conversation candid style," Condon recalled. "Wally had his legs
crossed and as the camera picked them up the audience
at home saw Marlon lean forward and inspect the sole
of Wally's shoe and then he said, 'Say, Wally, what's that
gook on the bottom of your shoe?' Now Wally leans forward, face a study of concentration, and he looks at Marlon and says, 'I don't know buddy—what do you think
it is?'

" 'I'll smell it,' Brando volunteered.

"The control room was in a panic when suddenly Marlon looked up with a demonic smile and said, 'It's only
chewing gum, Wally.' "

MARLON'S PILOT

According to Bob Condon, Brando also made a pilot film for a series to be called *Come Out Fighting!* "We were his guests on a trip to Brooklyn to see a fight card at a local club and meet the fighter who was to be the technical adviser," Condon recalled. "The evening went well and Marlon was enthusiastic as he has always admired pugilists and pugilism." The series was not picked up.

Marlon was making $550 a week of which $400 a week went to his father to invest. Marlon, Sr. had formed Marsdo, Inc. ("Marlon's dough") and was investing in his Penny Poke cattle ranch in Nebraska and oil fields in Indiana.

Yet with $150 a week pocket money, he was always broke. "I don't buy any clothes," he complained. "I don't go to nightclubs, I don't drink, I eat in cafeterias, I haven't got a car, I've never paid more than $65 a month rent—but I've never got any money." He was notorious for giving it away to acquaintances who hit him up for "loans." "I haven't made up my mind about money," he said, "I haven't decided what it *means.*"

Brando soon grew restless playing the same role night after night. "It's not that I didn't like it. It's that I HATED it," he said years later. "It was the worst experience in my life. I almost went out of my mind. . . . I thought it would be terrific, *Streetcar,* ah . . . awful. Awful to be in a play."

Marlon's *Streetcar* contract expired in June 1949 and with relief Marlon headed for Paris, his first time out of the country. Now he had a chance to soak up the heady intellectual atmosphere of the Left Bank. He also realized a lifetime dream: he yearned to meet Arletty, the star of *Children of Paradise*. He considered the film, "Maybe the best movie ever made. You know, that's the only time I ever fell in love with an actress, somebody on the screen. I was mad about Arletty. I mean I was really in *love* with her." He begged to be introduced to her, and recalled, "I went to see her as though I were going to a shrine. My ideal woman . . . wow! What a mistake, was that a disillusionment. She was a tough article."

Next, he headed for Rome and from there to Naples and Sicily. Back in Paris, he found a script waiting. It was for *The Men,* which he had already turned down via trans-atlantic telephone conversations with producer Stanley Kramer. Now, he looked at it more carefully.

It was a seven page synopsis of the story and he read it one day walking down the street. "It had what I felt was an important dramatic situation," he said later. Take this guy and his girl, the guy completely helpless, worse than a baby or an animal. It's impossible to realize such terrible frustration and hopelessness unless you live like that."

Up until now, Brando had refused all movie offers be-cause they involved multi-picture contracts. He wanted the freedom to make only pictures he cared about. Lured by the Carl Foreman script and a guarantee that Fred Zinneman would direct, Brando agreed to star as the paraplegic WW II veteran. Returning to the United States, he headed for Hollywood.

Three

Brando in Hollywood

"The only reason I'm here is because I don't yet have the moral strength to turn down the money."

—Marlon Brando

Immediately on arrival, Brando seemed determined to demonstrate his contempt for Hollywood and all it stood for. He declined to stay at a hotel, informing his producer, Stanley Kramer, that he would be at his Aunt Betty's modest home in Eagle Rock.

He also flexed his mischievous side: It's a talent agency tradition that all stars are met on arrival by one of the lowly trainees who are put at their beck and call. Thus, Brando was met at the airport by young Jay Kanter, a trainee at MCA, and a chauffeured limo. Brando insisted that Kanter, not much younger than himself, sit in back of the limo with him.

"And what do you do?" he asked.

"I'm in the mailroom," Kanter replied.

"Not anymore," Brando shot back. "From now on, you're my agent."

The next day, people were running up and down the halls of MCA asking "Who the hell is Jay Kanter?" "They had to give Jay an office and a secretary," a contemporary says.

"He was the hot young star, and he was always difficult to reach," Kanter recalls. "In essence, he said if anybody wanted to reach him, they'd have to talk to me. Suddenly, I was very popular."

(In 1989 Kanter's story inspired a TV sitcom, *The Famous Teddy Z*, starring Jon Cryer as a young bakery worker who becomes Hollywood's hottest agent overnight.) Kanter himself went on to become a powerful producer and remains Brando's friend.

"AS FAR AS I'M CONCERNED, HE CAN DROP DEAD."

He was openly contemptuous of the press, especially the two most powerful women in town, gossip columnists Hedda Hopper and Louella Parsons. To Brando, Hopper was "the one with the hats," and Parsons was "the fat one." "Lolly" Parsons returned the feeling, writing in her column that, "He has the manners of a chimpanzee, the gall of a Kinsey researcher, and a swelled head the size of a Navy blimp, and just as pointed—as far as I'm concerned he can ride his bike off the Venice pier." It was said that he sat through an entire half-hour interview with Hedda Hopper answering in nothing but grunts.

At his Aunt Betty's he slept on the living room couch

(his grandmother occupied the other bedroom) and seemed oblivious to the idea that his casual lifestyle or the reporters and photographers that followed him everywhere might be disrupting the Lindermeyer's tranquil household. He entertained a steady stream of press while wrapped in his grandmother's bathrobe.

Yet he was profoundly serious about his work. To prepare for the role of a paraplegic, he moved into the Birmingham Veteran's Hospital, sharing a ward with thirty-one paraplegic men. His seriousness never interfered with his childish sense of humor, however.

One day he startled some visitors by jumping out of the wheelchair and running across the lawn. It made him laugh every time he remembered the look on their faces. Others did not find it so funny.

Filming *The Men* was an ordeal, not just because of the emotional content of the subject, but because he was a complete newcomer to the technical aspect of moviemaking.

"None of it was easy," he recalled. "The hardest was where Theresa first comes to the hospital. I just didn't feel it. But old man Adler, old Jacob [Stella's father], taught me something once I've never forgotten: to hold back twenty percent and you're always being honest with an audience. They're the actors, you know. Try to show more than you have to give and they catch on right away."

As soon as *The Men* wrapped, Brando headed back to New York, moving in with Wally Cox, who was now living over a 52nd Street jazz club, Leon and Eddie's, and studying conversational French at the New School. Russell, his pet raccoon, accompanied him everywhere. Marlon had trained him to use a toilet.

BRANDO THE PRACTICAL JOKER

An observer at that time remembers that Brando was a notorious practical joker. Meeting a movie producer he had made up his mind in advance not to like, he held a fresh-laid egg in his hand while the producer shook it vigorously.

Brando was soon feuding with the management of Leon and Eddie's which objected to his blocking the entrance with his motorcycle and refused him admission in his T-shirt and jeans. To retaliate, he collected a bucket of horse manure and tossed it from his apartment window onto the front of the club, roaring, "Beware the flying horse!"

Much of his humor is scatological. There is the time a friend, a violist, noticed his instrument was heavier than usual. "Why, it's filled with horseshit!"

"Yes," said Brando, "that's precisely what it sounds like."

At the same time, he was wildly sentimental, especially when it came to sad scenes on screen. He cried throughout a showing of *The Yearling* and during a screening of *The Wizard of Oz*. Not having a handkerchief with him, he wiped his tears away on the face of the girl he was dating.

He was increasingly wary of the press. "I make a mistake in talking to anybody," he said. "What I have to say is either misinterpreted or misunderstood, and I always feel betrayed afterward. But I'm building up armor against this sort of thing, so they can't hurt me anymore."

The Men opened at Radio City Music Hall in June. It would never be a big box office winner, but Brando was hailed as an extraordinary new screen talent: "Brando

plays the crippled Wilozek with much the same sullen
tenseness that made his Kowalski a memorable figure,"
said *Newsweek.* "Broadway's Brando does a magnificent
job. His halting, mumbled delivery, glowering silences
and expert simulation of paraplegics do not suggest acting at all; they look chillingly like the real thing." The
picture and his performance were mostly ignored when
the Academy Awards were announced. The only nomination was Carl Foreman's for Best Screenplay.

When Brando and Russell (on a leash) arrived in Chicago on a cross country tour to promote *The Men,* they
were met by a United Artist's rep who asked if there was
anything he could do for the star. "Yeah," Brando replied,
"can you tell me where I can get my raccoon fucked?"

No one had huge commercial expectations for *The
Men,* but just everybody regarded the movie version of
A Streetcar Named Desire as pure gold. Kazin insisted
that Brando come with the package when the movie deal
was made, and managed to keep most of the cast together. Unfortunately, concerned about box office, the
studio insisted he drop Jessica Tandy and replace her
with Vivien Leigh who had played the role in London.
Russell was a familiar—and annoying—figure on the set.

Sometimes Brando could not restrain himself from a
bit of scene stealing, but when called on it he relented.
Karl Malden recalls that his own biggest scene came during the poker game and when filming began Brando kept
"horsing around," and stepping on Malden's lines.

"He was the star," Malden conceded, "and he could
get away with it. But I also knew that he was a nice guy
and was probably not thinking of what he was doing to
my part. I put it to him straight. I said, 'You've got fifty

sides [lines] and can toss them away and still register. If I lose one of mine, I've got nothing.' He understood right away. 'I never thought of it that way,' he said to me. And when that sequence was shot, I got more than was coming to me."

The movie was a brilliant transition from stage to screen and ensured that Brando would forever be associated with Stanley Kowalski. Associated? Or haunted? Sometimes it must be hard for Brando himself to decide. It is the role that made his career, but Stanley was in fact, his mirror opposite.

"Kowalski was always right, and never afraid. He never wondered, he never doubted himself. His ego was very secure. And he had the king of brutal aggressiveness I hate," he observed. "I'm afraid of it. I detest the character."

The film opened in September 1951. *The New York Herald-Tribune* lauded, "a remarkably truthful performance of a heavy-muscled, practical animal, secure in the normalcy of marriage and friendship, cunning but insensitive, aware of Blanche's deceits but not her suffering. This performance is as close to perfect as one could wish."

When the Academy Award nominations were announced the following January, *Streetcar* was nominated for Best Picture, and Kazan for Best Director, and Brando for Best Actor. Karl Malden won for Best Supporting Actor, Vivian Leigh won for Best Actress, and Kim Hunter won for Best Supporting Actress.

Sometime in 1951 he met Rita Moreno in Hollywood and began a tempestuous, headline-making love affair that would last on and off for eight years.

* * *

RITA MORENO

One writer has said that the first meeting of Rita Moreno and Marlon Brando in Hollywood "must have been like two exiles stumbling on each other in a strange country." Their backgrounds could not have been more different: where Brando had grown up in typical midwestern fashion in a family that was, outwardly at least, picture-perfect, Puerto Rico-born Rosa Dolores Alverio was the daughter of a seamstress who eventually married five times. She had been working as a professional dancer since the age of nine when at a bar mitzvah she picked up five dollars for clapping a basket of fruit on her head and imitating Carmen Miranda. Taking her current stepfather's last name, she became known as Rosita Moreno.

By thirteen she was on Broadway in *Skydrift* and at seventeen met Louis B. Mayer, who whisked her to Hollywood where studio types changed her name to Rita.

She made news, but too often it was the wrong kind. In 1954 the petite (five foot two, 100 pounds) Moreno was involved in assaulting two six-foot cops during a marijuana bust at the home of a boyfriend, meat-packing heir Geordie Hormel. By the time she met Brando, she was under contract to MGM and had appeared in small roles in films like *Pagan Love Song* and *The Toast of New Orleans.*

Rita Morena suited Brando's taste for exotic looks in his women. "Marlon has always liked Latin women," she said. "I don't think he ever went out with a blonde. He has the reputation of being tough or cold, but in reality he is a very gentle, loving man.

But she and Marlon shared much, including a loathing

for anything—or anyone—they sensed was phony. "Behind those big brown eyes there is a hidden radar screen," a friend once said of Moreno. "She can pick up an approaching phony at five hundred paces."

They were both moody, introspective rebels, disenchanted with the accepted values of the curious community in which they chose to live and work. Neither was afraid to take a stand. Rita marched in a demonstration against H-bomb testing. Marlon kept a vigil outside San Quentin to protest the execution of convicted rapist Caryl Chessman. Neither worried about the effect such stands might have on their careers. They had much the same tastes in books and films, the same detachment from the local social scene, the same antic humor.

The relationship with Moreno could have marked a turning point for Brando. They were both complex, passionate artists with promising futures. It seemed to be a match made in heaven, and had they married it might have been a union as successful as Paul Newman and Joanne Woodward or Jessica Tandy and Hume Cronyn. But Brando's inability to commit, professionally or emotionally, and his inability to control his impulsive behavior, both traits typical of the adult child of alcoholics, made such fulfillment impossible.

The first clue to the problems that lay ahead came during the filming of *Viva Zapata!*

Elia Kazan convinced Darryl Zanuck, head of 20th Century-Fox, to make *Viva Zapata!,* the story of the legendary Mexican revolutionary. John Steinbeck wrote the screenplay.

After two weeks of rehearsal at the Fox studios in Hollywood, the cast headed for location in Texas. By the time they returned to Los Angeles, Marlon was involved with Movita Castenada, a thirty-three-year old.

Born Maria Louisa Castenada in Mexico, Movita was a still-beautiful woman whose best-known role had been as the Tahitian girl in *Mutiny on the Bounty* in 1935. She had been married to an Irish prize fighter, Jack Doyle, but soon became Brando's favorite. Between six and ten years older than Brando, she was certainly more experienced in the ways of the world and Hollywood.

He was now seeing two beautiful Latin women.

To prepare for *Zapata,* Brando moved to Sonora, Mexico to study local culture and speech patterns. He altered his appearance with plastic bands in his nose and glued down the corners of his eyes.

On location in Roma, Texas, Russell was up to his old tricks, urinating on the leather upholstery in Jean Peters's new Cadillac, and was soon banished to the Illinois farm for good.

Kazan had had to fight to get Brando, his choice, as Zapata. Now, screening the first rushes, he roared: "Look at that face—that face! The brooding sadness of it, the poetry. Jesus, it's the face of an Edgar Allan Poe!" The studio and the world would come to agree.

Bosley Crowther of *The New York Times* said that Brando's portrayal had "power enough to cause the screen to throb."

His performance in *Zapata* would win him his second Oscar nomination.

"BRANDO WORKED HIS ASS OFF,
AND IT'S A VERY TALENTED ASS"

So far, Brando had established himself as the premiere film actor in the world. At least when it came to playing brooding, inarticulate, explosive types. Now it was time for him to try something new and more challenging.

The summer of 1952, John Houseman was planning to produce a film version of Shakespeare's *Julius Caesar* for MGM. Joseph L. Mankiewicz would direct, with Louis Calhern as Caesar and John Gielgud as Cassius. Brando was amazed and skeptical when he was approached about the role of Marc Antony. But, according to Mankiewicz biographer Kenneth L. Geist, he invited the director to his apartment ("a filthy pad on 57th Street that bore the remnants of many broads," Mankiewicz recalled) to play him the tape-recorded results of a months' intensive study of every recorded Shakespearean actor from Barrymore to Olivier. "You sound just like June Allyson," was Mankiewicz's dismaying verdict.

Columnist and night club comics had great fun at the prospect of Stanley Kowalski or the Wild One orating "Friends, Romans, countrymen." But they were in for a surprise because, Mankiewicz declared, "Marlon worked his ass off, and it's a very talented ass."

Using a tape recorder, he worked closely with Mankiewicz to perfect the modified British accent the director wanted. John Gielgud was impressed with Brando's work habits and with the way Mankiewicz managed to get their disparate accents to match. "Mankiewicz was somehow able to tone my accent down while heightening

Brando's," he recalled. "As far as the overall product is concerned, I was struck by how the script of the play was respected and adapted to the screen. Shakespeare would certainly be delighted."

He also studied with an MGM vocal coach, Gertrude Folger. When she was asked about her famous student she was protective: "The jibes about his diction are unjust. If he's playing a slovenly character, his diction quite properly fits. But his own is excellent."

The veteran coach was quite taken with him. "Such a dear boy, so punctual, so modest, so willing. I can't remember when I've had such a hard-working, keen, rewarding pupil. He's always prepared and considerate, and, unlike some big stars—who sometimes just don't show up—he always phones if he's going to be late."

Although still involved with Movita, Brando was still seeing Rita Moreno. But when filming ended and he headed back to New York it was with Movita. In fact, she moved in with him on 57th Street.

Director Joseph Mankiewicz praised Brando's work in the film: "When Brando goes into a role, he plunges in like a deep-sea diver. If he was going to play a blind man, he'd go around for weeks with his eyes shut. If he was going to play a man with his right arm missing, he'd do everything lefty until he got the hang of how it felt."

Julius Caesar made its international premiere in Sydney, Australia in May 1953 and arrived in New York the following month. Brando's classic performance was widely saluted. Bosley Crowther of the *Times* wrote:

"The delight and surprise of the film is Mr. Brando's Marc Antony, which is something memorable to see. Athletic and bullet-headed, he looks the realest Roman of them all and possesses the fire of hot convictions and the firm elasticity of steel. Happily, Mr. Brando's diction, which has been guttural and slurred in previous films, is clear and precise in this instance. In him, a major talent has emerged."

In fact, Gielgud himself was so impressed with Brando's work in *Julius Caesar* that he "begged" Brando to play Hamlet as part of a classical season, shared with Paul Scofield and himself in London. Brando declined, explaining that he was committed to go scuba-diving in the Bahamas. In any case, he never wanted to go back to the theatre.

Once again, he was nominated for an Academy Award for Best Actor, losing out to William Holden for *Stalag 17*.

"ONCE THE TROUBLE WAS ON THE WAY, I JUST WENT ALONG WITH IT"

Brando was besieged with offers. He still owed a picture to Fox on the two-picture deal he had signed for *Viva Zapata!*. Then Stanley Kramer came to him with an original script based on a short story, *The Cyclist's Raid* which was based on a real-life event when thousands of members of a motorcycle gang held their convention in the small town of Hollister, California in the summer of 1947. Who was more natural for the leader of the gang than Brando?

Some were puzzled by this move: the role seemed to clinch the stereotype of Brando as the brutal primitive. But it didn't start out that way. "We started out trying to say something about the hipster psychology, but somewhere along the line we ran off the track," Brando complained. "So, in the end, instead of showing why young people tend to join groups that seek expression in violence, we merely showed the violence."

Yet director Laslo Benedek had accomplished exactly what he set out to do. "The subject isn't juvenile delinquency," he explained, "it's youth without ideals, without goals, which doesn't know what to do with the enormous energy which it possesses." Benedek tried to show that "if you react with similar violence, you lose. That the vigilante attitude is useless, you just end up with an even greater problem. The film is not only about the cyclists, it's about townspeople, merchants, and policemen who behave badly and it's about the dangers of the white backlash mentality."

The film was banned by the British Board of Censors and not shown there until 1965. Brando regarded it as a failure.

The picture opens with an open, empty road and the sound of Brando's voiceover: "Once the trouble was on the way, I just went along with it." Seeing the direction, or mis-direction the film was taking, he chose to go along with it, a pattern that he would follow in other missteps throughout his career. It was the fatalistic, helpless character of the adult child of alcoholics.

In his black leather jacket, slouched over his motorcycle, Brando instantly established himself as an icon.

"What are you rebelling against?" a character in the film asks him. "What have you got?" he replies.

Hollis Alpert observed some of this in his comments in *Saturday Review:* "Lying behind his bravado, you see the crazy, hurt, messed-up child."

Although Brando was overlooked by the Academy Awards that year, his performance would influence two generations of actors, among them James Dean.

James Dean was among the many male stars who idolized Brando as the greatest screen actor of his generation. After seeing Brando in *The Wild One,* Dean started pestering him with phone calls and following him like a puppy. Finally Brando introduced him to a psychiatrist. Brando, later said he felt sorry for Dean, who died in a car crash in 1955. He described him as "just a lost boy trying to find himself."

"BRILLIANT, ONCE OR TWICE A WEEK"

Disenchanted with the experience of making *The Wild One,* Brando sought the solace of theatre with trusted friends, including William Redfield and Carlo Fiore.

Most fans believe that Brando left theatre after *Streetcar,* but he made one more appearance on the live stage the summer of 1953 in George Bernard Shaw's *Arms and the Man.* He took the role of the Bulgarian general Sergius; William Redfield was Bluntschli. Produced by Morton Gottlieb, and directed by Herman Ratner they opened that July in the Theater-by-the-Sea in Matunuck,

Rhode Island, moved on to Falmouth, Ivoryton, Framingham.

A young apprentice, Tammy Grimes, just sixteen at the time, was assigned to Marlon's personal props, like his cigarette holder and plume.

When the season was over in August, Brando and Redfield headed for Europe on the Liberté for a real vacation.

Movita had moved back to California, where Brando had no desire to go. Casting about for a new project, he talked to Kazan who recommended a script by Budd Schulberg: *On the Waterfront.* The producer, Sam Spiegel, had already decided that he wanted Frank Sinatra for the role of Terry Malloy, and the star was campaigning hard for it. When he learned that Brando had been cast, he sued Spiegel, unsuccessfully, for $500,000 for backing out of the deal.

This film would establish Brando as a movie star.

He hated *On the Waterfront* when he saw it and refused to cooperate in any publicity. "There were seven takes [of the big scene in the car] because Steiger couldn't stop crying. He's one of those actors who loves to cry. We kept doing it over and over. . . . The first time I saw *Waterfront* in a projection room with Gadge, I thought it was so terrible I walked out without even speaking to him." The picture wrapped in New York in December 1953.

While making *On the Waterfront,* Brando took up with Anne Ford, 24, a blouse designer who visited him on the set. She later described how he arrived at her door, "shirtless, danced the entire length of the room, made a demi-disappearance behind the opposite door, and exited with a graceful arabesque kick—without a word of greeting or glance my way." He took her to see *The Wild One* at a Times Square theatre. The affair was romantic, fun, and short-lived. She was later murdered and the crime was never solved.

After *Zapata,* Fox had an option on Brando and assigned him to *The Egyptian,* co-starring Bella Darvi, Zanuck's inamorata, and directed by veteran Michael Curtiz. After one rehearsal, Brando walked out, taking a train back to New York from whence word came from Dr. Mittelman that he was in no condition to work. "He is a very sick and mentally confused boy," said Dr. Mittelman. Zanuck prepared to sue.

In New York, Brando went to a party at Stella Adler's and was introduced to Josanne Mariani-Bérenger. The French fisherman's daughter had posed for Moise Kisling, famed painter of sensuous nudes, and was now working as governess for the family of a New York psychiatrist. At nineteen, she was petite, raven-haired, and barely five-foot-one.

"Two hours after meeting me," she recalled, "he asked, 'will you be my wife?' "

In March, when Brando raced to the side of his dying mother, Josanne accompanied him. Dodie had collapsed while visiting Betty Lindenmeyer in Pasadena and she died of liver and kidney disease at Huntington Memorial Hospital on March 31, 1954.

Back in New York Josanne left for France in June and he told her: "Go ahead, I'll see you soon."

That summer, he was caught up in the excitement surrounding the release of *On the Waterfront* which opened in July to huge critical acclaim. The *New York*

Times critic wrote that "Marlon Brando's Terry Malloy is a shatteringly poignant portrait of an amoral, confused, illiterate citizen of the lower depths." Brando and the film were heaped with international honors: saluted by the New York Film Critics Circle as Best Picture of the Year, the British Film Academy's Best Foreign Actor Award. The following year, the film would be honored with a slew of Academy Awards including to Eva Marie Saint (Best Actress), Kazan (Best Director), Schulberg (Best Screenplay) and Spiegal (Best Picture) and, finally, Best Actor for Brando.

But that was in the future. Brando sailed for Europe on the Ile de France that October for a reunion with Josanne, and rode into her home town of Bandol on his motor scooter.

On October 29 a Toulon newspaper ran the notice: "Madame and Monsieur Paul Berenger of Bandol are happy to announce the engagement of their daughter Josanne to Monsieur Marlon Brando."

Pandemonium followed as the press of the world descended on the fishing village.

Marlon and Josanne fled Bandol in her father's fishing boat for a little island off the coast. But newsmen caught up with them. "I want to get to know my parents-in-law," he told the press pack. "I want to live for a while under this beautiful blue sky where my fiancée was born."

"Sure," Marlon acknowledged, "we're engaged—there's no mystery about it."

Then he took Josanne by the hand and led her away fast for the boat trip back to the mainland.

In November, indicating he was anxious to see his fiancée but in no hurry to get married, Brando sailed for New York.

Reporters asked him if he was looking forward to seeing Josanne. "Oh, boy," he replied with gusto.

He was reminded that Josanne, who had left Paris by plane ten days earlier, had said they would be married in June.

"Well, we'll get married within a year," he said, gazing over the heads of a cordon of photographers and reporters at hundreds of wildly cheering teenagers blocking the gateways to his platform at St. Lazaire Station.

"I suppose we'll get married in the states," he added. "I don't know whether Josanne's folks will come over for the wedding."

Alas, there was never to be any wedding. Josanne joined Brando in Los Angeles and made the rounds of studios there in an attempt to start an acting career. Nothing came of it. The affair with Brando faded. Anna Kashfi says that Josanne posed nude for some skin magazines. Josanne finally gave up on Brando and the movies and returned to France and her childhood sweetheart.

Josanne declined to talk to the press about the end of the relationship. Years later she observed that, "Marlon is too independent to accept the discipline of marriage." But, like so many of the women in his life, she remained on friendly terms with Brando and he would sometimes visit her and her family when he was in the south of France.

The rest of the 1950s would be marked by a series of disastrous choices, beginning with *Desiree,* which he would come to regard as "a serious retrogression and the most shaming experience of my life."

Desiree, based on Annemarie Selinko's best-selling novel, would be directed by Henry Koster (*The Robe*). The story deals with the off-battlefield adventures of the Emperor (Brando), his inconstant consort Josephine (Merle Oberon) and a temptress named Desiree (Jean Simmons) who distracts him from his military and amatory path.

Brando agreed to settle with Fox and Zanuck. He would not have to make *The Egyptian* and instead would star in *Desiree.* Meanwhile, he turned down a starring role in *Picnic* that went to William Holden. Cameron Mitchell, who played Napoleon's brother Joseph, believed Brando needed a strong director, someone like Kazan, to control him and Koster was simply not that strong. According to Mitchell, Koster was reduced to pleading on his knees, begging "What have I done? What is it?" Mitchell said "He would walk on the set and go from chalk mark to chalk mark without the slightest show of interest. He flubbed and fumbled and fluffed his way through everything."

Marlon told Mitchell he was "trisexual." "What did that mean?" Mitchell asked. According to Mitchell, Marlon answered with a belch.

Certainly he went into *Desiree* with a negative attitude. "I wasn't going to break my neck playing in that picture," he recalls. "I got as many laughs out of the part as I could, and that was it. It was my own fault."

"I just let the makeup play the part," he said later, advice that Jack Nicolson would later repeat to Michael Keaton while they were filming *Batman.*

A *Time* magazine interview with Brando on the *Desiree* set quoted him as saying "I'll be damned if I feel obliged to defend myself, but I am sick to death of being thought of as a blue-jeaned slobbermouth and I am sick to death of having people come up to say hello and then just stand there expecting you to throw a raccoon at them." In a plea that would have poignant echoes throughout this career, he insisted on his right to privacy: "Well, I really did feel I have every right in the world to resist the stupid protocol of turning my private life into the kind of running serial you find on bubble-gum wrappers. You can't just take sensitive parts of yourself and splatter them around like so much popcorn butter."

When filming was completed, Brando left for the Venice Film Festival where *On the Waterfront* had its premiere.

His next role was in *Guys and Dolls,* the screen version of a long-running Broadway musical based on the colorful stories of Damon Runyon with Brando as the professional gambler Sky Masterson and Frank Sinatra as Nathan Detroit. At first Brando was wary of a song-and-dance role, but producer Sam Goldwyn, who had already paid $1 million for the film rights, and engaged Joe Mankiewicz to direct, was aware of Brando's confidence in Mankiewicz and sent the director an urgent cable: "CAN'T YOU HELP?" In turn, Mankiewicz wired Brando: "UNDERSTAND YOU'RE APPREHENSIVE BECAUSE YOU'VE NEVER DONE A MUSICAL COMEDY. YOU HAVE NOTHING REPEAT NOTHING

TO WORRY ABOUT. BECAUSE NEITHER HAVE I.
LOVE, JOE."

Brando was still trying valiantly to play the Hollywood
game. In February 1955 he even donned a tuxedo to
make his Hollywood social debut and accept an award
from the Hollywood Foreign Correspondents' Association and the Foreign Press Association for the best performance of a dramatic actor in 1954 for *On the
Waterfront*. He even announced plans to attend his first
Academy Award presentation on March 30. "I hope I'm
lucky enough to win it," he said.

Brando was accompanied by Celia Meredith, whom
he described as "my assistant." Other Golden Globes that
night went to Grace Kelly for best actress, Judy Garland
and James Mason, best in a musical film, *Carmen Jones*
as best musical; Jan Sterling and Edmond O'Brien as
best supporting actors, *Brigadoon*.

Brando was also becoming wise to Hollywood ways.
He was mastering the system and learning the game.
He had so far been nominated for an Oscar three times,
but lost out, mostly because he was perceived as an
outsider who had only contempt for the Hollywood system. This year, the Oscars came early in filming of
Guys and Dolls. Brando agreed to present the Oscar
for Best Director.

He showed up in the required tuxedo with his friends
Jay Kanter, Celia Webb, his Aunt Betty Lindemeyer, and
his father. Columnist Sidney Skolsky later reported that
he chewed gum throughout the evening, but he stopped
when Bette Davis came out on stage to announce the

name of the Best Actor. Besides Brando, the nominations that year were Humphrey Bogart (*The Caine Mutiny*), Bing Crosby (*The Country Girl*), James Mason (*A Star is Born*), and Dan O'Herlihy (*Adventures of Robinson Crusoe*).

When Bette Davis announced his name, Brando removed the chewing gum, shook hands with Bing Crosby, and raced to the stage to accept. He seemed genuinely pleased: "I can't remember what I was going to say for the life of me," he said. "I don't think ever in my life that so many people were so directly responsible for my being so very, very happy."

Later, he clowned around with host Bob Hope, posing for pictures in which Hope tries to grab his Oscar.

WHY SINATRA COULDN'T STAND BRANDO

Next day, Brando returned to the set of *Guys and Dolls* and a very un-amused Frank Sinatra. Sinatra had campaigned desperately for the role of Terry Malloy in *On the Waterfront,* but lost out to Brando. He was also the logical choice for Sky Masterson, but too, that role had gone to Brando, and Sinatra was left with the role of Nathan Detroit, the tart-tongued gambler who can always find a crap game.

Reportedly, Brando approached Sinatra for some acting tips. Sinatra turned him down. "Look, Brando," he said, "don't give me any of that method actor s===!"

Referring to Brando as "Mumbles," Sinatra said with a sneer: "He's the most overrated actor in the world."

Although he has always disdained the star treatment,

Brando has also shown himself no innocent when it came to asserting his status and protecting his turf. His style frequently clashed with Sinatra's. He was especially concerned when Sinatra sang. When he delivered his lines, Sinatra used Detroit's Bronx accent, but when he sang, he sang like the romantic balladeer he was. Brando took director Mankiewicz aside and confided, "Frank's playing his part all wrong. He's supposed to sing with a Bronx accent. He's supposed to clown it up. But he's singing like a romantic lead. We can't have two romantic leads."

"I agree with you," said Mankiewicz. "What do you suggest I do about it?"

"Tell him!" Brando said. "Tell him!"

The idea of telling Sinatra how to sing a song made Mankiewicz smile. *"You* tell him," he said and walked away.

Brando was stunned. Finally he turned to his friend Carlo Fiore and said, "It's not *my* job to tell him. It's the director's job. I'm never going to work with Mankiewicz again."

PENNY POKE DISASTER

By this time Penny Poke ranch had soaked up most of his money and would be sold at a loss. Marlon, Sr. moved into an apartment near his son's.

Marlon also took up with Alice Marchak, his father's blond secretary. This was never a romantic relationship. She would last with him for years.

* * *

Desiree was released in November. "I went to see it, expecting to be amused, but I was only depressed. If I'd had any sense, I would have handled the situation better," he said.

Brando has dismissed it as "the most shaming performance of my life."

In 1955, Brando and George Englund began work on a documentary for UNESCO about Southeast Asia.

Brando made plans to begin filming *The Teahouse of the August Moon*. He had seen John Patrick's Broadway hit four times. "Simply great," he raved, "I laughed so hard I almost ended up beating the lady's hat in front of me."

Teahouse satirized the American occupation of post-World War II Okinawa. The pompous Captain Fisby (Glenn Ford) is in command, but soon the villagers, led by the wily Sakini (Brando), are seducing him into their ways. This culminates with the construction of a teahouse. The message—a call for mutual understanding—appealed to Brando.

After the release of *Guys and Dolls,* Brando set up his own production company, Pennebaker Productions, backed by Paramount Pictures. Publicly Brando announced that he intended to spearhead his commitment to American film. Privately, he acknowledged that it was a means of providing financial security for his father. Marlon Brando, Sr. was named a director of Pennebaker Productions. The other three directors were George Englund, George Glass, and Walter Seltzer. All four directors were delegated to find properties for Marlon Brando, but Brando himself showed little interest in Pennebaker and his next venture, *Teahouse of the August*

Moon, would come via MGM. Marlon hoped to make a film version of a Louis L'Amour western.

The Pennebaker operation would produce two interesting failures: *Shake Hands With The Devil* (1959), directed by Michael Anderson, a gripping drama of war-torn Ireland in the 1920s, with Don Murray as an American student reluctantly drawn into the rebel army under the command of James Cagney, and *Paris Blues* (1961), directed by Martin Ritt, an offbeat account of two musicians on the Left Bank of Paris, played by Paul Newman and Sidney Poitier, romancing two tourists played by Joanne Woodward and Diahann Carroll.

His father handled the business end, with Marlon controlling creative affairs. Pennebaker offices were on the Paramount lot, and it was while there, stopping in at the Paramount commissary for lunch, that Brando asked the fateful question: "Who is that good-looking broad in the red sari?"

Four

1955—The Marriage From Hell

"Marlon leaves a lot to be desired as a romancer."
—Anna Kashfi

In October 1955, at thirty-one, Brando was introduced to Anna Kashfi in the Paramount Studio commissary. She had a small role in *The Mountain.* He asked to be introduced. She claims she had never seen any of his films and did not recognize him. He followed up with a phone call to Paramount publicist Harry Mines, looking to date her.

In her memoir, *Brando for Breakfast,* the demure Miss Kashfi recalls that she declined—unless she could bring a traditional *amah* or chaperone. Brando agreed. But it was Brando who brought the chaperone, his friend producer George Englund. (One wonders why, if Miss Kashfi felt she needed a chaperone on her date with Brando, she would feel safer with another bachelor along. Perhaps it can be attributed to the strange ways of the east.)

In her memoir, Miss Kashfi claimed to be the product of "an unregistered alliance" between Devi Kashfi, "a professional architect," and Selma Ghose, and was born September 30, 1934 in Calcutta. When she was two years old, she says, her mother married an Englishman, William Patrick O'Callaghan, and she was educated at a convent school in Darjeeling in the north of India. She further claimed that at eighteen she briefly attended the London School of Economics, and her mother and stepfather relocated to a small seacoast town in Wales.

She was discovered at a party in London by a Paramount scout and soon found herself acting opposite Spencer Tracy in *The Mountain,* which was filmed in the French Alps. When the production moved to the Paramount lot in Hollywood, she moved with it.

According to Kashfi, she and Brando had dated for several months before they made love. One night, in her apartment, he carried her into the bedroom. When she asked if he had rape in mind, she claims he answered: "Rape is just assault with a friendly weapon." Kashfi reports that he "is not well appointed" and refers to his sex organ as "my noble tool."

In January 1956, Kashfi signed for *Battle Hymn* opposite Rock Hudson, while Brando left for Japan.

MARILYN MONROE

In 1955 he also drew close to Marilyn Monroe. After his blazing success in *On the Waterfront,* she had pressed Samuel Goldwyn for a part in his next film, *Guys and*

Dolls. She hoped one of her first independent projects would star Brando and Charles Chaplin.

Asked to define sex appeal, Marilyn said, "There are people to whom other people react and other people who do nothing for people. I react to men, too . . . personally, I react to Marlon Brando." Marilyn never fulfilled her desire to work with Brando, but, according to biographer Anthony Summers, they did have an affair.

Marilyn spoke of him to a friend as "sweet, tender." A photograph taken of them together at an Actors Studio benefit in December 1955, after the world premiere of *The Rose Tattoo,* shows Marilyn and Brando looking dreamily happy together.

The friendship faded, but Summers claimed that in 1962, in the last days before her death, Marilyn would spend hours talking on the telephone with Brando.

Anna had been hospitalized with tuberculosis at the City of Hope Medical Center in Duarte, California. "Marlon was there constantly," recalls columnist Cindy Adams. "No dark glasses, no back doors, no hiding. Spoke to patients, gave autographs, hit the cafeteria. Yet [he] lied to reporters that he even knew Kashfi."

Something about seeing Kashfi laying there in bed, weak and helpless, seemed to stir memories of his mother. According to Kashfi, he began bringing her some of his late mother's possessions—"earrings, a brooch, her Bible; on one visit he brought the pillow she had died on (two years earlier)." He also shared memories of Dodie, including, according to Kashfi, a tale of urging his friend Carlo Fiore to seduce his mother while they were living together in New York.

Fiore himself was there when Brando told her: "I wish

my mother were alive. . . . I wish she was here to meet you. . . . I'm sure you'd both love each other. . . . You are so much alike." And the ominous words: "Yet—it's better that my mother is dead. If she had lived, I could never have loved you. She wouldn't have let me go." Kashfi later discovered that the latter thought was not original, but lifted from a letter from D.H. Lawrence to Frieda.

Had she known that the thought was not original, she might have understood that this is a man for whom the line between authentic emotion and *acted* emotion often seems blurred.

While she was hospital-bound, Kashfi claims, Brando asked her to marry him and she accepted. Ultimately, she would come to believe that "Marlon yearned to share himself with another person but that he could not and cannot."

That March, Brando left for a research tour of Southeast Asia for his film for the United Nations Assistance Program. He visited Hong Kong, Singapore, Manila, and Bangkok to scout possible locations for the documentary. After that he was to report to Japan in the spring to begin filming *Teahouse.*

At his press conference in Singapore, Brando called the fan magazines "scavengers, against whom the libel laws give no protection." He complained "I have enemies in the film world, because I don't want to follow the dictates of certain companies or give interviews to columnists I don't know." He criticized America for being "shoddy, vulgar, and commercial." He also met with local government and film dignitaries. He praised Asian reporters for their "intelligent questions instead of the foolish emphasis on my sex life which I have to tolerate in the United States." The UNESCO movie never happened.

On April 23, 1956, Brando arrived in Tokyo to begin filming *Teahouse*. His co-stars were Glenn Ford and Louis Calhern. Brando played Sakini, the Oriental houseboy.

Brando and Glenn Ford loathed each other. Louis Calhern died during filming. Calhern was found dead in his hotel room on May 12.

While filming some scenes in Manila, Brando met an eighteen-year-old dancer, Marie Cui, and began a romance with her.

When Kashfi was released on Thanksgiving Day 1956 they celebrated with dinner at the home of Marlon's sister Jocelyn and her second husband, Eliot Asinof. Marlon moved Anna into an apartment in the same West Hollywood building where Marlon, Sr. was living.

A week later, while in New York for the premiere of *Teahouse,* he bought Anna an engagement ring of four clusters of pearls on a platinum band. But when he brought it back to California and slipped it on her finger, he asked her to keep the engagement a secret from his family and reporters.

He found an apartment in West Hollywood for her, across the courtyard from Marlon, Sr. They shared a mutual dislike and rarely spoke.

According to Kashfi, Brando has always kept two cars. In their courting days, he took her out in a battered and unkempt Volkswagen. The white Thunderbird convertible that Sam Goldwyn gave him for *Guys and Dolls* was reserved for "private occasions behind the public eye."

In California, Anna Kashfi had been bounced from the cast of *Don't Go Near the Water* because, she claims, star Glenn Ford hated anyone who had anything to do with Brando. Kashfi had hoped to be cast opposite Brando in *Sayonara* but he vetoed the idea and the role went to Miiko Taka.

According to Kashfi, Brando returned from filming *Sayonara* in Japan having completely embraced the Japanese way. He wanted her to wear kimonos, to dress and behave like a geisha, especially when it came to attending him.

And about a month after he returned from Japan, she found a woman's black wig on his bedroom headboard. He admitted it belonged to Rita Moreno. There was a quarrel, a separation, a reunion. A renewed engagement. And Brando was soon off to Europe for preproduction on his next Fox film, *The Young Lions,* while Kashfi began filming *Cowboy* with Jack Lemmon and Glenn Ford.

Around this time, Carlo Fiore, concerned about Anna's jealousy, tried to discourage the relationship. Brando wouldn't hear of it, but he wasn't willing to give up any of the other women he was seeing either.

"With women, I've got a long bamboo pole with a leather loop on the end of it," he told his friend. "I slip the loop around their necks so that they can't get away or come too close. Like catching snakes."

In late September, Anna Kashfi discovered she was pregnant and they decided to marry. One night she and Marlon were awakened in bed by violent banging on his front door. It was Rita Moreno. Anna said, "It's her or me. Make a choice—right now."

The wedding on October 11, 1957 was at his Aunt Betty Lindemeyer's house in Eagle Rock. Screenwriter Peter Berneis and his wife Ina were the witnesses. Among the guests were his friends Kathy and Louis L'Amour. But his father was barred. A few months later, Marlon, Sr. married Anna Parramore, a widow six years younger than his son. Marlon, Jr. did not attend the wedding.

Anna recalls that her friends the L'Amours drove her to Betty Lindemeyer's house. She had a premonition that she shouldn't be doing this, and L'Amour assured her that she could still back out. But she went forward.

But not immediately. First, she decided, she had to have a nosegay of Madonna lilies. But the closest place for the lilies was San Francisco, and that took two hours. Meanwhile, everyone drank champagne and "By the time the lilies arrived," Kashfi recalls, "I was tipsy enough to have said 'I do' to a baboon."

Anna yearned to be married in a Buddhist ceremony because she admired its simplicity and symbolism. Marlon claimed that no Buddhist monk could be found in Los Angeles and offered to arrange for a Zen ceremony, which, Kashfi "felt to be ill-suited to my temperament." They compromised on a Presbyterian minister, Reverend J. Walter Fiscus, pastor of the Little Brown Church in the Valley in North Hollywood.

The groom wore a dark suit, opera cape, and homburg, the bride wore a green and gold sari.

She discovered that Brando had not made any plans for a honeymoon, but his friend Jay Kanter offered them the use of his Beverly Hills house. There they spent their wedding night, until she contacted her friends the L'Amours and arranged to spend the next week with them at their house in Palm Desert. L'Amour and Brando spent hours target shooting with a .38 revolver.

In the outside world, news was breaking that a William Patrick O'Callaghan was claiming to be Anna's father, a claim that she vehemently denied. According to her, he was her stepfather, her name was always Anna Kashfi and she only adopted Joan O'Callaghan for immigration quotas.

Although Marlon stood by her, she grew to feel that she saw less of him now than before they were married.

She did manage to have his father removed from managing his business affairs and replaced by a professional management firm.

Anna grew rapidly disenchanted with her movie star husband. She told Hedda Hopper: "Marlon leaves a lot to be desired as a romancer. He's just plain clumsy, and that's the truth. If he were not a film star, he wouldn't get to first base with women."

Kashfi seemed to revel in belittling her husband in the press. She told another reporter: "Living with Marlon is like an afternoon at the races—short periods of orgiastic activity followed by long periods of boredom and anticipation. He's almost never home." She added: "He attracts women like feces attract flies."

She found them a small Japanese-style house on Mulholland Drive, with a view of the San Fernando Valley to the north and the canyons to the south.

* * *

Brando attended the 1958 Academy Awards with friend George Englund. Anna, eight months pregnant, stayed home. She did not get to see him lose.

Domestic life *chez* Brando was tumultuous. The staff, consisting of a cook, two gardeners, a chauffeur, and Anna's personal maid, turned over frequently. They discharged one cook when they found out she was raising extra money by offering guided tours of their house, with dinner, for fifty cents a head. "Fifty cents per person!" Marlon said, "I should think the traffic would bear a dollar."

According to Carlo Fiore, when the Brando's quarreled, Anna displayed a "frightening" rage. "During one argument, she came out of the bathroom with a huge bar of soap in her hand and let it fly at Marlon," he recalled. "It got him between the eyes and cracked in half. Stunned, he staggered back and almost fell." On another occasion, Fiore says, Anna left baby Christian alone in her car parked on Wilshire Boulevard while she confronted Brando in his office, "beating at him with her fists, in a frenzy of rage."

On May 11, Mother's Day, 1958, Anna gave birth to a son, Marlon named Christian for his friend Christian Marquand. She wanted to name him Devi, after her father. They compromised on Christian Devi. He called the boy Christian or Chris, she called him Devi.

According to Kashfi, when she was breastfeeding the weeks-old baby, Brando returned home with the eighteen-year-old France Nuyen, who berated her for eating curry while breastfeeding, and took her last mango from the refrigerator. Kashfi ordered him to get her out of the house. The two of them left.

According to Brando biographer Charles Higham, Nuyen denies the episode described by Kashfi.

Nuyen told Higham that "Anna was completely out of the picture in Marlon's life when I met him again. For six months, I resisted him, but his humor, cleverness, and little-boy qualities finally succeeded in winning me over. He made me laugh. He was very sweet."

Trapped in her unhappy marriage, Kashfi began to abuse alcohol and barbiturates. She also lashed out at Brando himself, pulling his hair, throwing dishes at him, heaping him with verbal abuse.

The Brandos were headed for an eventual divorce, but according to Kashfi, their respective studios, MGM and Paramount, prevailed on her to delay any action so as not to affect their current films.

Kashfi made one more film, *Night of the Quarter Moon,* with John Barrymore, Jr. and Julie London, at MGM in 1958. Her Japanese maid, Sako Milligen, looked after Devi. One afternoon in September, on a break from filming, Anna was napping at home while Sako swam in the pool. Anna awakened to find Sako floating face down in the water. She summoned the police, fire department, and Brando's business manager. Somehow in the confusion word got out that it was Anna who had drowned. Brando raced home, walked into the house and came face to face with his wife. "Good God," he said, "you're still alive."

The death of Sako and her husband's reaction crystalized Anna's feelings and she fled that night, with her son. She soon moved into a house in Coldwater Canyon.

One afternoon, she received a call from Jay Kanter who claimed that Brando had taken some kind of pills and was about to throw himself into the pool. Convinced he planned suicide, she raced up to Mulholland Drive, only to find Brando and Kanter lolling by the pool. Furious at their idea of a joke, she screamed, "No, you son of a bitch! Now, jump!! I want to watch you drown!"

According to Kashfi, Brando soon surrendered himself to a parade of women, video-taping the encounters via a camera at the foot of his bed.

Halfway through the production of *One-Eyed Jacks,* Anna filed for divorce in Santa Monica Superior Court. She charged Brando with causing "grievous mental suffering, distress, and injury." Anna's friend Kathy L'Amour supported her claims of mental anguish. She flew with Devi to stay with friends in Hawaii.

Anna's petition for divorce was uncontested and became final April 22, 1959.

The settlement was a relatively generous $60,000 cash with $500,000 to be paid out over the next ten years. She also received $1,000 a month for child support until their son was of age, and medical and dental coverage of over $500 a year. She could request additional support if she had not remarried after ten years. She received permanent custody, but Marlon had visitation rights on alternate evenings, Thanksgiving, Christmas, and Christian's birthdays. Salaries for all servants were to be paid by Brando.

"SHE FLUNG HERSELF ON THE BED
AND BIT ME THREE TIMES"

In mid-August, at two in the morning, Brando would later tell the Santa Monica court, "while I was home in bed, [Anna] came in and flung herself on the bed and bit me three times and slapped me. I tried to restrain her and got her out of the house, but she went to get in her car and tried to run over me. I went back in my house and locked the doors. She threw a log through one of the windows and came back into the house through the windows. I held her down on the bed and tied her up with the sash from my dressing robe. I then called the police. I told them I would not press charges and asked them to escort her home. She refused but the police persuaded her."

He later testified in court, that he was in bed with a female friend "when all of a sudden I was awakened by the person I was with. Then I saw Anna.

"She had broken into my house and jumped on the bed and started pulling the girl's hair out.

"The girl, terrified, beat it. Then Anna started wrecking the house. I let her do it. I thought it would be good to let her get it out of her system. The house was rented and I didn't own the furniture anyhow, and it was all insured.

"Then Anna heard the taxi drive up which the girl had called and Anna ran down to try and catch the girl. I followed along, with Anna biting me, hitting me, scratching me, and swearing at me.

"Finally I said: 'Anna, this is enough. Go home.'

"She refused, so I took her and turned her over and spanked her as hard as I could. I put her in her car and hid behind a wall as she drove off. I went back to the house and locked all the doors.

"It wasn't long until she came back again and threw a log through the window and started wrecking the house all over again."

Anna herself would later tell the court that, "I came up to Marlon's house, found the door open, went up to the bedroom and found a nude girl in bed with Mr. Brando. They both jumped on me. Furniture started flying. I'm not strong enough to fight two people, so I ran."

"HE JUST WANTED AN EXCUSE TO BE A LITTLE BOY"

On the eve of beginning *The Fugitive Kind,* he focused his attention now on France Nuyen. She told Brando biographer Charles Higham that he insisted they travel in disguise. "I lost count," she said, "of the false noses, wigs, makeup, false names, and accents we both had to use, most of which failed to work with the paparazzi. I even wore blond wigs, which looked ridiculous on my Asian head." Once, posing as "Dr. Miles Graham of Omaha" Brando wore a false nose. "He wasn't so much afraid of the press," Nuyen recalled, "he just wanted an excuse to be a big little boy and dress up and be someone else and see how long he could fool everybody."

They traveled in disguise to Haiti, but to Marlon's chagrin they were greeted in Port-au-Prince by a brass band and a banner saying "Welcome Marlon Brando." Eager to soak up the culture, he arranged for them to attend a voodoo ritual. They traveled in a tiny, rickety plane into the mountains. "I was petrified, thinking we would crash at any minute as we jolted through air pockets," Nuyen told Higham. "I clung to him in fear. All I remember of the voodoo ceremony was fire, and drums, and dances."

When Brando and Nuyen arrived in Miami after their two-week vacation, they were besieged by reporters. France tried to beat them off with her purse. Photographs of her attacking the photographers made news around the world.

Back in Hollywood, Brando became embroiled in more battles with Anna Kashfi. On November 28, they were back in court. Judge Aggeler ruled that Marlon could visit Christian three days a week from 5:00 P.M. to 7:00 P.M. and that Anna could not be present during these visits. But when Anna took off for London with Christian, Brando went back to court, charging that she had violated the order.

Marlon arrived at her home on Christmas day 1959 with presents for his son. Anna ordered him off her property. In his subsequent complaint, he charged that, "Anna became emotionally disturbed when she saw me and my companion and heaped vilification upon us. She deprived me of the opportunity of seeing my son, and slammed the door against me. I put my Christmas gifts on the front porch and left."

Anna herself admitted that she barred him from her home that Christmas, insisting she had court permission to have "undisturbed enjoyment" of the boy that day.

His companion was actress Barbara Luna. France Nuyen was filming *The World of Suzie Wong*. Reportedly distraught over the collapse of her relationship with Brando, she was dismissed from the film and replaced by Nancy Kwan.

Five

Sayonara, Etc.

"Marlon's the most exciting person I've met since Garbo."

—Joshua Logan

Veteran producer-director Joshua Logan (Picnic, Bus Stop) had been looking for years for a story that would try to explain the East to the West and vice versa. Michener's romantic tale of a Korean War pilot (Brando) who falls in love with a Japanese entertainer (Seattle-born Miiko Taka) struck him as one that contained a lot of fascinating information about Japan and Japanese culture. Now he and producer Bill Goetz were going to co-produce it. They agreed that they wanted Brando for the lead.

Brando said he would be willing to discuss the subject, but warned them that he didn't like the book's patronizing attitude to the Japanese. But he saw a chance to send a message about racial tolerance. It was also a chance to revisit Japan.

Logan assured him that screenwriter Paul Osborn would change all that. Brando accepted a salary of $300,000 and a percentage of the gross.

Brando arrived in Tokyo on January 12, 1956, to begin filming. The film returned to California that April and he balanced relationships between Kashfi and Rita Moreno who had visited him in Japan.

Marie Cui also visited him in Kyoto.

As usual, Brando was up to his childish practical jokes. He nearly gave director Josh Logan a heart attack. "There were just a few days left when he came to work with his right arm in a heavy sling. Broken. Marlon told me. We would have had to close down."

It was Brando's idea of a joke. He laughed and laughed. Logan did not laugh with him.

But after working with Brando for two weeks, Logan raved: "Marlon's the most exciting person I've met since Garbo. A genius. But I don't know what he's like. I don't know anything about him."

There were also the first hints of problems to come. The weight was becoming an issue. Told he had to lose ten pounds before filming, Brando had managed to trim off seven by the time he arrived in Kyoto, only to gain that back and seven more. By the end of filming, his weight was approaching two hundred pounds.

Sayonara opened in New York in November 1957. The *New Yorker* critic, noting that Carlo Fiore was credited as Brando's dialogue coach, wrote that, "Instead of mumbling along in his customary Middle Western style, Mr. Brando, under the guidance of Mr. Fiore, mumbles along with a corn-pone-and-chitlin accent that seems absolutely legitimate, even to the generic drawback of occasionally—particularly when he is cracking jokes—making him sound like the end man in a minstrel show." According to Fiore, Brando was not as distressed at the slam as at the fact that the *New Yorker* had credited Fiore—not him—with devising the accent. *Time's* reviewer wrote that his accent sounded "strained through Stanislavsky's mustache."

Sayonara was a huge financial success and nominated for nine Academy Awards, including Best Picture, Best Screenplay and Marlon's third nomination for Best Actor.

TRUMAN CAPOTE

Over the objections of Joshua Logan, Brando agreed to be interviewed by Truman Capote for *The New Yorker* while the *Sayonara* company was filming in Kyoto. Afterwards, realizing that he had opened up too much, Brando sent Capote a lengthy letter pleading with him to delete all references to friends and family. Capote never replied and his interview finally ran in October 1957, weeks before the film's premiere. The portrait "The Duke in His Domain," was devastating and Brando felt betrayed. The incident would shape his attitude to print media and he would in the future avoid those interviews.

Years later, Capote himself said: "Though not claiming any inaccuracy, he apparently felt it was an unsympathetic, even treacherous intrusion upon the secret terrain of a suffering and intellectually awesome sensibility. My opinion? Just that it is a pretty good account, and a sympathetic one, of a wounded young man who is a genius, but not markedly intelligent."

THE YOUNG LIONS

By the time Anna Kashfi was giving birth to their son, Brando was deep into the making of *The Young Lions,* a film for which he had "higher hopes for this than I have had for any picture I have ever done."

Brando soon clashed with his co-star Montgomery Clift. From the beginning Brando had made it clear that his Nazi officer would be a sensitive, sympathetic character. Clift, on the other hand, was playing a Jewish GI who is the martyr of the story.

His co-star was Maximilian Schell, a Swiss who could not speak a word of English and played the entire role by memorizing the language phonetically.

Six

Brando Directs!
One-Eyed Jacks

"With this film I intend to storm the citadel of cliches."
—Marlon Brando

Pennebaker Productions had spent an impressive amount of money but had so far not yielded any great roles for Brando.

Paramount had turned down Brando's beloved *Burst of Vermillion* project, but he had not lost his enthusiasm for doing a serious western. Producer Frank P. Rosenberg brought a script to his attention. It was an adaptation by then-unknown television writer Sam Peckinpah of Charles Neider's novel *The Authentic Death of Henry Jones*. Brando liked the basic story but called in Calder Willingham to totally re-write the script. He still didn't like the results, which by that time had been renamed *One-Eyed Jacks*.

The new title appealed to Brando because it had a double meaning: in poker, the two one-eyed jacks are usually wild cards, just as to Brando, "some men show only one side of themselves, and they're wild."

Numerous story conferences among Brando, Willingham, and the director Brando had hired, Stanley Kubrick, followed. (Brando had admired Kubrick's *Paths of Glory* and *The Killing*.) Willingham was soon discarded.

Recognizing that Brando wanted to control the picture, Kubrick left the project and Brando decided to direct it himself.

Production began in Monterey on December 2, 1958. Although he was a first-time director, he showed no lack of confidence.

"It's been trying," he acknowledged. "The first few days were very difficult, but it improves as we go along. I work fourteen hours a day. Directing by itself is hard enough. But I've found that there are no divisional lines between an actor becoming a director. Things are so subtly interlaced it is hard to know where one begins and the other ends.

"I've directed myself to a large extent in most of the pictures I have been in," he added. "My most difficult role was Sakini in *Teahouse of the August Moon*. I don't think I did it well at all. In *Guys and Dolls* I wanted to effect a frothy farce style, but I'm heavy-footed with high comedy. I liked *The Young Lions,* but I wish I could have done it better. I gave up in the middle of *The Wild One* because I was discouraged and disgusted. It was depressing and fruitless. I think I liked *On the Waterfront* and *Sayonara."*

Producer Frank P. Rosenberg went to Mexico City to find Brando a leading lady. His star-director had only one requirement. "No tits," he ordered. "I don't want my leading lady heaving big boobs on that wide screen while I'm trying to get an important point across to my audience."

Rosenberg discovered Pina Pellicer in Mexico City that August where she was appearing in a Spanish-language production of *The Diary of Anne Frank*. Jet-haired, tawny-eyed Pellicer was promoted as "Hollywood's new Cinderella." And *Jacks* publicists announced that "with no prior screen experience, she had been selected from hundreds of actresses. But to Fiore, "She was like an exposed nerve, thin, frightened, and full of a kind of anger." She kept her distance from everyone but Brando.

Brando began an affair with her. "I was afraid when I began to work for him," Pellicer said in an interview. "I am still afraid when I go on the set, but I try to do the best I can. Mr. Brando is very kind and patient with me. He is that way with everybody. He takes as much time with an extra as he does with the stars, and he is teaching me many things about acting."

Brando approached his first directorial effort with gusto. "With this film I intend to storm the citadel of cliches," he announced.

One-Eyed Jacks is a classic revenge story. Brando plays a bandit whose only purpose in life is to kill his former partner, now a border town sheriff. Karl Malden played the partner, Kathy Jurado, the wife, and Pina Pellicer, the daughter.

Filming began at Big Sur and Monterey and at the end of the first day of filming they were five days behind schedule. After Christmas they moved to Death Valley. There Brando met Red Arrow who taught him to use a bow and arrow and may have begun his interest in the American Indian movement.

Journalist Joe Hyams, one of the few reporters Brando trusted, was on the *Jacks* set to observe personally Brando's directorial style. One scene called for Malden to punish Brando for getting into a shoot-out by tying him to a hitching post and flogging him with a horse-whip. When director Brando couldn't get the right reaction of shock and horror that he wanted from the crowd of extras, he convinced Malden to fake a heart attack. The reaction still wasn't right.

He offered $200 for the best performance by an extra, with himself to be the judge. But the scene still wasn't right. He increased the prize to $300. Still not enough shock and horror. He resorted to a lecture on acting: "Very often," he said, "it's beneficial to bring in something from your own life. . . . It can help. . . . Pray, perhaps just try and feel something . . . revulsion, pity, something. There'll be a couple of minutes of silence. . . . Remember, the best acting comes from preparation."

As Brando lectured, the cameras slowly panned the extras, searching each face. He continued: "One of the old cliches, they say, is that there are no small parts, only small actors. It happens to be true. Some of the best performances given are the small touches, the vignettes. 'Let it come out of you now . . . don't hold the emotion back . . . let it flow. If you hate this sight of a man being horsewhipped, hate it. . . . If you like, really enjoy it. If you're sorry, let your heart break. Think it, really feel it, make it a part of your own life." Brando stopped talking and called "Cut." Then he declared, "That was wonderful. . . . I really applaud you all." Ironically, one young extra became so hysterical she could not be calmed for twenty minutes.

But this personal approach cost money and a picture originally budgeted at a generous $1.8 million soared to almost $6 million. Filming finished June 1959, having taking six months instead of the originally planned sixty days.

Brando's "first cut" lasted six hours. When Brando showed his final version running four hours and forty minutes to Frank Rosenberg, the producer emerged speechless. Marlon pressed for his opinion of the picture. "What picture?" said Rosenberg. "That's not a picture, Marlon, it's just an assembly of footage."

By the time Brando would finish editing *Jacks* and the picture was released, he would have already begun and completed the starring role in another picture, *The Fugitive Kind.*

When *One-Eyed Jacks* was finally released on March 30, 1961, it ran two hours and twenty minutes. *Time* magazine called it "just a big, slick commercial horse opera. The film, to be sure is meticulously produced, directed, acted, and edited, and is often startlingly beautiful to see." *Newsweek* called it "one of the most intriguing westerns ever made."

Typically, Brando distanced himself from it, labeling it a "potboiler," and stating: "It is not an artistic success. I'm a businessman. I'm a captain of industry—nothing less than that. Any pretension I've sometimes had of being artistic is now just a long, chilly hope. *One-Eyed Jacks* is a product like—a news item. News makes money, not art. Movies are not art."

Pina Pellicer received the Best International Actress award at San Sebastian for her work in *One-Eyed Jacks,* and returned to Mexico City where she appeared in two

Mexican films before committing suicide in December 1964.

"WHEN I WORK WITH HIM IT IS LIKE I WORK WITH A STRANGE ANIMAL THAT IS READY TO POUNCE."

Brando was soon deep into plans to film Tennessee Williams's *Orpheus Descending*. Williams had written the play with Brando and Anna Magnani in mind for the leads. But Brando had turned down the role of Val Xavier, who drifts into a Southern town and romances a middle-aged woman and a rebellious young girl several times.

"I can explain very easily why I didn't do *Orpheus,*" he said. "There are beautiful things in it, some of Tennessee's best writing, and the Magnani part is great; she stands for something, you can understand her—and she would wipe me off the stage. The character I was supposed to play, this boy, this Val, he never takes a stand. I really didn't know what he was for or against. Well, you can't act in a vacuum. I told Tennessee. So he kept trying. He rewrote it for me, maybe a couple of times. But—well, I had no intention of walking out on any stage with Magnani. Not in that part. They'd have to mop me up. I think—in fact, I'm sure—Tennessee had a fixed association between me and Kowalski. I mean, we're friends and he knows that as a person I am just the opposite of Kowalski, who was everything I'm against— totally insensitive, crude, cruel. But still Tennessee's image of me is confused with the fact that I played that part. So I don't know if he could write for me in a different color range. . . . There aren't any parts for me on the stage. Nobody writes them."

Yet Brando finally agreed to take the role of Val Xavier, a man described as "the fugitive kind—the kind that don't belong no place at all." Brando was stressed out and burdened with financial worries from *One-Eyed Jacks* and his divorce. His agent, Jay Kanter, aware that Brando needed money, approached producers Martin Jurow and Richard Shepherd. They offered Brando one million dollars to star in the screen version of Williams's play, now re-titled *The Futitive Kind* and also starring Magnani.

In the beginning, the two stars approached each other cautiously. "When I work with him it is like I work with a strange animal that is ready to pounce," said Magnani. "Yet it is a wonderful experience to see him be so realistic . . . so completely all man."

Brando was equally enthusiastic: "This explosive woman is the type I like to play opposite," he said. "She is real. Of course she is crazy like me and we have our differences. But actors have a way of understanding these things. We forget very quickly."

Filming of *The Fugitive Kind* began in Milton, New York, near Poughkeepsie, in July 1959, with Sidney Lumet directing, and a cast that also included Joanne Woodward as a wayward rich girl and Maureen Stapleton as the mousy wife of the bullying sheriff.

Seven

Brando Enters Tabloid Inferno

"Most people don't know it, but there's money in gossip."
—Marlon Brando

The 1960s would be marked by a debilitating and distracting custody battle for his son Christian, a devastating experience with the filming of *Mutiny on the Bounty,* and finally, a measure of self-empowerment when he committed himself to the struggle for civil rights. But the stress took a toll physically and his weight ballooned to 195 pounds.

"BRANDO SAYS EX SHUTS THE SON OUT OF HIS EYES"

The first shot in the Brando vs. Kashfi custody battle was fired on January 8, 1960, when Brando obtained a court order directing his former wife to show cause why she should not be held in contempt of court. He filed a nine-page affidavit charging that she "willfully violated" his visiting rights with their eighteen-month-old son. He also charged that she had "heaped vilifications" upon him and his female companion on Christmas Eve.

Back in Los Angeles that February, he and France Nuyen made a hurried exit after newsmen discovered them on a midnight date at the New Ginza cafe, a Japanese nightclub in the Little Tokyo section. To a customer's question of "Where's Barbara Luna tonight?" Brando did not even grunt.

In June Anna filed a complaint that Marlon had "misjudged the best interests of our child," and charged him with acts that "tended to degrade himself and his family in society," earning "public contempt and scorn and ridicule." During one hearing she retreated to the courthouse ladies' room and refused to come out. She charged that Marlon was "an immoral man" and he countered that she had refused eight times to let him see his son. He was granted additional visiting time. Outside she screamed, "You criminal! You slob!" That summer, Marlon married Movita in Mexico. (Court papers filed when they were divorcing indicated that Brando married Movita on June 4, 1960.) She later gave birth to his son Michael, whom they nicknamed "Miko."

A STRANGE RELEVATION

The following October, Brando sent Anna a telegram asking her to come to Tahiti with Christian. "I vaguely remember," Brando acknowledged when questioned on the stand, "I think I asked her to come out with the baby."

Anna received the message and replied that she could not go because Brando already had "a family" there.

WALLY COX

There were rumors Brando had leaped into the marriage to Movita to dispel rumors about his close relationship with Wally Cox.

"THE SECRET WIFE OF MARLON BRANDO"

Before leaving for Tahiti for location shooting of *Mutiny on the Bounty,* Brando ducked rumors that he had married Movita. "I will neither confirm nor deny it," he said.

In April, Anna revealed that Brando had married Movita and was the father of a nine-month-old son. Anna appeared in court to answer Brando's charges that she refused to allow him to visit Christian, now three years old. Brando, stuck in Tahiti filming *Bounty,* did not appear in court himself.

"Marlon told me weeks ago that he was secretly married to Movita and that they had a baby," she said. "He also asked for my help, saying he was going to get a divorce from her. Marlon wanted to know if I would allow his new baby to visit with our son, Devi. I told him I would have to think it over."

Anna said that Marlon had told her the name of the new baby, but she had forgotten it. "I still haven't made up my mind about letting the children visit one another," she said.

Newspapers were full of stories of "The Secret Wife of Marlon Brando."

ANNA SLAPS BRANDO'S FACE

The next bitter court hearing came in late December in Santa Monica Superior Court. In an affidavit Anna charged that her former husband had ideas "contrary to present established society." During the hearing, Brando, his hair long and slicked back in a tight ponytail for his role in *Bounty,* testified that he was "tired of always playing the heavy" in the prolonged court squabbles with Anna over his son. On December 28 Judge Benjamin Landis ruled that Brando could have Christian every third weekend in addition to the twice weekly visitations previously permitted. He also gave the actor added summer visiting rights.

Outraged, Anna waited for him outside and delivered a stinging slap across his face when he emerged from the courtroom. Reports said that "the sound of the blow was like a pistol shot in the corridor." Brando ducked to avoid another slap and hurried away without saying a word.

Anna turned to photographers who had recorded the scene and remarked: "Don't ever say I didn't give you a good picture."

All the publicity about Anna and Brando upset Movita. She announced that Hollywood was not a fit place to raise children and returned to Mexico in April. But she and Brando remained on good terms.

"MOST PEOPLE DON'T KNOW IT, BUT THERE'S MONEY IN GOSSIP"

On April 19, Brando tried to put his message out with an exclusive interview on the *Today Show* with Hugh Downs.

Brando lashed out at what he called "irresponsible sections of the press" which sought to "exploit your personal life for money."

Declaring that he had been "demeaned and maligned in a lot of ways," Brando said he felt that his remarks and his position had sometimes been distorted because he tried to avoid contact with those publications and writers that dealt primarily in gossip.

"Most people don't know it," he said, "but there's money in gossip, it's a multimillion-dollar industrial complex.

"If you don't kowtow, if you don't call up every time you get an attack of gas," he said, ". . . you don't describe the most intimate details of your life, and when you presume to keep some vestige of self-respect and independence, you are considered an enemy of the people by Hollywood columnists and people like Dorothy Kilgallen."

Brando also attacked *Time* magazine, saying the publication apparently maintained a "blacklist" of people it didn't like, and that this list seemed to influence the magazine's reviews of their work.

"I won't see any *Time* correspondent because I don't like the magazine," he said, "and I think it misrepresents the news unfairly and often dangerously," he said.

Brando's appearance on the *Today Show* was just part of a five week media blitz during which he logged more than 30,000 miles in what one columnist called "the town's most talked about about-face since Garbo clammed up."

Perhaps recognizing that he had kept himself cooped up for too long, Brando had set out to set the record straight.

The promotional tour for *The Ugly American* became a personal mission, an opportunity to show that he was not a monster or libertine at all, but a serious man with serious concerns.

Brando took to the skies to cooperate in endless press conferences from Bangkok to Hong Kong, Tokyo, Honolulu, Boston, Chicago, New York, and Washington, D.C.

Besides the *Today Show,* he appeared on the *David Susskind Show* and a full four-hour session with Chicago talk-show host Irv Kupcinet.

BRANDO, FLAT ON HIS BACK, IS HIT WITH PATERNITY SUIT

But his image-repair campaign took another hit when on July 20, while he was confined to his bed in St. John's Hospital in Santa Monica, where he was suffering from a kidney ailment, Brando was slapped with a paternity suit.

Maria Cui was suing him, claiming that he was the father of her five-month-old daughter and that he refused to see her after he discovered she was pregnant.

A slim, 25-year-old dancer from the Philippines, Maria Cui charged that she had met Brando in Los Angeles, while he was filming *The Ugly American,* but when she found out she was going to have a baby he merely referred her to his doctor and would have nothing more to do with her.

She returned to Manila where her daughter, who she named Maya Gabriela Brando, was born on February 27, 1963.

"Marie used to be the typical geisha-type, quiet and subservient," her attorney, Bernard B. Cohen, said, "but now she's a woman scorned. She's alone with the baby in a little apartment on Sunset Strip and she's angry. She insists she wasn't intimate with any other man during the period of conception."

On August 6 a judge dismissed the paternity suit. Blood tests showed that Brando could not be the father of her daughter, Cui's attorney said. He added, "Under California law, this requires us to dismiss the action, which has been done."

Yet Brando's behavior remained puzzling: "Brando said 'Hello, Marie' in the hospital when his blood was being tested Monday like nothing happened," her attorney reported, "and two hours after we got the results he called her and said none of this business would make any difference."

Her lawyer told the press that in the past, when Brando wanted to reach Cui in Manila, he would send a cable from Hollywood which read: "Call an American at _____"

"Brando would put whatever unlisted number he was at and wait."

After a moment, the lawyer added: "You know, it's just possible he hasn't sent her the last cable like that."

According to Brando biographer Charles Higham, Cui

later remarried, but continued to claim that Brando was the father of her child.

April 19, 1961, Rita Moreno made headlines when she took an overdose of sleeping pills at the home of Brando's secretary, Alice Marshak. Marshak took her to Brando's house. He wasn't home, but they went inside and called a doctor. An ambulance soon arrived and rushed Moreno to a hospital. Doctors pumped her stomach and released her. The incident was widely reported as a suicide attempt.

Three days later, Brando and Moreno reunited to discuss their relationship. According to Charles Higham, "while they were driving it began to rain, Marlon lost control of the wheel, and they ran off the road. Rita's head smashed against the dashboard, and her face was cut severely." She said: "When I got to the emergency room, I was bloody and hysterical. The nurses almost had me calmed down when a bunch of photographers surged into the cubicle, shouting questions, popping flashbulbs. I was screaming, fighting them out of the room . . ." Later, after another quarrel with Brando, she slashed her wrists. To rid her life of the specter of Marlon Brando, she entered psychotherapy.

"PLEASE COME TO MY HOUSE. MOMMY IS SICK"

Although she fought tirelessly for custody of her son, Anna was not totally successful as a mother. Christian attended a Montessori pre-school run by Tom Laughlin and Delores Taylor, later famous as the team behind *Billy Jack*. Recently they recalled their experiences with five-year-old Christian. Taylor told of rushing to Kashfi's house one day after receiving a call from a neighbor, and discovering the little boy standing alone at the edge of the swimming pool. Inside the house she found Kashfi, "passed out, lying in her own vomit."

A year later, on December 7, 1964, Anna Kashfi was rushed to the emergency ward of the UCLA hospital. Brando informed the press that his former wife had suffered injuries in a fall, but Los Angeles police told a different story.

They said that shortly after midnight six-year-old Christian called police and pleaded: "Please come to my house. Mommy is sick."

On arriving at Kashfi's Brentwood home, they found her "incoherent." Rather than turn the child over to juvenile authorities, the police called Brando who took charge of Christian. At the hospital, a doctor diagnosed Kashfi's condition as "a possible overdose of barbiturates," police said.

Brando would later testify in court that Anna talked officials at the medical center into letting her leave. She then turned up at Mulholland Drive with a gun. Brando testified that she "broke into my house, assaulted and struck my secretary, threw a table through a plate glass window and ran off with our son."

In his subsequent petition for custody Brando charged that Anna "keeps a fully loaded revolver in her home and carries it around and plays with it while under the influence of barbiturates . . . She is capable of doing great physical harm to herself and our son."

Within hours Brando had obtained a court order granting him custody of Christian. But when he went to Anna's home, both mother and child were gone.

Christian's disappearance set off a dramatic search throughout Los Angeles. They were found at the Bel-Air Sands Hotel in Brentwood.

Police knocked at the door of Anna's two-room suite.

The door was opened by Anna's maid, Mercedes Lucar, and Brando and his attorney and police and private investigators entered the room. They presented Anna with the custody papers. She ripped them up. Brando took Christian and left.

Then, according to a witness, "Miss Kashfi became hysterical when she realized the child was gone. She screamed obscenities and ran through the halls dressed in her nightgown and robe screaming: 'I want my child.'

"She ran down to the manager's office and threatened to sue him. Then she hit him. She also hit the private investigator."

According to the police officer: "When I tried to restrain her, she hit me in the face. I put cuffs on her and arrested her."

Still dressed in her pink nightgown and white robe and wearing thirty-four bracelets on her left arm, Anna Kashfi was taken to the West Los Angeles police station to be booked for assaulting a police officer. After she was released on $276 bail, she posed for a photographer, showing off the bruises on her arm which, she said, she incurred during her ride to jail in the police car.

THE NEW BRANDO . . . BUT AN OLD PROBLEM

Reporters began to note evidence of a "new Brando," as he sought to polish up his image before he went back to court on December 22 to seek permanent custody of his oldest son.

The following February, the battling Brandos made their fourteenth appearance in Santa Monica Superior Court to decide custody of their child. Brando testified that "on one occasion she attempted to stab me; this occurred in front of the boy. On several other occasions, she threatened to kill me, the child, and herself." A psychologist testified that Christian had become "a tense, fearful, terrorized youngster who is very hypersensitive and is unable to maintain attention or relate well to most adults. . . ."

Representatives from Christian's Montessori school testified that he was, "emotionally disturbed, totally incapable of facing reality, experiencing behavior problems, and working far below his intellectual potential."

"He was working far below his intellectual potential because most of the disintelligence was being channeled off to motor activities," testified one instructor. Tom Laughlin, principal, testified that, "since Mr. Brando took custody of the boy in December, there has been a behavior change that is marvelous. He is simply a different boy."

Citing Kashfi's dependence on prescription drugs and alcohol, the judge placed Christian temporarily with Brando's sister Frances Loving and her husband. The boy went to live on their farm in Mundelein, Illinois.

An outraged Anna told reporters outside the courtroom, "This baby is my whole life. I bore him. Where in hell was Marlon Brando when the child was being brought up? I am not through fighting. I will subpoena the judge and the whole goddamned court."

Frances Loving later told Brando biographer Charles Higham that Christian was "a charming little devil of a kid. His main impulse in life was to win over the adults to his side. When you caught on to that, it encouraged him to try harder."

Brando was marked by the first public revelation that he was the father of a child born out of wedlock. When Alice Marchak was forced to take the stand, Anna's attorney asked her: "Mr. Brando has another child, hasn't he?"

"Yes," she answered.

"What is his name?"

"Tehotu."

"Do you know who the mother of this child is?"

"Yes, it is Tarita."

Simple enough statements, but the revelation Brando had committed the then-shocking sin of fathering a child out of wedlock made headlines.

The situation was even more complicated, for he was still married to Movita Castenada, and the father of *her* son, Miko.

"BRANDO TESTIFIES HE MARRIED BOTH WIVES IN A FAMILY WAY"

Brando himself made headlines when he testified that both of his wives were pregnant when he married them and that he was the father of a child born out of wedlock to Tarita.

Testifying in a hesitant monotone, he stated that he had married Anna Kashfi with "the primary purpose of getting a divorce within a year." As for Movita, mother of his No. 2 son, Miko, now five, he stated that he had not lived with her since marrying her and "I've had no sex relations with her since the baby was conceived." He further stated that Tarita's son, Tehotu, now two years old, was also his.

"Tarita stayed with me [in Los Angeles] on numerous occasions and I have explained to Christian that Tehotu was his brother," he said.

This was heady stuff for Americans in 1965, but it got even wilder.

"I HAVE LADIES IN MY HOME FOR MANY PURPOSES, INCLUDING SEXUAL"

Anna's attorney asked Brando if he was in the habit of having ladies in his home for sexual purposes.

"I have ladies in my home for many purposes, including sexual, but I would not like to give the impression that people are invited to my home primarily for sexual reasons," he said.

Anna, wearing a white fox turban and a tailored suit, stared fixedly at her ex-husband as he recounted previous violent episodes such as the time in 1959 when she found him in his bedroom with a female friend and "started wrecking the house."

Later, when she took the stand to give her own version of events, she testified that Brando had urged her to go to Hawaii for the birth of their son. "He told me," she said, "since you are an Indian and I am an American, how in hell do I know what color he's going to come out?" She also testified why she did not want Christian to visit Tarita and Brando's No. 3 son, Tehotu in Tahiti: "It's very disturbing with illegitimate children and mistresses."

But the bulk of the testimony was ultimately more damaging for Anna. Her own doctor testified that she had a history of epileptic seizures, saying: "She has a wide, swinging personality—episodes of deep depression to normal elation, all with hysterical overtones."

The judge put Anna on probation for six months and ruled that she should have psychological and neurological care. "Unfortunately . . . she is not well," he said. "Miss Kashfi's reliance on drugs and alcohol contributed to her uncontrollable temper," the judge declared. "With her own problems I feel that she will have enough trouble taking care of herself, let alone taking care of her son." Anna, tears streaming from her dark eyes, dashed from the courtroom, slamming the door behind her.

In July 1965 Anna went on trial for assault and battery for attacking the policeman at the Bel Air Sands Hotel. A reluctant Brando was forced to testify and said that his ex-wife suffered from "psycho-neuroses, which at times caused hysterical blindness . . . barbiturate poisoning . . . occasional malnutrition . . . a psychological and physical addiction to barbiturates, alcohol, and suffered from tuberculosis." Anna was convicted and sentenced to pay a two-hundred dollar fine or spend thirty days in jail. She paid the fine.

BRANDO LOSES CUSTODY OF HIS SON

On October 2 Anna was vindicated. Superior Court Judge A.A. Scott awarded her custody and said: "If this lady is left to lead her own life with her own son and without fights and obnoxious matters put in her way, she will be a good mother." In returning custody to Anna, the judge ordered that Brando be given reasonable visitation rights. He warned Anna and Marlon that if they could not agree on visitation days for Brando, he would set them himself.

According to columnist Sheila Graham, Brando once boasted that he could have any woman he wanted. It was probably true. But it is one thing to have an affair, and quite another to have a good relationship with a woman or a happy marriage.

"WHAT DOESN'T WORK OUT AS A MARRIAGE SOMETIMES SHAPES UP ALL RIGHT AS A RELATIONSHIP BETWEEN A MAN AND A WOMAN"

In June 1967 Movita filed for divorce, charging Brando with causing her "great mental suffering," and asking $5,000 per month for herself and $3,000 per month for her two children, Miko and Rebecca.

Movita stated: "Marlon is a nice guy, but he'll never change. He can't help being what he is. I'm just tired of sitting alone all the time. I want to go out and have a little fun in life."

The marriage was annulled in 1968, on the grounds

that Movita was still legally married to her first husband. Brando continued to pay alimony and child support and he and Movita remained on friendly terms. At that time it was revealed that Brando and Movita had a second child, a daughter Rebecca, then two years old.

If his relationship with Anna Kashfi was a disaster, Brando was more successful in maintaining cordial relations with his second ex-wife, Movita. "What didn't work out as a marriage," said Brando, "sometimes shapes up all right as just a relationship between a man and a woman.

"I still want to be with Movita and she with me. Nobody seems to have any objection, so we'll keep seeing each other. I find her very good for me. She's a very understanding woman. A lot of times when I was blue, she'd bring me out of it. I still feel quite a bit for her."

Eight

The Turkey Parade

"The nadir of my creative resources has been reached."

—Marlon Brando, on the ordeal of filming
Mutiny on the Bounty.

By April 1960, when *The Fugitive Kind* opened, Brando
was deep in discussions about his next project, a remake
of the 1935 epic, *Mutiny on the Bounty.* Brando was
scheduled to play Fletcher Christian and Trevor Howard
would play Captain Bligh. The film would be shot in Tahiti, produced by Aaron Rosenberg, directed by Sir Carol
Reed.

The idea of a group of simple, sympathetic sailors who
mutiny when subjected to the brutality of Captain Bligh
appealed to Brando, as did the tragic ending: the muti-
neers sail to Tahiti only to destroy themselves within two-
and-a-half years.

On October 15, Rosenberg arrived in Tahiti with a
company of more than a hundred people, at a cost of

roughly fifty thousand dollars a day, but with no script. Neither Rosenberg, Brando nor MGM liked Eric Ambler's script. Charles Lederer was brought in to revise and complete the screenplay. Meanwhile, there was no H.M.S. Bounty. Construction delays would delay its arrival for two more months.

Although Brando arrived in Papeete, Tahiti, on November 28, shooting did not begin until December 4. With time on their hands, crew members befriended local females and Brando himself took up with Tarita Teriipaia, a beautiful Chinese-Tahitian waitress, 19, who had a small part in the film. By then Tahiti was in the middle of rainy season and after a few wet weeks the entire company was ordered back to the MGM studios in Hollywood. Brando had brought Tarita back and she was staying at the Bel Air Sands Hotel.

Next, Sir Carol clashed with Rosenberg over his conception of Captain Bligh. Sir Carol Reed was fired and replaced by Lewis Milestone, who had directed *All Quiet on the Western Front*.

Shooting resumed February 11, but the *Bounty* company did not return to Tahiti until March. Production dragged on for the next four months, and in October, when the final scene, Christian's death, was shot at the MGM studio, Milestone sat in his dressing room while Brando himself directed the scene.

"THE NADIR OF MY CREATIVE RESOURCES HAS BEEN REACHED"

But *Bounty* was rapidly becoming one of the most controversial as well as most expensive movies in film history. It was now estimated that the final tab would be $18 million, which, as journalist Joe Hyams put it, was "enough to run Tahiti for the next six years."

In the eighteen months that *Bounty* had been before the cameras, there had been thirty different screenplays plus five separate versions of Brando's character, Fletcher Christian.

MGM contended that Sir Carol was dismissed because he was too slow and at a production cost of $32,000 a day the budget would have been staggering. Brando contended that Sir Carol "couldn't in all conscience go ahead without a full concept of the nature of the story, so he delayed shooting crucial scenes."

There were other rumors, however, that Brando himself had insisted that Sir Carol be removed. These stories so disturbed Brando that he called an evening meeting in the office of Sol Siegel, head of MGM, with the director, producer Aaron Rosenberg, and agents for the people involved.

"I told Sir Carol the meeting was to be called because his agent had been told I was responsible for his being fired," Brando recalled. "It was decided then and there in that room that Sol Siegel fired him, not me. That was the first incident of blame-shifting."

Brando also called a meeting of the other members of the cast, and with Sir Carol present, said: "I don't give a damn what the press says about me concerning this matter, but I do care what you people think." Brando was in a difficult position: he was fond of Aaron Rosenberg and Sir Carol, but their argument with the studio did not concern him and he had nothing to do with the studio's decision.

Sir Carol's dismissal was the first public hint of trouble on the *Bounty* set.

By now the shooting script was a complete reversal of the picture Brando had signed up for. Since he had a contractual "right of consultation," he believed that the studio was in breach-of-contract. Still, he had gone ahead with the film because "I visualize the fight as hopeless."

"HE WOULD PUT EAR PLUGS IN SO THAT HE COULDN'T HEAR MY DIRECTION"

There were also stories that Brando did not get along with his new director. "Before he would take direction," Milestone complained, "he would ask why. Then, when the scene was being shot, he would put ear plugs in so that he couldn't hear my direction." One MGM executive on the set acknowledged that Brando did not pay much attention to Milestone. "But then," he added, "no one else did either."

In late September, Brando was summoned to a meeting with Sol Siegel. Siegel threatened to sue his star for throwing his performance in *Mutiny* in an effort to force the studio to accept his ending of the picture rather than theirs. This was the final break in Brando's relations with Siegel.

"THERE'S ONLY ONE COMPENSATING FEATURE—I WENT TO TAHITI"

"My version of the ending is not available to them under any circumstances and I have never worked harder in a picture in all my life," he told journalist Joe Hyams. "When my agents told me the result of the meeting with

Siegel my morale cracked. The nadir of my creative resources has been reached. Obviously the studio is going out after me to lay the blame for this fascinating saga of failure at my feet.

"From the beginning they've been blaming me and I've been the goat. But I'm not going to be without a few butts back."

After Siegel threatened to sue him, Brando declared: "I wanted them to offer some reasonable solution to this impending disaster. I have had five different character attitudes in the film and in the final one my character dies a slow death of ambiguity and inconsistency. On top of everything else I find I'm being blamed generally for the total disaster. There's only one compensating feature in the year and a half I feel I must write off as an actor—I went to Tahiti."

Brando would later acknowledge his own part in *Bounty*'s problems. "Sure, I staged my own rebellion," he told columnist James Bacon, "But it was an artistic rebellion—the only kind an actor can stage. There is one simple fact—MGM sent a full company to Tahiti at a cost of $32,000 a day at a time when neither the script nor the ship itself was finished.

"When the ship (costing $750,000) finally arrived, we were in the midst of the monsoon season. Those decisions were not mine.

"Several top executives who made those decisions are no longer with MGM. I still am. There's a lesson to be learned there."

He even admitted to wearing the ear plugs during his scenes. "Acting is an illusion, a form of histrionic sleight-of-hand, and in order to carry it off well, an actor must have intense concentration.

"Before I go into a scene, I study it, almost psycho-analyze it, and then I discuss it with the director, then rehearse it.

"When the actual shooting commences, I put in ear plugs to screen out the extraneous noises that inevitably prick at one's concentration."

It was probably *Bounty* and the resultant publicity that did the most to damage Brando's reputation and saddle him with the reputation for being profligate and undisciplined.

Brando recognized that the bad press surrounding *Bounty* could damage his career and bankability, and characteristically he went to a friend in the media to put out his side of the story.

"I'VE BEEN IN SOME PICTURES BEFORE IN WHICH I JUST FELT HOPELESS—*DESIREE, THE WILD ONE, THE FUGITIVE KIND*"

"These stories about the high cost of the picture being in any way attributable to my whims are outrageous and false," he told Joe Hyams. "What's going to happen when I go to the bank or to studio people some time in the future to get a loan for a picture? The bankers who have read these stories are not going to consider me a good investment and studio people won't want a troublesome actor."

What especially rankled Brando was that he was being blamed for the expensive delays. "In spite of the fact that there have been some thirty scripts and my character attitude has changed five times in the writing, I've kept playing each version of *Mutiny on the Bounty* with the fullest amount of enthusiasm and optimism, even under enormous handicaps as an actor."

For the first time, he acknowledged a measure of the pain and disappointment he had felt in his movie work: "I've been in some pictures before in which I just felt hopeless—*Desiree, The Wild One, The Fugitive Kind*— but I've done my best in this picture, and for me to be blamed for any of the executive confusion that has characterized it is amazing, unfair, and comedic. I'm so hurt and angry about all this I don't know what to do—and I know it's only the beginning."

Hyams revealed the true costs of *Bounty:* the property itself—the right to remake the 1935 film—was carried on the books at $500,000. The boat, the *Bounty,* had cost $700,000. Salaries for the cast, apart from Brando's, totalled $2 million. He was receiving $500,000 against ten percent of the gross. Sets were another $1.5 million, California property tax on the uncompleted negative was $780,000; insurance for $3.5 million was divided among six companies for $175,000. And on and on. As of September 28, Hyams reported, *Bounty* had been before the cameras for two hundred and fifty one days and it was still only two-thirds finished.

Producer Aaron Rosenberg dismissed Brando's fears that he was being made the goat. "Nonsense," he insisted. "I want to go on record now. I'll take full responsibility for the picture. If it's a flop we're not going to blame Marlon Brando. We made the investment, selected him for the role. Until a week ago he was undisputably cooperative and we couldn't be more appreciative about it. Now he's emotionally upset about the ending of the picture. We think this is going to be one hell of a film if we can just get through the next few weeks."

"WHERE DOES A REPORTER DRAW THE LINE?"

Bounty took most of 1962 to edit and package and was not released until November of that year. But months before it was released, a devastating article appeared that purported to tell the inside story of the making of *Bounty*.

In June 1962 the *Saturday Evening Post* ran a story about the making of the movie. The article claimed that "the childish antics of Marlon Brando cost the producers of *Mutiny on the Bounty* an extra $6,000,000. The magazine listed "some of his shenanigans: He tried to switch roles halfway through the picture. He sided with 'every punk extra' who had a gripe. And he even turned up with ear plugs—so he wouldn't have to listen to the director." The story claimed that "Brando antagonized the other stars on the set," "deliberately muffed his lines," and "threatened to jump out a window in front of sixteen Polynesian girls." One director was quoted as calling him "a ham actor, a petulant child."

Brando initiated a lawsuit against the magazine, complaining, "Where does a reporter or writer draw the line between legitimately dramatizing a subject and plainly distorting the facts to fit a preconception?" He also said, "A publication that prattles about morality on its editorial page is being two-faced by toying with the truth in news and features." For once, Brando responded to the baiting of the press and filed a $5 million libel suit against the *Saturday Evening Post*. (It was later withdrawn.)

When Bounty finally did open, in November 1963, reviews were mixed, but most of them praised Brando's performance. "This *Mutiny* has action, hilarity, beautiful color photography of Tahiti and the open sea—and, above all, sex," said James Bacon.

But some critics could not understand why Brando chose to speak in a prissy, tight-lipped British accent that came out as a caricature of English upper class.

Brando himself had the last word: "If you send a multimillion dollar production to a place when, according to the precipitation records, it is the worst time of the year, and when you send it without a script, it seems there is some kind of primitive mistake. The reason for all of the big failures is the same—no script. Then the actor becomes the obvious target of executives trying to cover their own tracks."

In 1962, with *Bounty* still incomplete, Universal Pictures signed Brando to a long-term contract, beginning with the leading role in *The Ugly American*. He had already acquired rights to the bestselling novel for his Pennebaker Productions.

"NO STAR COULD HAVE BEEN MORE PROFESSIONAL THAN MARLON"

Between the time Brando completed *Mutiny* and the time a decision was made to reshoot the ending, he completed *The Ugly American* at Universal-International.

Although his reputation had been damaged by reports of self-indulgence and ego attached to *Mutiny,* it was the commercial failure of the string of pictures that followed that took some of the luster off his star power by the early 1960s. Fortunately, he still had the loyalty of friends like Jay Kanter. Government anti-trust decisions had required MCA to give up its talent agency business and focus on production. It acquired Universal Pictures and moved into full-scale film and television production. Kanter became an important figure at Universal and arranged for release of *The Ugly American,* the first of five Pennebaker productions Brando appeared in at Universal. (A year later, Pennebaker was sold to MCA-Universal for $1 million.).

The producer-director was his friend George Englund who had been working on the property since 1959, waiting for Brando to complete his commitments to *One-Eyed Jacks* and *Mutiny.*

"The role is really a departure for Marlon," he said. "He plays an American ambassador, and that means wearing suits and all that. He's even growing his own mustache for the part."

The material was controversial: based on a bestselling novel by William J. Lederer and Eugene Burdick which criticized American mistakes in foreign aid to Southeast Asia. Senator John F. Kennedy reportedly sent a copy of the book to each of his colleagues in the Senate.

Universal executives were naturally concerned about the prospect of following *Mutiny.*

"But we had to go through with it," said a Universal executive. "Our deal was made before *Mutiny* and all the horrible publicity started. All I can say is that our picture started and finished on time and on budget. No star could have been more professional than Marlon.

"Even if half of the *Mutiny* stories were true, I can't believe that we had the same Marlon Brando working here that we read about at MGM."

Universal backed up that statement by immediately signing Brando to another picture, *King of the Mountain,* a comedy about an aging Don Juan who turns over his trade secrets to a younger protege.

Brando acknowledged that his own attitude might have caused his bad press. He spoke only to a trusted group of journalists that included James Bacon of the Associated Press, Joe Hyams of the New York *Herald-Tribune,* and Army Archerd of *Daily Variety.*

"As to the gossip columnists and the slashers," he told Bacon, "I ignored them. Their beat is the boudoir, and they tried to make me their hot-copy boy.

"Most people I've met out here had a preconceived notion of what I was like. Only a few ever bothered to find out about me for themselves. Most just mutter a frightened 'Hello' and duck, expecting me to hit them with a custard pie."

Kazan had recently observed that Brando had yet to fulfill the promise of his early years. "He's probably right," Marlon acknowledged, "I need to go back to the stage and sharpen up my tools."

BRANDO AS ACOA

Brando's relationship with Anna Kashfi often reflects the classic behavior of the adult child of alcoholics. She has acknowledged bursting in on him long after they were divorced, and creating violent scenes throughout their relationship and after the divorce. But his tender letters to his ex-wife while she was going through treatment for what she describes as "epilepsy and incipient alcoholism" in 1963 are touching and encouraging. While she was undergoing the treatment, he hosted her, her lawyer and his wife, and their two children, on Tetiaroa.

"I HAVE REACHED THE POINT OF NO RETURN"

Marlon returned to Bangkok with George Englund for the world premier of *The Ugly American*. After his audience with King Rama IX, he said, "One tends to think that the system of monarchy belongs to an old, decadent, useless world. I was especially privileged and impressed that His Majesty not only is a king, but that he is alive to even the subtlest and ordinary kinds of information. He certainly is concerned with the state of the world and the preservation of democratic ideals. He is not a man full of platitudes and drowned in formalities."

In a press conference, he was his playful self. Asked about how he anticipated the reaction to the film, he said, "Some people will react as Barry Goldwater might. Some people will react as President Kennedy might. And the spectrum of reaction will depend upon the individual. There will be a wide variety of reactions within the State Department."

He and Englund proceeded to Paris and on to Los Angeles for the American premiere. On April 15, 1963 he appeared at a press conference in Chicago for the local premiere.

On April 21 he appeared on David Susskind's live interview program, with Eugene Burdick and George Englund, *Open End* to slam reporters like Truman Capote of *The New Yorker, Time,* and *The Saturday Evening Post.* "I have two children growing up in this community, and I think that they deserve protection, as do their mothers." In rare form, Marlon raged on. "I have withstood raps, justified and unjustified—wrath, hatred, disregard, vulgarity, insults—for years and years." He slammed "claptrap scatological journalism," and announced "I have reached the point of no return, and it might be a fruitless, stupid and vain effort, but I cannot, will not, tolerate this kind of thing anymore." He even taunted Susskind because he was sponsored by a cigarette company.

That April, Marlon became involved in *King of the Mountain,* which became *Bedtime Story,* co-starring David Niven and Shirley Jones. Screenplay by Stanley Shapiro, director Ralph Levy.

On June 11, he and Paul Newman joined CORE demonstrators in the Capitol Rotunda in Sacramento where CORE was staging a two-week sit-in in support of Governor Brown's bill to end discrimination in housing which was stalled in a Senate committee.

In July he spoke at an ACLU meeting at the Beverly Hills Hilton, and slammed the lack of blacks in movies. "We can refuse to work in a picture if the Negro is not represented in it," he told his colleagues. "Somebody said it was going to be a long, hot summer. We can do something now or let the situation get away from us and have it end tragically," he said.

At a press conference on July 16, Brando announced plans to go to Maryland to take part in integration demonstrations in Cambridge and Baltimore. He said that if he had to go to jail for defying the National Guard in Cambridge, "then I guess I'll go." He stressed that he would participate "as a private citizen—not as a representative of the NAACP, the Civil Liberties Union or any other organization." Asked about the possibility of physical danger, he said: "I wouldn't fight back if I were attacked."

From Cambridge, he said, he planned to go to Baltimore's Gwynn Oak Amusement Park, where 383 persons, including several clergymen, had been arrested two weeks earlier for an integration demonstration.

Suddenly on July 18, Brando was stricken with an acute inflammation of the kidneys while working at the Universal-International studios filming *King of the Mountain*. He was taken by ambulance to St. John's Hospital in Santa Monica, where it was said he was suffering from "acute pyelonephritis."

His doctor said that the actor's kidney and bladder were badly inflamed. His illness forced Brando to cancel his plans to participate in the Maryland demonstrations.

The following day, Brando was reportedly "uncomfortable but in satisfactory condition." He was released the following Tuesday.

BRANDO PICKETING DESPITE HIS DOCTOR

Stung by rumors that he fell conveniently ill because he was afraid to march in Maryland, Brando authorized his doctor to release his confidential hospital records to prove that he had really been sick. He next disregarded his doctor's orders to rest and insisted on joining a local integration demonstration.

He declared he was determined "to make my first march in behalf of Negroes' civil rights." On July 28, he joined a massive picket line at an all-white housing tract in the Los Angeles suburb of Torrance where forty demonstrators had already been arrested that month.

In answer to movie colony skeptics, Brando insisted that integration should be Hollywood's special cause.

"There is a lot of muscle represented by the stars, if only because of the money involved," he said. "We can do something now or let the situation get away from us and have it end tragically. There is little to be said and a great deal to be done."

Spectators jeered when Brando joined 125 picketers in Torrance, but he ignored their taunts and continued marching. He was joined by actor Pernell Roberts, then starring in television's *Bonanza*.

Instead of a placard, he carried a notebook, scribbling in it as he was followed by a trio of neo-Nazis with a sign stating, "Brando is a stooge for Communist race mixture." Brando told reporters, "I hope this demonstration will communicate to others the truth that discrimination does exist. Many people are not aware of what's going on, and anyone who believes in civil rights should take part in this." When neighbors protested that the demonstrators where stomping over their lawns and gardens, he responded, "Some of the flowers are being stepped on today. But so are some people's civil rights."

The new, activist Brando went to New York in August to join Paul Newman at a benefit at the Apollo theatre in Harlem to raise money for a planned march on Washington. At a subsequent twelve-hour rally at the Polo Grounds, they were picketed by neo-Nazis and segregationists.

Muckraking columnist Jack Anderson revealed that the FBI was wiretapping Brando's telephone. Brando appeared on *The Tonight Show* and *The Today Show* to give his side.

"WE'VE BEEN INTRODUCED TO THE MOST SHOCKING FACTS I'VE HEARD"

August 21 found Brando in Birmingham, Alabama, with Paul Newman, Anthony Franciosa, and Virgil Frye to protest unfair hiring practices at the local Republic Steel and Goodyear Rubber factories. "We are here as devoted and peaceful representatives of good will, not as agitators, interlopers, or interferers," Brando said at a press conference outside the Goodyear gates. "Southerners can point to the North and accuse us of hypocrisy, insulated and restricted thinking just as easily as the finger can be pointed the other way."

The next day, they traveled by bus to Gadsden which had been the scene of steadily mounting racial protests, since mid-June. More than 500 black people had been arrested for defying state court injunctions against demonstrations.

In Gadsden, Brando and his colleagues participated in an unforgettable round of conversations, interviews, and visits with rank and file of the civil rights movement.

They showed him what it felt like to be jabbed with a cattle prod. They showed him their scars and shared their stories.

"We were told about 133 prisoners who were forced to run two miles after they were released from jail," Brando reported. "They were beaten while they ran. One fellow had his shoes removed and he ran on the hot asphalt in his bare feet. The blisters were punctured by cattle prodders."

"It's so hard," he told a reporter, "to express it in words without being emotional. It's one thing to read about the South. It's quite another to be here. It's like walking into an underground world."

But in the end, Brando was optimistic about the results of the trip. "We've witnessed here something that's very special, the renaissance of a grassroots democratic spirit," he declared. "You can mark the time of its beginning from the moment Rosa Parks stood up in the back of the bus in Montgomery and moved forward."

By now he had three families to support in California, Mexico, and Tahiti respectively, and was paying alimony to Anna Kashfi and Movita. He needed money, and his film choices showed it. At least the lamentable *Morituri* gave him the opportunity to work with old friends Wally Cox and William Redfield again.

He started 1964 off by addressing the National Congress of American Indians' executive council meeting in Washington on January 18, with a headline-making charge that Indians had been blackmailed into submission.

"Most people in this country don't know that United States treaties with the American Indian have been broken," he charged. "They don't know the Indian has been blackmailed into keeping quiet."

Brando got even more aggressive: "The Bureau of Indian Affairs of the Interior Department has followed a nearly consistent policy to obliterate the Indians," he said. "The bureau hit its depths during President Eisenhower's Administration. There was a slight upswing during the Kennedy Administration.

"The Indian has five more years to win a battle of understanding, or he faces extinction.

"People say the Indians are uneducated. The Indians are over-educated. They are over-educated in suffering and denial."

He concluded by promising to produce and act in "a movie that would tell the story of misery of the American Indian today." Then he sat down and listened to the chieftains spell out their troubles.

JACKIE & BRANDO DINE OUT

On January 29, Jacqueline Kennedy dined out with Brando in a plush Washington restaurant, the Jockey Club, to plan a dinner for the Kennedy Foundation. They were joined by her sister Lee Radziwill and his longtime friend George Englund.

"A KEY FIGURE IN THE BATTLE FOR CIVIL RIGHTS"

That February *New York Post* columnist James A. Wechsler announced that "Brando has become, despite modest personal disclaimers, a key figure in the battle for civil rights." It was already well known that he had participated in demonstrations in the South. But that

month he secretly went to Washington to lobby privately
for Senate Majority Leader Everett Dirksen (R. Ill.) to
support a civil rights bill. "I went to Washington trying
to play the role of Mr. Citizen, as if I were a dentist from
Duluth," he said. "I did it as a matter of personal conscience—I had to do it, but I don't want to seem to be
standing on a soapbox. I regard my conversations with
Mr. Dirksen as private ones, but I did want him to know
that a lot of us will praise him if he helps get the bill
through."

At the same time, Wechsler reported, Brando had assumed leadership of a movement of Hollywood stars re-
quiring that all their contracts include a provision that
would prevent the showing of any of their films in any
segregated theatre. "Except for a few rednecks, I really
believe most of the theater-owners in the South are eager
for an excuse to desegregate their houses," he said.

BRANDO RISKS SECOND ARREST

In March Brando starred in a real-life drama on the
Puyallup River near Tacoma, Washington.

It began with Brando, a young Puyallup Indian and
an Episcopal priest taking a traditional dugout canoe on
the river. The young Puyallup leaned over the side of the
canoe with an illegal fishing net. Brando stood up and
paddled.

"I tried to tell him you can't stand up and paddle a
canoe, but he grinned and said, 'This is the way they do
it in Tahiti.'

"I said, 'Well, the water's a lot warmer down there.' "
When they returned to shore, Brando and the priest

were arrested for breaking a state law against drift-net fishing. Released on $500 bail each, they said they would hold another fish-in the next day.

"It's a matter of survival for the Indians," said the priest. "Some of the forty-seven tribes in this state derive eighty-five percent of their income from commercial fishing. That income includes food for their families. Without it they can't exist."

More than 1,000 tribal leaders—some from as far east as New York's Algonquin and Mohawk Nations—were converging on Tacoma to protest. According to the protesters, the state was abrogating a 100-year-old treaty with the Indians, who gave up three-fourths of their lands in return for perpetual fishing rights.

Brando was there to dramatize the protest.

"I've only known him forty-eight hours, but Brando has certainly done his homework," said the priest. "He's well-read on Indian affairs, knows all the treaties and side issues and spent an hour answering questions for reporters today. He's more conversant on the issue than I am."

"Mr. Brando's capacity to get attention is very much appreciated here. It is providing the only hope the Indians have had in a long time."

"A LIBERAL SADO-MASOCHISTIC FANTASY"

Brando went to work on *The Chase,* directed by Arthur Penn, that May at Columbia, produced by Sam Spiegel. Jane Fonda, Robert Redford, and Angie Dickinson co-starred. Lillian Hellman adapted Horton Foote's short story for the screen, then later disowned the project.

Sam Spiegel conceived *The Chase* as a big-budget, all-star effort. The story centers on a Saturday night in a small Texas town as the residents wait for the return of Bubber Reeves (Redford), who has escaped from the state penitentiary where he was probably wrongly imprisoned. The whole town is corrupt; the one decent man is the sheriff (Brando) and even he is compromised.

Jane Fonda, then in the middle of her marriage to French director Roger Vadim, was thrilled at the opportunity to work with Brando, whom she had long admired.

"Marlon was a tortured man in the early days," said Spiegel who had produced *Waterfront,* "and he was great on the screen. When he ceased being tortured he had to pseudotorture himself in order to function."

Brando unwittingly confirmed Spiegel's insight. "You have to upset yourself," he said. "Unless you do, you cannot act. And there comes a time in one's life when you don't want to do it anymore. You know a scene is coming where you'll have to cry and scream and all those things, and it's always bothering you, always eating away at you . . . and you can't just walk throughout it . . . it would be really disrespectful not to try to do your best."

At least director Arthur Penn welcomed Brando's suggestions. "We had a good interchange of ideas," Penn said. "Marlon told me at the onset that he would present his ideas and that if I didn't like them I should tell him so."

"WHEN A MAN OF CHAPLIN'S STATURE WRITES A SCRIPT FOR YOU YOU CAN HARDLY REFUSE"

In December 1965 Brando arrived in London to begin *The Countess from Hong Kong.* He was thrilled to be working with the seventy-seven-year-old director and he had long admired Chaplin's classic silent films. He said he took the role, "because Chaplin asked me. When a man of his stature in the industry writes a script for you, you can hardly refuse. Why he should think of me for comedy, I haven't the faintest idea. But he said I was the only one who could play it."

Brando celebrated the arrival of 1966 at his flat in Berkeley Square, deep in *Countess* which Chaplin had written in the 1930s and described as "a romantic comedy—high, delicate comedy, I hope. And it's about real people, human, happy, touching, funny."

According to Anna Kashfi, he was so thrilled about doing a film with his idol that he did not even bother to read the script Chaplin had written. But Brando himself insists he not only read it, "then read it again, then tried reading it upside-down."

They worked a grueling seven-days-a-week schedule. Chaplin's directorial style included the dreaded "line-readings" that are anathema to method-trained actors like Brando.

"For the first few days," Brando acknowledged, "I thought I'd gone raving mad, Charlie had gone raving mad, and it was impossible. I can't do 'faces' and triple-takes—stuff like that. I was afraid both of us had made a big mistake. But then, suddenly, it all started to work. It was like chess—chess at ninety miles per hour."

But insiders claim Brando was openly unhappy, and by the time *Countess* wrapped he and Chaplin were barely on speaking terms.

"TOO BAD WE CAN'T RELEASE THE PARTY INSTEAD OF THE PICTURE"

By the time *Countess* opened in New York in March 1967, reviewers were lukewarm. Bosley Crowther of the *New York Times,* dismissed it as a "painfully antique bedroom farce," and recommended that, "if an old friend of Mr. Chaplin's movies could have his charitable way, he would draw the curtains fast on this embarrassment and pretend it never occurred."

Brando, fresh from the exclusive Buxted Park fat farm, was svelte and charming, helping make the London gala so successful that Jules Stein, chairman of Universal-MCA openly regretted, "Too bad we can't release the party instead of the picture."

As for Chaplin, he dismissed his critics: "If they don't like it, they're bloody fools. Old-fashioned? They are old-fashioned. . . . I am not worried. I still think it's a great film, and I think the audiences will agree with me rather than the critics."

MARCHING FOR CIVIL RIGHTS

On June 25, 1966 Brando joined Anthony Franciosa, Rafer Johnson and Sammy Davis, Jr. to fly to Mississippi to support the James Meredith Civil Rights March.

TETIAROA

In 1966 Brando purchased his own atoll, Tetiaroa. The chain of thirteen atolls formerly known as the Society Islands were thirty-eight miles north of Papeete, the capitol of Tahiti, and came complete with coconuts, lobsters, turtles, a bird sanctuary, 100-foot palms, a five-mile lagoon, 300-year-old trees, twenty-five archaeological sites dating back 700 years, pawpaw, and breadfruit trees growing wild.

Tetiaroa also had trade winds, brilliant sunshine, starry skies, white beaches, tropical flowers, and Tahiti only twenty minutes by prop plane or one and a half hours by motorboat or five hours by sail.

Onetahi Isle had an airstrip, six-room school, beach bar, water for three-hundred-and-fifty people and a sixteen-bungalow hotel.

"YOU SIMPLY CAN'T GET PAST THE 'B' IN CONVERSATIONS WITH BRANDO"

The Appaloosa was the third in Brando's Universal commitment. Like *One-Eyed Jacks,* it is set in the Mexican border country circa 1870 and tells of a loner out for revenge.

The title refers to a select breed of horse, with distinctive markings similar to a pinto. His Appaloosa is the one cherished possession of Matt Fletcher (Brando), a wandering buffalo hunter who wants to settle down and raise Appaloosas. Anjanette Comer is the girl who steals his horse and John Saxon plays a sadistic bandit.

Brando and director Sidney J. Furie, fresh from his

success with *The Ipcress File,* did not get along. "He's disorganized," Furie complained "No discipline at all. A procrastinator. One little scene that should have taken us a few hours took ten days."

According to Furie, "Every day he had another complaint—his tummy ached, his head ached—you should have heard the moans. What a performance! Then he'd be searching for his lines. Anything to procrastinate."

Clearly, Furie and Brando were mismatched. "He loves chaos," Furie recalled. "You simply can't get past 'B' in conversation with Brando and you can't get him to discuss a script rationally."

The breakdown in communication between star and director showed on the screen. "Brando broods and suffers a multiplicity of physical humiliations," Pauline Kael observed in her review. "Presumably out of despair, the director Sidney J. Furie abandoned himself to closeups of tequila bottles, decayed teeth, and bloodshot eyes."

A few years after *The Appaloosa* flopped, Brando ran into Furie in London. He was warm and friendly to the director. "It takes me a long time to get to know people," he told him. "I thought you were a phony, a liar, a dirty double-crosser. I discovered you've got the great visual sense of good directors. Let's do another film."

"Never!" Furie replied. "Never!"

REFLECTIONS IN A GOLDEN EYE: "THE APPEAL TO ME? $750,000 PLUS 7 1/2% OF THE GROSS"

Reflections in a Golden Eye, was based on the novel by Carson McCullers. Director John Huston wanted

Brando. He came to see Huston in St. Clerans, Ireland. He had read the book, but wasn't sure he was right for the role of Major Penderton, a latent homosexual married to the luscious Elizabeth Taylor. While they talked, the final screenplay was being typed, so Huston suggested that Brando wait and read it. Marlon did so, then took a long walk in a thunderstorm. When he came back, he said simply, "I want to do it."

Taylor also had a hand in the casting.

"I had heard that they were interested in me," Brando said, "and I let it be known that I was quite interested in the role. The trouble was that there were studio people who weren't too keen on having me in the film. They figured I'd be more trouble than I was worth."

Taylor did not agree.

"I insisted on Marlon," she admitted. "I told them I didn't care how much money they had to pay, I wanted him."

"It was a great gesture," said Brando. "I'm grateful to Liz."

But he also had to emotionally distance himself. When asked what appealed to him about the role, he replied: "The appeal to me of a neurotic role like Major Penderton? $750,000 plus seven and a half percent of the gross receipts if we break even. That's the main reason. . . . Then the attraction of a book by Carson McCullers."

Filming began in November 1966. Although set in Georgia, *Reflections* was filmed in Dino Di Laurentiis's studio in Rome because Elizabeth Taylor did not want to leave her new husband, Richard Burton. Brando stayed on the island of Tiberia with Tarita and their son

Tehotu, then three. Relations with the Burtons were friendly enough so that at the conclusion of filming, he stayed at their chalet in Gstaad for several months while making two more films in Europe, *Candy* and *The Night of the Following Day.*

During their preliminary conversations, Huston had asked Brando if he could ride a horse. Brando assured the director that he had grown up with horses. But when filming started, Huston noticed that Brando seemed to be so afraid of horses that Taylor, an experienced rider, began to show fear also. "I wondered then," said Huston, "if Marlon got this fear because he was so immersed himself in his role. The character he played had a fear of horses. It could well be."

Huston recalled Brando's statement that, "if you care about it it's no good." Meaning, Huston explained, that, "you have to get into a role to the point that you're no longer acting. You shouldn't give a damn about giving a 'performance' or winning an audience's approval; you had to be the character you're supposed to be."

On the set, everyone commented on Brando's good spirits.

"Yeah," he said, "you might say I'm sort of sticking my head above ground for the first time in awhile."

Even his social life revived. He was seen in nightclubs and at parties. He was frequently seen with Faye Dunaway, who had just made a splash in *Bonnie and Clyde.*

"It's funny," he said. "Your work goes well and it changes your whole life. Yeah, a year ago, I was down in the dumps. What I'd done in the movies just hadn't lived up to what I felt I could do. But with *Reflections,* I came back into circulation."

"IT'S BEEN A WHILE SINCE PEOPLE'VE BEEN FUSSING ABOUT OLE BRANDO"

"I still enjoy being with Faye Dunaway. She's bright and full of humor and digs the things I like to do. I think she's a great talent. Did you see her in *Bonnie and Clyde?* Great. It really touched me."

It was said his relationship with Dunaway was more than casual. Brando only smiled and said: "It's really only my concern, mine and Faye's, isn't it?"

Everyone noticed the positive change in Brando. "He seemed to be coming out of himself," said Taylor. "When we first started talking about *Reflections,* he obviously had a lot of hostility in him. Not that he directed it at me. But with others in the same room, you could see it."

Brando acknowledged that his career was at a crossroads. "It's been a while," he said wistfully, "since people've been fussing about ole Brando. Been a long time."

"I think," he said, "that I wasn't discreet enough about the roles I chose for myself. I guess I thought I could transcend whatever mediocrity I sensed in the script. It never happened, though, did it? Well, that's life, huh?"

Yet he had always felt that he would come back as a star.

"Of course!" he said. "I figured that I'd hit again. What the hell, I did it before, why shouldn't I be able to do it again? I'm the same Brando!"

And Elizabeth Taylor fully supported him. "I'm sure that this is going to be the film that gets Marlon back on the right track. I certainly hope so."

Brando truly believed that *Reflections* was his comeback film. Shortly before it opened, he enthused: "I feel like I've changed since my performance in *Reflections.* . . . it's kind of like a new life. You know what I mean. I'm not jumping around and doing cartwheels. I don't mean that sort of thing. I'm not the cartwheel kind of guy. I just feel like, baby, my day is here again."

He was eagerly looking forward to his next film, *The Night of the Following Day* which was soon to be released, and *Candy* which he would also produce. "It's like an excitement in me. I try not to let it get away from me. I want it working for me in the films I have coming up. No sense wasting the raw material I use in my business. Emotions, man, that's my business."

Alas, reviews for *Reflections* were lukewarm. Pauline Kael did praise Brando's work: "This is one of Brando's most daring performances: the fat, ugly Major putting cold cream on his face, or preening at the mirror, or patting his hair nervously when he thinks he has a gentleman caller is so pitiful, yet so ghastly, that some members of the audience invariable cut themselves off from him by laughter."

"ONE IS GLAD TO SEE HIM ON THE SCREEN IN ANYTHING"

Brando's next career misstep was *Candy* and once again he courted disaster by acting out of the noblest of methods: friendship.

His old friend Christian Marquand, best known for his role *And God Created Women,* was determined to direct the film version of the 1960s satirical porn classic by Terry Southern and Mason Hoffenberg. Once Brando agreed to take the cameo role of Candy's Jewish/Indian guru Grindl, Richard Burton came on board, followed by a line-up of stars that included James Coburn, Walter Matthau, Ringo Starr, and Charles Aznavour.

When screenwriter Buck Henry (*The Graduate*) was asked what direction the movie would take, he answered: "Every one conceivable away from the book." As for the ending, none of the actors was told beforehand, Henry explained, "We're keeping it a secret from them."

Candy opened to unanimous pans in December 1968. Renata Adler of *The New York Times* declared that it, "manages to compromise, by its relentless, crawling, bloody lack of talent, almost anyone who had anything to do with it." But she did have some kind words for Brando who, was "less unendurable [than Burton] because one is glad to see him on the screen, in anything."

THE NIGHT OF THE FOLLOWING DAY

The Night of the Following Day marked the end of Brando's five-picture commitment to Universal. His old friend, Jay Kanter was now MCA-Universal's British production head, and at his request, Brando agreed to star in the low-budget thriller, filmed in Europe.

Disguised as a chauffeur with long blond locks, Brando plays the leader of three men and one woman (Rita Moreno) who kidnap a rich girl (Pamela Franklin) upon her arrival in Paris, then take her to a remote beach cottage and proceed to fall out among themselves.

Director Hubert Cornfield clashed with Brando and midway through filming was replaced by co-star Richard Boone who shared Brando's method training.

The picture was not released until March 1969 and was considered a failure.

On April 4, 1968, Martin Luther King, Jr was assassinated in Memphis. Brando went to the funeral and saw King's children and widow. "It was then I decided to quit making movies and to find out what I could do to help," he declared.

The tragedy had a profound impact on Brando. He had been scheduled to star in the film version of Elia Kazan's novel, *The Arrangement,* and a western, *Butch Cassidy and the Sundance Kid,* but in July he bowed out of both. His commitment to civil rights took precedence over the movies.

"I don't feel I can do two things successfully at one time and there are issues facing us today which I think everyone ought to concern himself with first and foremost," said Brando.

On April 15, he was the only white man to attend the funeral of Bobby James Hutton, a seventeen-year-old officer of the militant Black Panther organization, who had been fatally shot by Oakland police. He was photographed observing members of the Party perform a close order drill before the funeral and memorial service for Hutton. A speaker at the funeral called it a "political assassination."

"You have been listening to white people for four-hundred years and they said they were going to do something," he told the gathered Panthers. "But they have done nothing as far as I'm concerned. I'm going to do something right now to inform the white people what it's all about. Time is running out for everybody."

True to his word, a few weeks later, he appeared on the *Joey Bishop Show* to criticize the Oakland police and was sued—unsuccessfully—for slander by the Oakland police.

Brando had reportedly donated $5,000 and helped raise $20,000 more for a scholarship fund for the children of Medgar Evers, another slain civil rights leader.

"I've asked all my friends to turn over one percent of their earnings to help black people get food, housing, and job training," he told the Panthers. "In some measure we are all responsible for the present situation and we must begin to do something about it."

"MY GOD, IT'S MARLON BRANDO!"

"Is this flight to Cuba?" was all the heavily bearded man with the pigtail asked the young flight attendant as he boarded the National Airlines plane in Los Angeles on December 5. The next thing he knew, he was being ordered off the Miami-bound plane because she feared he intended to hijack the airliner and fly it to Cuba.

There had been more than twenty hijacking incidents in recent months and they took even the hint of a threat seriously.

On the way back through the ticket gate an airline representative looked at the culprit and exclaimed: "My God, it's Marlon Brando!" He was told he could return to the airplane, since he had a ticket to Miami, but he declined.

His lawyer issued a statement: "Needless to say, Marlon is very upset and we may sue the airline."

He was actually on his way to Colombia to begin filming *Queimada.*

The attorney explained: "It was the only flight with direct connections to Colombia. However, we finally got him on a plane to Jamaica and then he will have to go by chartered plane to his destination."

A spokesman for National Airlines claimed that Brando was dressed like a "hippie" and hard to recognize.

BURN!

Maybe he should have stayed home, instead he went forward with his commitment to star in *Queimada,* directed by Gillo Pontecorvo. The Italian director was best known for *The Battle of Algiers* (1966) which Brando regarded as a significant step in political cinema. He had met Pontecorvo in Italy, they hit it off, and the director created the film with Brando in mind.

Quiemada—Portuguese for "burn"—was supposed to be an attack on nineteenth-century Western colonialism, depicting a slave uprising in a fictitious, Spanish-speaking Caribbean island. Brando would play a British agent provocateur who instigates the revolt, to enable the British to break the Portuguese control of the sugar business, then cynically crushes it.

The *Queimada* company was filming in Colombia for seven months. Pontecorvo had never worked with a star

of Brando's caliber and was of the European school in
which directors have total authority over the actors. Not
only did Brando feel neglected, but it seemed to him that
the way Pontecorvo treated the black extras was as ex-
ploitative as anything in the nineteenth century.

"RIGHT NOW I WANT TO KILL HIM— HE HAS NO FUCKING FEELING FOR PEOPLE"

Brando, in the tradition of Fletcher Christian, re-
belled, demanding that the company be relocated. The
Brando/Pontecorvo honeymoon was over.

"American actors are spoilt," the director complained.
"Just because they are often good they think it gives
them the right to interfere where no one has asked them
to interfere."

Producer Albert Grimaldi, best known for Clint East-
wood's spaghetti western period, agreed to move the unit
to Marrakesh for the final ten days of filming.

Even so, Brando remained angry. "Right now I want
to kill Gillo," he said. "I really want to kill him . . . he
has no fucking feeling for people."

On his side, Pontecorvo repeated that Brando was, "a
great artist. . . . But—I never saw an actor before who
was so afraid of the camera. . . . Brando is also a little—how you say?—paranoid. He thinks when I take
forty takes it's because I want to break him. Why should
I break him?"

He remained admiring of Brando's gifts. "There are
many moments when there is no time for dialogue," he
explained, "and then we need the synthesis of Brando's

acting and his face. When things are psychological, we trust the face of Brando."

Released in late 1970 as *Burn!,* it received little support from United Artists and vanished quickly. According to Pauline Kael, "The film is large-spirited, and it might have reached a much wider audience if the Spanish government, sensitive about Spaniards being cast as heavies, hadn't applied economic pressure against the producing company, United Artists.

And *New York Times* critic Vincent Canby observed that, "in the course of production, *Burn!* turned into a kind of mini-*Cleopatra,*" but "I must add that I wasn't bored by the film for even a minute."

Nine

The Comeback

"People were always so ready to say 'he's had it.' It makes me furious. Talent is delicate. It can hide for a while, go underground, get discouraged. It's human . . . but it doesn't go away."

—Elia Kazan

The new decade of the 1970s began with the disastrous *Burn!* and continued with *The Nightcomers*. This version of Henry James's short story, "The Turn of the Screw," was filmed in England under the direction of Michael Winner. It was an independent production and languished for almost a year before it was picked up by an American distributor. Even after it was released in a few major cities it attracted little attention.

After four unqualified disasters, Brando had been written off by many in the motion picture community. Only those with unqualified faith in his talent could have believed that he would ever come back. But come back he did, boldly and beautifully in two very different films, *The Godfather* and *Last Tango in Paris*.

THE GODFATHER: "I DON'T THINK THE FILM IS ABOUT THE MAFIA AT ALL"

Although Mario Puzo, author of *The Godfather*, claimed that he had Brando in mind when he created his bestselling novel, executives at Paramount were loathe to cast the fading star in the leading role in their multi-million dollar epic. But throughout his career, Brando had never been the first choice for any of his greatest roles and *The Godfather* would be no exception. Producer Albert Ruddy and director Francis Ford Coppola originally sought Sir Laurence Olivier who was unavailable. Brando was their second choice, but Paramount management resisted.

Brando had read the book and decided he wanted the role of Don Corleone. He and Coppola created their own "screen test," a video of Brando in make-up and in character. Not even Paramount's normally astute head of production, Robert Evans, recognized Brando underneath. He only learned who the actor was after he approved the casting.

Brando had his own surprising reasons for making the picture: he saw it as an allegory for corporate America. "I don't think the film is about the Mafia at all," he told an interviewer. "I think it is about the corporate mind. In a way, the Mafia is the best example of capitalists we have. Don Corleone is just any ordinary American business magnate who is trying to do the best he can for the group he represents and his family."

Years later, Brando blamed his ballooning weight on Coppola. "He made me the pig I am," he said. "Coppola not only makes the best pictures but the best spaghetti in the world."

But Coppola had a good reason for cooking for Brando. He recalls that the rest of the cast of *Godfather* was so uptight around Brando they could not perform. He broke the ice by cooking dinner at his home for James Caan, Al Pacino and Robert Duvall and having Brando drop in after the meal. "They were nervous and intimidated," Coppola says. "Caan told jokes. Pacino sulked. And Duvall was just making crazy noises."

When filming began, Al Pacino could only whisper: "It's like acting with God." But the awe of Pacino and co-star James Caan turned to laughter when Brando showed his prankish side. Journalist Lester David recalls that in a limo, Brando would suddenly drop his pants, pull down his shorts and "moon" passersby. Caan soon caught the spirit. On subsequent occasions, he mooned from the other side of the limo, which purred along majestically with bare backsides protruding from opposite windows.

Brando and Duvall became the unofficial champs when they mooned the hundreds of extras gathered for the wedding scene.

At one point, on location at New York Eye and Ear Infirmary, Brando was in a hospital bed, lying wounded while an assassin waited to finish him off. Between takes, a real doctor took his blood pressure. The doctor couldn't believe it. In spite of the lights, people, tension, Brando's pressure was *better* than normal.

"Know why?" Brando said. "Because I don't give a [deleted] about this film." The staff was horrified. Twenty-one years later, relating the story to columnist Cindy Adams, the doctor still remembered it.

"HE IS A MAN WHO IS STILL A CHILD"

Even as *The Godfather* was about to premiere on March 11, 1972, Brando was deep into what would become his most controversial film. Together with *The Godfather,* Bernardo Bertolucci's *Last Tango in Paris* would revitalize Brando's career and restore him to the pantheon of acting immortals.

But his beautiful co-star, newcomer Maria Schneider, was not intimidated by his reputation. "He's a man who is still a child," she said. She acknowledged his impact on her own work: "In the movie, his character takes that girl and teaches her a lot of things, makes her stretch, makes her explode," she said. "That's what he did to me as an actress."

Encouraged by Bertolucci's improvisational style, Brando put everything he had into his work. "Forty years of Brando's life experiences went into the film," said his friend Christian Marquand. "It is Brando talking about himself, being himself. His relations with his mother, father, children, lovers, friends—all come out in his performance as Paul."

Ironically, it was not the exposure of his most intimate sexual feelings that would give Brando the greatest challenge. Rather, it was the long monologues in which his character reflects upon his past. Brando simply could not remember his lines. For one extended scene, he reportedly asked that his dialogue be written on his co-star Schneider's bare backside where he could refer to it easily.

Tango premiered at the New York City Film Festival in October 1972 and was lauded by critic Pauline Kael as a monumental step in modern filmmaking.

CHRISTIAN

Brando's battles with Anna Kashfi over the custody of Christian continued to sap his strength and command his attention. In 1970 a judge had placed the boy in the custody of both parents, and by 1972 he was a boarding student at the Ojai Valley Military Academy near Santa Barbara. According to Anna Kashfi, he had adjustment problems there and was reported by the headmaster to have set a fire in a dormitory. While his father was away filming *Last Tango,* she had Christian taken to Mexico where an investigator whom Brando hired found him in the care of a group of American hippies. They claimed Anna had promised them payment for hiding the boy.

DEATH OF WALLY COX

Just as he was once again flexing his acting muscles, Brando was hit by the loss of his oldest and dearest friend, Wally Cox, who died on February 10, 1973. He flew to Los Angeles from Tahiti for the funeral. Cox was cremated and Brando was given custody of his ashes. It has been variously reported that he scattered them over a mountain stream in northern California and off Tetiaroa. Either way, it left a great empty spot in his life.

Perhaps Brando was thinking of his friend when he gave a revealing interview to a European journalist, Adrano Botta, in *L'Europeo* that March. "I have loved a lot in my life. I still do," he told her. "I have had many women. I like love. I insist on enjoying sex. Should sex and desire die in me, it would be the end. It doesn't matter if I have almost never been happy with a woman. Nor does it matter that with every woman my relationship has ended up in nothing. I face love every time as a necessary good or a necessary evil. Sometimes I even approach sex and love with boredom. But I must make love and give love, whatever the price. It is a matter of life and death."

He also told Botta: "I don't like people. I don't love my neighbor. Every time I put any faith in love or friendship I only come through with deep wounds. Today I am truly a person not open to relationships; this isn't a lie, but a very true fact. I am deeply lonely: alone. I enjoy life, up to a point, but I no longer have dreams. Death and old age are events which I accept and await with all feasible serenity. To a certain extent at times I make of them the purpose of living: I work toward the point at which I can accept them with equanimity."

OSCAR NIGHT SENSATION

It began to look like Brando had learned to play the Hollywood game and was being rewarded with two critical and artistic blockbusters: *Last Tango* and *The Godfather.* He was even honored with his first Oscar nomination in years, for his role as Don Corleone. But at the Academy Awards ceremony that March he demonstrated that he was the same old rebel.

The Academy cannot say it wasn't warned. He had already declined the Golden Globe and the Reuters News Agency World Film Favorite awards with a lengthy statement that boils down into the proclamation that "There is a singular lack of honor in this country today."

Then, at the last minute, he sent his personal representative to the Academy Awards ceremony. And when Brando was announced as the winner of the Oscar for Best Actor, a beautiful young woman in white buckskin costume and elaborate feathered headdress strode to the podium. After introducing herself to the gathered luminaries as Sacheen Littlefeather, an Apache and president of the National Native American Affirmative Image Committee, she explained that Marlon Brando could not accept his award because of the treatment of American Indians in the film industry.

Shock waves went through the hall that night and through the industry for days later. Brando had challenged the sanctity of Hollywood's holiest night. In the end, however, it was not he who suffered from his daring, but his delegate.

Years later, Littlefeather told author Jim Pinkston: "I felt exploited . . . period! By everything and everyone. I don't think that Mr. Brando meant to exploit me or hurt me in any way. It just happened that I was exploited in a cruel and vicious way." Brando himself was criticized for using the event as a soapbox. Littlefeather's

friendship with him dissolved as her personal life started
to come apart. Her Indian heritage was challenged when
it was revealed that her real name was Maria Cruz. A
former "Miss Vampire 1970," she had been introduced
to Brando by Francis Ford Coppola. She discovered she
was under scrutiny by the FBI and had trouble getting
acting jobs. "I was suddenly considered undesirable . . .
there would be trouble if I was hired. I traced these rumors to their sources and realized I was on some kind
of blacklist." One night in 1974 she was shot at by men
in a car. She eventually went to work for a public broadcasting station in San Francisco.

Littlefeather found her dreams of an acting career
thwarted. "I went up there thinking I could make a difference," she recalls. "I was very naive. I told people about
oppression. They said, 'You're ruining our evening.' "

In 1986 she was reportedly teaching nutrition.

It was assumed that Brando was in Wounded Knee on
the big night, but according to Anna Kashfi, he and
Christian Marquand, visiting from Paris, had driven to
Trona, California, on the edge of Death Valley and reg-
istered in a motel there as Mr. Marquara and Mr. Christian. Presumably they watched the show on television
along with most of America.

Back in the public eye with his two hit films and his
Oscar, Brando continued to try to bring attention to the
plight of Native Americans. He even agreed to be interviewed on television by Dick Cavett. On June 12, Brando

Marlon Brando,
age 6.
(*Everett Collection*)

Marlon at 6 with his sisters, Frances (left) and Jocelyn
(center). Their happy expressions belie the tumult inside
their home.   (*Archive Photos*)

Marlon, age 8, in Evanston, before he embraced the cause of the American Indian. He grew up with guns and learned to shoot at an early age. (*Archive Photos*)

With Jessica Tandy in *A Streetcar Named Desire.* Brando's performance in the play revolutionized acting in America and established him as an overnight star. (1947) (*Everett Collection*)

Despite movie censors, Brando blazed even hotter
on screen than on stage in *A Streetcar Named Desire,*
opposite Vivien Leigh. (1951)   (*Everett Collection*)

The icon of a generation: Brando as *The Wild One.* (1953)
(*Everett Collection*)

Brando with his parents on the Hoboken set of
On the Waterfront. From left to right: Marlon Brando, Sr.,
producer Sam Spiegel, Dodie and Marlon Jr. (1954)
(*AP/World Wide Photos*)

A rare picture of Brando and his would-be successor,
James Dean, on the Fox lot. Brando is in costume
for *Desiree.*   (*Archive Photos*)

Almost unrecogniz-
able as Sakini, the
Oriental interpreta-
tor in *The Teahouse
of the August Moon.*
(1956) (*AP/World
Wide Photos*)

Brando with Marilyn Monroe at a benefit for The Actors
Studio in 1956. (*Archive Photos*)

Walking the streets of Rome with fiancée Josiane Mariani-Berenger. (1954)   (*Everett Collection*)

One-Eyed Jacks was Brando's first and last directing effort. Here he is with co-star and lover Pina Pellicer. The Mexican actress was another Brando lover who chose suicide. (1961)   (*Everett Collection*)

Embracing Tarita while making *Mutiny on the Bounty.* They had no inkling of the tragedies that lay ahead. (1962) (*Everett Collection*)

Wedding portrait of Marlon Brando and Anna Kashfi. Note Brando's body language, perhaps the first clue that the union was doomed. (1957) (*Archive Photo*)

Arriving at the west coast premiere of *Mutiny on the Bounty* with second wife Movita, the Mexican actess who starred in the original version. (1962)   (*AP/World Wide Photos*)

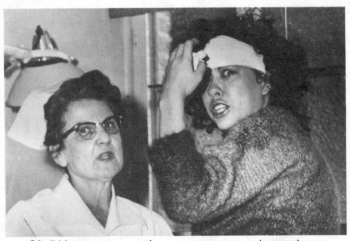

Of all his romances, perhaps none was more tempestuous than his eight-year, on-and-off relationship with Rita Moreno, during which she twice attempted suicide. Here she is treated for injuries after her car went out of control on a winding road and hit a tree. (1960)   (*UPI/Bettmann*)

The serene
France Nuyen,
another longterm
Brando relationship.
(1959)
(*Charles Bonnay/
Black Star*)

France Nuyen tangles
with news photogra-
pher after returning
from a Caribbean idyll
with Brando. (1959)
(*UPI/Bettmann*)

Brando's marriage to Anna Kashfi lasted barely a year, but the custody battle over son Christian Devi went on for more than a decade. Here Anna attacks Brando as they leave a Santa Monica courtroom hearing. She slapped him across the face, but he continued on without a word. (1961)
(*AP/World Wide Photos*)

Brando as a sexually confused Army officer married to Elizabeth Taylor in *Reflections in a Golden Eye.* (1967)

The nadir of a roller-coaster career: Brando in *Candy*,
directed by good friend Christian Marquand. (1968)
(*AP/World Wide Photos*)

Brando made the
comeback of his career
in *The Godfather*, yet
producers were so
dubious they forced
him to audition for the
role. Shown here with
Al Pacino who said:
"It's like acting
with God." (1971)
(*Everett Collection*)

Some things about Brando would never change. Here, at his request, Sacheen Littlefeather accepts his Oscar for *The Godfather*. (1972) (*Everett Collection*)

Brando solidified his comeback with his brilliant, heart-breaking performance in *Last Tango in Paris*. Here he embraces Maria Schneider. (1972) (*Everett Collection*)

Brilliant, beautiful, but oh, so vulnerable. Caught off-guard on the set of *Last Tango.* (1972) (*Everett Collection*)

In his shadowy quarters in a remote outpost of the Vietnam War, Brando's Colonel Kurtz discusses philosophies with Martin Sheen in *Apocalypse Now.* (1979)
(*Everett Collection*)

Brando's greatest tragedy occurred in May 1990 when his oldest son, Christian Devi, killed his daughter's lover and went on trial for murder. Here Brando poses outside court with Christian (center) and No. 2 son, Miko (right). (1990) (*Kevin Winter/DMI*)

With attorney Robert Shapiro who arranged for Christian to plead guilty to voluntary manslaughter. Last minute revelations about Christian's previous violent history blew hopes that he would receive merely a suspended sentence. Brando kept his eyes closed to discourage photographers, a tactic he often uses. (1990)   (*Kevin Winter/DMI*)

Seldom-seen No. 3 son Tehotu rarely leaves Tahiti where he looks after Brando interests. (1984) (*Sipa/Special Features*)

Troubled daughter Cheyenne shown leaving a Tahiti courthouse. She fled the U.S. during her half-brother's trial for the murder of her lover. Without her as a witness, L.A. prosecutors were unable to try him for first degree murder. (1992) (*AP/World Wide Photos*)

Brando's longest-lasting relationship has been his open
partnership with Tarita, mother of two of his children. The
agony of the trial brought them even closer. (1990)
(*Bob Scott/Galella, Ltd.*)

The world's greatest actor in his greatest and most heart-
wrenching performance: testifying on behalf of his son at
Christian's sentencing hearing. In spite of Brando's efforts,
Christian received the maximum: ten years. (1991)
(*AP/World Wide Photos*)

arrived at an east side heliport with two aides, then departed for the ABC studio taping by car. Dressed casually in a denim jacket, black shirt and pants, and a jaunty silk scarf tied around his neck.

After the taping, photographer Ron Gallela followed Brando and Cavett to Chinatown. After he'd shot about a dozen pictures, Brando signalled to Gallela. "What else do you want that you don't already have?" he demanded. Gallela asked him if he could remove his sunglasses. Suddenly Brando threw a punch and the surprised Gallela later said, "If you've seen Marlon throw a punch in the movies—in say, *On the Waterfront,* you know the man knows what the hell he's doing. Few stars could throw more punches that looked as if they meant it and knew what they were doing."

On November 3, he spoke at a rally supporting Ramsey Clark at Harlem's Apollo Theatre, and later in the month he joined Yakima Indians at a "First Americans" gala at the Waldorf's Starlight roof. It was a benefit for the American Indian Development Association, which encouraged Indian economic development. He was chairman of the organization's national board of sponsors and said the purpose of the gala was to focus attention on the dire economic plight of many Indians. Also at the gala: Ethel Kennedy and Jean Kennedy Smith.

THE MISSOURI BREAKS

Brando's artistic and commercial roll would come to a screeching halt with his next film choice, *The Missouri*

Breaks, and it is difficult to say what went wrong. His co-star was Jack Nicholson who was eager to work with the actor he regarded as the master, the director was Arthur Penn who had worked with Brando on *The Chase,* and the original screenplay was by Thomas McGuane.

When filming began in Montana in June 1975, all three parties approached the project with enthusiasm. "You know, you make so few movies in the course of your life," said Penn, "and so many of them have to do with nursing actors through them, that when you get a chance like this to go with two really superb heavyweights, why not go for them, if for nothing else than to be present and participating in it. That's why, in a sense, there is no thesis in this film. It was much more of an event. And it certainly shows, I think."

The picture is set in Montana in the 1880s and Brando plays a "regulator," hired by ranchers to get rid of cattle rustlers. His character is a charming Irishman and a cold-blooded killer. The critical consensus was that the movie was pretentious and muddled and Brando had been given way too much freedom by his director.

While most of the cast and crew was stationed in nearby Billings, Brando and Christian made their home in a mobile trailer. When his five weeks of shooting were up, he and the boy stayed on, avoiding the production, but reveling in the outdoor life.

APOCALYPSE NOW

Brando next bounced back with a part that was little more than a cameo yet one that would imprint itself on moviegoers forever. Francis Ford Coppola's epic *Apoca-*

lypse Now sought to portray the entire panorama of the Vietnam War through a screenplay based on Joseph Conrad's novella *The Heart of Darkness.*

Brando, who had grown physically huge since *Last Tango,* shaved his head to give himself an even more frightening look. When he whispered "The horror, the horror," viewers recognized that he knew of what he spoke.

Although Brando's small but pivotal role was filmed in 1977, *Apocalypse Now* would not be released until 1979. Meanwhile, Brando would take on another role that would create a modern icon.

SUPERMAN

In the early 1970s the colorful English father-and-son production team of Alexander and Ilya Salkind announced that they would film the classic comic strip Superman. Credibility came when they announced that they had signed Marlon Brando to play Jor-El, Superman's father, for $3.7 million, the largest sum paid to any actor up to that time.

"Marlon must have been paid by the pound," quipped Tennessee Williams. But the Salkinds were on to something: signing Brando gave them instant clout in the international market. Brando completed his part in a mere twelve days of filming in England.

"I had heard about his eccentricities and I was expecting the worst," acknowledged director Richard Donner. "But he turned out to be a treasure and I was really pleased with him. He was disciplined and he was willing to work all day. He never came late and his humor was good. It wasn't easy for him because his costume weighed about thirty pounds and the heat in the studio was always high. He never complained."

THE FORMULA

Brando would close out the decade with one more confusing film, this time teaming with another Academy Award rebel, George C. Scott. *The Formula,* which writer-producer Steve Shagan based on his own novel, was bound to appeal to Brando. It concerned international energy cartels with Brando playing an American oil tycoon who matches wits with a dedicated cop (Scott) investigating the murder of a friend who was killed because he knew the location of a formula for a synthetic fuel devised by the Germans during World War II.

Released in 1980, *The Formula* failed to catch fire with the public or critics.

BRANDO FOR BREAKFAST

For all his film activity in the 1970s, Brando remained passionately committed to the American Indian movement. Yet his personal life did not seem to be any more fulfilling than it had ever been.

At the end of the decade, Anna Kashfi finally took her revenge by publishing a memoir, *Brando for Breakfast.* In it she wrote: "He can be brutal. He has punched photographers with the temerity to request a pose. He's slapped and beaten women and shown callous unconcern at the death of a friend or employee. Within his being lurks the unregenerate soul of a Cro-Magnon."

Kashfi also revealed that in the years she knew him he "collected and pored over a number of books detailing the customs of ancient phallus-worshiping civilizations."

She revealed that far from being bored by his own career, he owned prints of his films and might sit for hours, watching them.

It was also in 1979 that Brando returned to dramatic television (and the ABC Network) for the first time in thirty years. That February 25 he appeared in the final episode of *Roots: The Next Generation*, also known as *Roots II*. It was a small but significant role as George Lincoln Rockwell, leader of the American Nazi Party, and it garnered Brando an Emmy as Outstanding Actor in a Limited Series or Special.

But he was beginning to pay a price for his excesses. In November a friend found him at Mulholland Drive hemorrhaging on his pillow after a midnight food binge. Later, a haggard, bloated and almost unrecognizable Brando was photographed leaving St. John's Hospital in Santa Monica where he had reportedly been treated for obesity.

In spite of his comeback, Brando was still a man wrestling with personal and professional demons.

Ten

The Roller Coaster 1980's

"The unholy turmoil in the man—the vanity, cruelty, and arrogance of a prodigiously gifted child—destroys what he's been trying to create."

— a longtime Brando friend.

After the disappointing reception for *The Formula*, Brando retreated. His children were growing up. Christian had married longtime girlfriend Mary McKenna in 1981. Brando was delighted because he loved Mary like a daughter.

"I know he sees a lot of projects," said British producer David Puttnam, who spent time with Brando on Tetiaroa, and who tried, without success, to lure him back to the screen during this period. "He's very courtly. He generally seems to read what you send him, and then says: 'No, thanks, I'm not ready to go back to work yet.' "

According to one television executive, Brando spent at least some of his time ordering up women and filming himself bathing with native women on Tetiaroa.

Brando bragged that getting women into his bed was not difficult. "It's like ordering Chinese food," he boasted to Brandon Tartikoff, former head of entertainment at NBC-TV, who recalled the conversation in his book, *The Last Great Ride.* According to Tartikoff, Brando told him he would be sitting home, "getting stoned, watching the news, see somebody, call the station, get her on the phone and, a half hour later, I'd be in bed with her."

The television executive also said Brando shocked him with a "great" idea for a TV film. Brando pitched for, "home movies of myself, in the water, with beautiful, naked native women. I've got thousands of minutes of the stuff." Brando was so excited he showed up early for their meeting, "wearing a dark business suit" and "sat on the couch in the waiting room looking like a banker."

CLAVELL PATERNITY CASE

On April 16, 1982, Brando appeared in Santa Monica Superior Court with his longtime friend Caroline Barrett Naylen who was suing novelist James Clavell for child support for her ten-year-old daughter Petra. He identified himself as the child's godfather.

According to Brando biographer Peter Manso, Brando "masterminded" his secretary's 1982 $15 million paternity suit against novelist James Clavell.

Manso told columnist George Rush: "[Brando] regarded Clavell as an irresponsible parent."

In Brando's deposition, according to Manso, "he said all men have a responsibility to acknowledge their children. He also said it wasn't unusual for him to have sexual relations with his female employees."

That September it was revealed that Brando is the largest financial contributor to a school for over one hundred orphans in Papeete, Tahiti. For years he had shown up faithfully for Christmas to personally deliver presents.

MARLON'S SECRET TORMENT

In January, 1983 it was reported that Marlon had asked a Japanese beauty young enough to be his daughter to marry him, but she could not accept and it broke his heart.

"I love Marlon very much and he loves me," twenty-seven-year-old Yachio Tsubaki told a close friend. "He has asked me to marry him and spend the rest of my life with him and he's even given me a beautiful diamond ring."

But Yachio's parents—who were very traditional and old-fashioned Japanese—would disown her if she married the twice-divorced American actor who at 58 was 31 years her senior.

"My parents have no idea that Marlon is my love and they'd die if they found out but we are engaged," Yachio confided to the friend. "They have their hearts set on my marrying a Japanese man. In their eyes, marriage to a man like Marlon Brando would dishonor them."

The dilemma had turned Brando into a "tormented" man said a friend of the actor. "He can't marry the woman he loves and it's driving him crazy."

"Marlon told me, 'She's my life. I can't imagine living without her.'"

Yachio had jetted from Los Angeles to Tetiaroa the previous November to spend three weeks with him there. A friend of his said the couple "love it" in Tetiaroa "because they can walk on the beach hand in hand undisturbed. It's a very romantic place."

The relationship began almost six years earlier—but only in the past year and a half had it bloomed into intense love.

They met when Yachio and her wealthy, aristocratic parents accompanied mutual friends to a party at Brando's Los Angeles home.

"They discovered mutual interests in music, art, and history," said a source close to Yachio. "As time went by their friendly relationship developed into something deeper."

Yachio lived with her sister Yoshiko, 25, in Los Angeles' Coldwater Canyon, two and a half miles from Marlon's home on Mulholland Drive.

"Marlon and Yachio have a wonderful loving relationship," said Brando's friend. "He calls her 'my princess' and 'my love.' Most of the time they spend quietly together at his house."

Concerned about his health, Yachio had put him on a very strict diet of Japanese food, which she cooked herself. The result was that he had lost thirty pounds in just over six months and even started to exercise.

Yachio was very proud of the stunning ring Marlon had given her, a magnificent three-carat flawless pearshaped diamond in a beautiful gold setting.

But the love affair was causing both of them torment, Brando's friend said.

Because of her strict upbringing, disobeying her parents would be unthinkable to Yachio.

He confided to a friend: "Without Yachio, my life would be empty and cold. I can't give her up!" And Yachio told the source close to her, "Our hands are tied. If I marry Marlon I will lose my parents' love and respect and I can't bear the thought of being cast aside by them. But I can't imagine life without Marlon either!"

DOCUMENTARY

In February 1983 it was reported that Marlon was producing and starring in a sixty-minute TV special filmed on Tetiaroa. Shooting was supposedly already underway and two major networks plus several cable companies were supposed to be interested in airing the film.

That month journalist R. Couri Hay reported that Brando would make a whopping $10 million for writing, directing and starring in *Fan Tan,* a hot love story about female pirates. And in June it was reported that he would play Al Capone in *The Assassin* and he would walk off with an almost criminal six-million-dollars-plus for just three weeks' work.

THE HURRICANE

In September two hurricanes devastated Tetiaroa and a heartbroken Marlon learned that his gorgeous tropical paradise had been destroyed. He immediately flew Tarita and their children to Los Angeles to live with him and Yachio. They lived as one big happy family, a family that also included Tarita's mother, his former "mother-in-law."

"The South Seas that I have loved so much have broken my heart," Brando mourned.

"Living there was my escape from reality, but those terrible winds ripping apart my home and my hotel have made me realize there is no escape from reality!"

Said the friend, "I have never seen Marlon so distraught.

"He's proud of his toughness and independence, but this setback broke his spirit.

"His only solace was his family. He said he needed them with him to help him over the heartbreak of what happened to his island.

"Brando was the uncrowned king of the island," said an insider. "He waddled around dressed in an immense flowing white robe, with bare feet and a huge large-brimmed white straw hat festooned with shells."

But then came the hurricanes.

"First in mid-March, Cyclone Rewa hit the island destroying Marlon's house, the administration building of the hotel, all the chalets, and seven bungalows," said the insider. "Where Marlon's house and some of the hotel buildings used to be there was only sand. Guests had to be evacuated by air just before the storm hit.

"Winds close to 100 m.p.h. were sending waves crashing right into the tiny island, literally washing buildings away!"

Workers had started to rebuild when on April 12, a

second hurricane, Cyclone Veena, came roaring through, destroying another bungalow and doing further damage.

"Marlon burst into tears when he learned that his island paradise had been destroyed," said his close friend.

"The second disaster just broke Brando's heart," said the insider. After the hurricanes, his home, the guesthouses and trees along the shoreline were gone, but not the hotel.

"The two hurricanes have cost him more than one million dollars, and those losses were only partly covered by insurance."

Marlon, said his friend, "sank into a deep depression, sitting around for hours on end. He was so hurt that he couldn't bring himself to fly down there and see the devastation. "Fortunately both Yachio Tsubaki, his girlfriend, and Tarita knew how to handle his grief. They just sat quietly by, tending to his needs, until he was ready to come out of it."

Still another source recalled, "It was so sad to visit Marlon at his house in Los Angeles and see him in such deep depression!"

But Brando pulled himself out of his depression—and moved forward with plans to rebuild his island paradise.

Finally, Marlon announced, "I'm not going to let this thing beat me. I'm just not going to give up. Tetiaroa will be rebuilt!" Then he leaped back into action, summoning architects to the house to draw up new plans.

It was wonderful to see the old Brando again, bustling around and brimming over with new ideas for his island. Tetiaroa had broken Marlon's heart. But now his love for the island has returned. He talked constantly about going back there—but not until it had been restored to its original glory.

Brando told the insider, "Tetiaroa will rise again!"

CHILDREN

That February he was reportedly upset that twenty-year-old Tehotu had joined the French Air Force.

But in March it was another son, Christian, whom Marlon kicked out of his house, telling him to get a job—and his own place to live. Chris was now working as an independent contractor doing pipe and structural welding. He also did artistic welding, creating bizarre metal sculptures, as a hobby.

In June, he gave Christian a $13,000-plus Chevy Camaro for his twenty-sixth birthday. It was the first brand-new car that Christian had ever owned. But by September a careless driver ran Christian off a winding road in the Hollywood hills. Christian smashed his new car into a tree, escaping with cuts and bruises.

MICHAEL JACKSON

In March, Michael Jackson got Marlon to meet with him and advise him on how to make it in acting. Michael said that Brando was the best actor in the world.

PETS

That summer Marlon was heartbroken over the disappearance of another dog, Winky, and had posted neighborhood signs offering a "generous reward for the dog's return. He was even consulting psychic Peter Hurkos in an effort to find the dog.

He was not immune to the troubles of real life, nor from the penalties of superstardom. He was only mildly shocked when a stranger suddenly climbed over the eight-foot wall surrounding his Los Angeles estate and handed him a screenplay. Marlon only persuaded the intruder to leave by promising to read it.

TURNING SIXTY WITH YACHIO

Marlon shed tears of joy that April when Yachio feted him with a surprise sixtieth birthday party at a posh Beverly Hills hotel. But he told friends that October that she refused to marry him until he shed some weight. He had already tried karate to get in shape, and had shed fifty pounds in six months. He also quit smoking. Dining out in London, he nibbled only on broccoli, telling other diners: "I'm on a strict diet." But on the way home he was seen stopping off for take-out pizza. He was up to 300 pounds. By November they were fighting furiously. He returned from a business trip in New York with some nice clothes for her but driving home from the airport they got into a huge fight and he ended up throwing all the stuff out the car window.

CHRISTIAN'S BRUSH WITH DEATH

True to his word, Marlon had begun to rebuild Tetiaroa. He told friends that he was spending five to ten million dollars to build "the ultimate resort" on his island. He would replace the old hotel destroyed by hurricanes with ultramodern facilities.

But the return nearly ending in tragedy for Brando's No. 1 son when he was attacked by seven savage man-eating sharks.

An urgent prayer ran through Christian's mind over and over as he treaded water in the ocean 100 yards from shore—completely surrounded by huge, hungrily circling sharks.

Each time one of the horrible monsters closed in on him, he shouted at it with all his strength and slapped the water in its direction. That was all he could do to keep them from him. He was trapped.

Only that morning, Christian and one of his father's employees, Johnny, and he had been towing a barge loaded with logs from a smaller island to the main island where they would be used to rebuild the hotel.

They had overloaded the barge and it began to sink.

Christian told Johnny to stay in the boat while he swam to the main island about 100 yards away to get help. He didn't want to cut the barge loose and risk having it swept out to sea.

He dove overboard and started swimming. After he had gone about halfway to the main island, he saw a silvery flash in the water nearby.

Then came a gut-wrenching sight he would never forget—the shark's distinctive fin broke the surface about ten yards from him. It was about four feet long, and it slowly circled him. He treaded water, for a while, trying not to splash much.

"I looked frantically for Johnny to help me, but the

barge was drifting away and there wasn't anything he could do anyway. The boat was disabled and he had no weapon.

"Then I saw more sharks coming toward me and before I knew it, I was surrounded by about seven man-eating monsters. The biggest one looked about nine feet long. They kept circling around him, closer, closer."

"I could have reached out and touched them. One raised its head out of the water and I was horrified to see row after row of razor-sharp teeth staring me in the face.

"One bite from those teeth and I'm a goner," he thought.

Once the other sharks smelled blood, all of them would tear him up like a pack of wolves. He couldn't take a chance.

Terrified, he slapped water at the closest one. Then he remembered a trick a Tahitian native told him about. He said that if you shout underwater it frightens a shark and keeps it from attacking.

Each time a shark came closer, he'd slip under the water and yell with all his might. They stayed about four feet away from him.

"I kept spinning around, trying to watch all of them at once, afraid one would attack. I'd been treading water for about forty-five minutes and was getting exhausted.

Then suddenly, he heard a purring sound, like the humming of a bee. He looked around—and saw an outboard motorboat heading straight toward him.

The sharks scattered as the boat drew near and he saw the face of his friend Bill Cable. He had spotted the barge with his binoculars, realized there was trouble, and came out to help them.

Just as Christian swam toward the boat a shark darted at him. And as he threw himself in the boat, Cable grabbed his spear gun and fired at the shark. A spurt of blood came gushing out and all the other sharks ripped the wounded one's body apart in a feeding frenzy.

"I was afraid to tell my father about my adventure—fearing he'd scold me for being foolish. Pop never was one to mince words.

"But after I finished the tale, he took a deep breath, and said, 'Hey, kid, you take care of yourself—it's a dangerous world out there. I know you're a man now, but you're still my son. I don't want anything to happen to you.' "

Brando gave his son a big hug. And Christian could not help thinking how close he'd come to never feeling that hug again.

PROJECTS

In February Brando was offered five million dollars to play Pope John Paul II but he turned down the offer after learning he'd have to shed 100 pounds.

In June he was mulling a $3 million offer to play the late FBI boss J. Edgar Hoover in *Seven Silent Men*.

He continued to record events in the weekly diary he had been keeping for decades, but he said he would never publish it, even though he had been offered five million dollars. "My life story will be given to my children, so they will know the truth about me," he said.

Over the years, many had tried to convince Marlon to write his memoirs. In 1986 he reportedly met quietly with Jacqueline Kennedy Onassis to discussing writing it for Doubleday.

In November friends said that he had ended his romance with Yachio, who turned down his marriage proposal, and moved out. Now he planned to marry his former secretary, Caroline Barrett.

Brando was quoted as saying: "I'm going to marry Caroline. It's going to be a big wedding at my house in L.A. All my friends will be invited."

Caroline, forty-three, had served as Brando's secretary on and off for several years.

Brando had wanted to marry Yachio, but her "very traditional" parents objected, saying it would be a disgrace for a Japanese woman to marry the divorced actor. Friends said Brando even offered to live in Japan for six months of every year and said he would sign a premarital agreement offering her millions if the marriage should end.

The four-year romance over, Brando began telling his problems to Caroline. "Caroline began to comfort him, but their friendship soon turned into romance. Marlon is constantly showering Caroline with gifts and flowers. I've never seen him so happy," his friend said. "He's making wedding plans, but no date has been set."

The truth was that there would be no wedding. "He couldn't get Yachio out of his mind," said a friend. "He was miserable."

"CHRISTIAN HELD A LOADED RIFLE POINTED RIGHT AT MY MOTHER"

In the late 1980's Brando's troubled children began to act out the simmering problems that would eventually explode into tragedy.

Cheyenne had emerged as a beauty every bit the equal of her mother, Tarita. She yearned for a career in show business and wanted her father to help her. He resisted her pleas, convinced that Cheyenne, sheltered most of her life, was not tough enough for the movie world. In September 1985 he refused to let fifteen-year-old Cheyenne accept the lead role in a movie in which she would have played a wild twenty-year-old. He said she was too young for the part. She stopped speaking to him.

The following August, Cheyenne danced up a storm in a show put on by her dance school troupe in Papeete and photographs of her in costume appeared around the world. He had to recognize that his little girl was growing up and was now a woman to be reckoned with.

Christian seemed even more troubled. He and his wife Mary McKenna had first separated in June 1983. For the next three years, Brando tried frantically to salvage the marriage. In March 1985 he reportedly invited them both to dinner—without telling either one the other was invited. For a time it worked. They reconciled.

"I don't want them to divorce because I think eventually they can be happy," Brando told a friend. "He'll never find a better girl."

At times Brando seemed to be successful in reuniting the couple. But the same problems plagued them and no matter how much he did, he couldn't keep them together long enough to fulfill his dream of becoming a grandfather.

"In the five years of their marriage there were constant fights over Christian's lifestyle," a friend recalled. "he stayed out nights and Mary became furious, warning him she would end the marriage."

In January 1986 Brando even bought Christian an early birthday present: a $200,000 house in the Hollywood Hills just a mile from Mulholland Drive.

But in April 1986 twenty-eight-year-old Christian filed for divorce in Los Angeles Superior Court. Deeply distressed, Brando angrily told his No. 1 son that he would cut him off without a cent unless Christian dropped the proceedings.

In a bitter confrontation at Mulholland Drive in mid-July, the sixty-two-year-old actor issued an ultimatum to his son:

"Be warned. I want you to drop the divorce proceedings—and if you don't, I'll disinherit you.

"I'll cut you out of my will. You won't get a penny!

"Why don't you make your marriage work and give me the grandson I desire?"

But according to a friend of Christian, the confrontation ended with the son storming out of his father's home screaming: "You've had all sorts of women in your life. You've been married three times—where do you get off telling me what to do?

"I don't give a damn about your money. I have the right to live my life the way I please!"

Mary retaliated by hiring famed divorce lawyer Marvin Mitchelson to represent her—and in her response, filed in June, she accused her husband of assaulting her repeatedly.

Mary said in her court papers that in March Christian told her she would have to sign some papers for a divorce because his father's lawyers were "pressuring me to get it over with."

When she refused, Christian "became angry and worked himself into a rage, and said, "You better call the police or get out of the house because I'm going to kill you if it's the last thing I do . . . even after the divorce you better look behind your back."

Mary said she took Christian's "verbal threats literally because he has on many occasions physically assaulted me and my family."

"Petitioner [Christian] has come home many times and for no reason become enraged and started breaking furniture and throwing me across the room."

Although Christian told his father he didn't care about his money, he was upset over Marlon's threat to disinherit him, the family friend said.

"Christian just doesn't have much money and relies heavily on Marlon in many different ways."

A source close to Brando confided: "If Christian goes ahead with the divorce it will break his father's heart."

According to her lawyer, Marvin Mitchelson, Mary McKenna accused Christian of adultery and obtained restraining orders against him. In court papers she said Christian threatened to kill her if she didn't agree to his demands during their court battle.

She also charged that he slapped her, threw her across

the room, jumped on top of her car, and, "held a loaded rifle pointed right at my mother."

"Even Marlon told me that the next time he tried to lay a hand on me, I should call the police," she said.

MANDELA PROJECT

In October Harry Belafonte announced that Brando would star with Jane Fonda and Sidney Poitier in an ABC-TV miniseries dramatizing the last forty years in South Africa. Belafonte would produce the series.

It would depict the nation torn by apartheid as seen by Nelson Mandela who had been imprisoned for twenty-four years, and his wife, Winnie. Poitier was to star as Mandela and Fonda as Molly Blackburn, recently deceased leader of a white women's support organization. Brando's role, it was said, had not yet been decided, nor had a director been engaged.

EDDIE MURPHY

Eddie Murphy was at his Los Angeles office one day in June when the phone rang. The voice on the line claimed to be Marlon Brando. "I've seen all your pictures," he told Murphy, and then invited him to dinner. Murphy accepted but, convinced it was some kind of joke, promptly forgot about it. The day came, and at the appointed hour Murphy was informed that a caller was waiting. Sure enough, there was Brando, in a beat-up Volkswagen. But it turned out he had more than dinner on his mind. He wanted to remake *Robinson Crusoe* and wanted Murphy to play Friday. Murphy, insulted, declined.

Brando also emerged from seclusion to attend a weekend solar energy exposition in Phoenix, Arizona. He was primarily interested in seeing the experimental cooling towers created by his friend Carl Hodges, the director of the University of Arizona Environmental Research Laboratory. He said Hodges first told him of the idea during a trip to Tahiti and he decided to come to Phoenix to see the towers for himself. "We are one planet. We are five races, but one people," Brando told an impromptu news conference. "I'm just a tag-along at the moment, just rubbernecking like you are, fascinated with all of it."

"I feel Chernobyl and Three Mile Island have made us adequately aware that we face planetary problems because radioactivity doesn't have any friends or enemies anyplace. It just goes where it wants to go."

PROJECTS

In July, after supersecret huddles with ABC brass, Marlon agreed to make a rare TV appearance—he would get a record $1.5 million for a three-hour movie, plus complete creative control. The picture, which would air in 1988, was titled *Legend* and would chronicle the rise and fall of a Brando-like star who makes a comeback late in his career. A search was underway for a young actor who looked like the early Brando because the movie would feature clips from his favorite pictures like *On the Waterfront* and *The Wild One*. Brando would play himself from age forty on and vowed he would get his near 300 pound frame down to about 220. He had already lost twenty-three pounds by strict dieting, riding his bike eight miles a day, and bathing in algae goo to tighten his skin. But like so many Brando projects, *Legend* never happened.

He did clash with photographers when he joined friends at an Orthodox Jewish restaurant to break the Yom Kippur fast. "Hey, you. Wadda you doin? You think I'm some kinda ape?" he snapped.

WEIGHT

Marlon was seen weekly at a Beverly Hills ice-cream parlor where he bought five gallons of vanilla almond every week. And he confessed he was eating it all himself.

CHILDREN

The year started with some good news: he was about to become a grandfather. His son Miko and housemate Giselle were expecting the stork in April. They planned to marry soon. But happiness turned to sorrow when Giselle lost the baby, then she and Miko split. "Marlon lived for the day he could play with his grandchild," said a friend. "He's taking it badly."

By November Miko was working for Michael Jackson as "Artist's Assistant." He was named to the key position after rushing to Jackson's rescue when the star's hair caught fire during the making of a Pepsi commercial.

Brando made peace with Christian by making an offer his son could not refuse: a co-starring role in his next movie. Soon they were excitedly discussing Chris's role in Marlon's upcoming film about downed flier Eugene Hasenfus's ordeal in Nicaragua.

A few months later, it was Marlon who rushed Christian to a hospital after he fell fifteen feet from a tree. Chris was out on a limb trimming branches and he needed knee surgery.

"TO MY BELOVED YACHIO, MY NEXT WIFE?"

In September it looked as if Marlon had finally convinced the girl of his dreams to marry him. And he was telling friends that he and Yachio would wed around Christmas.

"I'll be getting the greatest Christmas gift of my life this year—I'll have Yachio as my bride!" the sixty-three-year-old Brando said.

And a close friend confided: "Marlon is walking on air. I haven't seen him this happy in years."

She had turned him down in January 1983, but over the next two years, Brando repeatedly asked Yachio to marry him. She kept refusing—and in the fall of 1985 he ended the romance and began dating his ex-secretary, Caroline Barrett.

Brando broke up with Caroline after only a few months—and won Yachio back by showering her with gifts, calls, shopping sprees, and flowers, said insiders.

"Marlon was still thinking of marriage that time. But he knew that mentioning it would cause problems between them, so for a long time he never brought it up," confided a source close to Brando.

Recently he had noticed Yachio looking at photos of her Japanese girlfriends with their husbands and children—and he knew she was beginning to wonder if she would ever have a family of her own.

So he decided the time was ripe to pull a little surprise.

He gave her a gorgeous eighteen-karat gold bracelet engraved with beautiful designs on the outside. On the inside he had engraved: "To my beloved Yachio, my next wife?"

That was Brando's way of proposing, a friend said.

When she saw the inscription, Yachio began to laugh and cry at the same time. She threw her arms around Marlon and held him tightly.

The next day she rushed down to Beverly Hills and purchased an expensive Italian ostrich leather briefcase for him.

On the gold clasp she had engraved the word "YES!"

When he saw it, Marlon's face lit up and he began dancing a jig. "He gave her money to go to New York City on a shopping spree," said a friend. "She was gone two weeks and bought up a storm, buying all the clothes she'll need for her wedding plus new household items like china and silver."

Marlon told a friend: "We're planning a Christmas wedding. I can't believe this is happening to me.

To Brando, Yachio was the most beautiful, sweetest woman in the world and she was going to marry him. He was always afraid that Yachio's fear of being disowned would keep her from marrying him.

The fact that she was willing to risk rejection from

her parents has made him unbelievably proud. "I'd do anything for her," he said.

Yachio's parents had warmed a bit to the idea of their daughter marrying Brando, said insiders. In Japan a woman is considered an old maid if she's not a wife by age twenty-five and Yachio was six years past that.

Brando told a longtime friend: "We're not planning anything big. After the ceremony we're going to go on a honeymoon—and hopefully we'll start in Japan, visiting Yachio's friends and family there."

But once again, Yachio's parents back in Japan refused to give the union their blessing, because of Brando's previous divorces. As the year 1987 drew to a close, Marlon was heartbroken when thirty-one-year-old Yachio Tsubaki called off their December wedding.

CHARITY

That year he offered $5,000 to help keep a prison arts program afloat in Springfield, South Dakota. "It looked like we were going to have to close it down because of the lack of funds," said Lynne DeLano, superintendent of the Springfield Correctional Facility. "So one inmate, Ruth Packard, who is involved in the program, wrote to Marlon Brando and he was so touched by her letter that he said he would send us a check for $5,000 to keep the art project going."

LAUGHS

Although he was living with Yachio, Marlon still indulged his twin loves: flirtation and comedy. Smitten with one beautiful gal seated near him in a Los Angeles eatery, he rose to his feet and burst into song, warbling "Falling in Love Again," in German.

CHRISTIAN

Christian seemed determined to follow in his father's footsteps after all. According to Walter Baran, he was working as a welder in Rome, "where he can cultivate his film industry connections and be near his fiancée, actress Laura Fuino."

"I'm sure my father loves me," young Christian told Baran. "But to tell the truth, he's never really looked after me very much. When I was born he was very involved with his career, so he was never really a father to me.

"I envied my school friends—some of whom weren't as rich as me—because at least they had their fathers there," he added. "I saw him rarely. He didn't have much time to play with me."

His twenty-two-year-old girlfriend said: "Christian is very proud of his father. He says that Marlon is the greatest and most handsome actor of all times—though he does make fun sometimes of his weight problem."

According to Christian, his father had promised to make a movie in Honduras, with Christian playing a CIA agent.

"But Marlon keeps postponing shooting it," Laura said.

"People say Christian is not as handsome as his father,

that he'll never be the actor his father is. They're wrong. In time I believe he'll rival Marlon Brando."

"I NOTICED THAT WHEN CHRISTIAN IS NEAR HIS FATHER, HE SEEMS TO SHRINK, HE BECOMES A GNAT."

In 1988 film producer Carmine De Benedittis persuaded Christian to play the role of a hired assassin in the Italian film *What's at Stake.*

"I saw his picture and I knew right away I had found the killer for my movie," said De Benedittis. But no sooner did Christian arrive in Rome than Brando summoned him and the producer back to Los Angeles to discuss the project.

"When I met Marlon Brando, I noticed that when Christian is near his father, he seems to shrink, he becomes a gnat," De Benedittis recalled. "He seems to be crushed by the force of his father's character. It's a very heavy load, to be called Christian Brando."

For one thing, Christian had to endure endless advice from his father. It was said that while he was in Italy Christian received daily phone calls from his father saying: "Why don't you ask them for more money? They should have signed the contract in Hollywood and not in Italy. See about it." A furious Christian finally blew up at his father and asked him to leave him alone. "I have the greatest respect for my father, but I've overcome the complex of being an artist's son," he said.

Finally, after suggesting Christian be written into more scenes, Brando gave his blessing. But Christian had mixed feelings about the $30,000 job. "Christian is so sensitive and against violence," said his friend Bill Cable, who played a bit part in the film, "that he didn't even want to do that role."

But in making the film *La Posta in Gioco (The Stake is High)* Christian played a mob hitman who shoots his victim in the head at point-blank range. The scene deeply affected him and he told friends he suffered nightmares afterwards.

"MARLON GETS INSPIRED PERIODICALLY TO DO MOVIES. FORTUNATELY FOR THE INDUSTRY, HE'S NOW IN THAT MODE"

Brando chose his first project in eight years: *A Dry White Season,* based on the anti-apartheid novel by Andre Brink. He was attracted by its message, but it also helped that Jay Kanter was involved. The agent who represented him in his salad days was now a powerful producer and remained one of his closest friends and his principal representative in his dealings with the film community.

At first, the idea of making *A Dry White Season* revitalized Brando. The director was thirty-two-year-old Euzhan Palcy, a black native of Martinique, who lived in Paris. "When I saw how black people were being portrayed in American films, that upset me so badly," she recalled. "How will people have respect for black men or women tomorrow in the street when they meet them if the pictures they have of them from movies are without dignity? That's why I decided to be a filmmaker myself."

Season depicted the shattering impact of apartheid on two South African families, one white and one black. Taken by that idea, and impressed by Palcy's first film, *Sugar Cane Alley,* Brando agreed to take a small but important part for scale.

"He's a man who loves to take his time," she said shortly before the film opened. "I wouldn't say that he has no sense of time, but he doesn't want to let time interfere in his life. He's following his own rhythm. He's very curious about people's lives. What are your interests? Do you love animals? Do you remember your dreams?

"Before I started working with him, many people called to warn me that he is terrible with directors," Palcy added. "In fact, on the set the man was fantastic. He hadn't worked for ten years, and he was very courageous, knowing that all the other actors were considering him their god in acting."

Most of *Season* was shot in Zimbabwe in April, but when Brando's scenes were filmed in England, co-stars Susan Sarandon and Donald Sutherland became virtually speechless, barely able to say "hello."

In the new film, Brando played a lawyer who reveals the horrors of apartheid after a young boy dies in police custody. The Pinewood Studios set was closed to outsiders, but an insider told journalist Lester David that, "Working with Brando is not like working with the average person. He knows what he wants. Marlon worked hard. He created the character with great respect for the material."

He did not leave London without one embarrassing incident. After completing his scenes, he visited a longtime female friend and accepted her invitation to use her private sauna—not realizing the thing was the size of a small closet. The door jammed as he tried to exit. Soon the friend was putting in an emergency call: "I've got Marlon Brando stuck in my sauna!" His rescuers had to take the door off its hinges to free the star. Poor Marlon was stuck for twenty minutes.

Far more devastating was an incident with Yachio, who visited him on the set and found him with Vietnamese Mei Lai, who was on vacation from San Francisco. He could not convince Yachio that Mei Lai was just a fan he'd invited to the set. She turned around and went back to Los Angeles without unpacking.

That fall, when a friend confided that Brando's recent "business trips" were really excuses to sneak off to Tahiti and Mei Lai, Yachio moved out. But when his relationship with Mei Lai ended, Brando's answering machine was soon collecting messages from Yachio who wanted him back. Still furious that she had left him because of Mei Lai, however, Brando would not return her calls.

After completing filming *Season* in London, he returned to Los Angeles. Soon gossip emerged about an intriguing new friendship. Brando had moved into Michael Jackson's Santa Ynez ranch and was said to be particularly delighted with the pop star's zoo.

Brando and Jackson soon teamed up to write and co-produce a TV movie based on the dramatic rescue of two famous whales off the coast of Alaska. Marlon would star as the head of the rescue team. Michael would direct. Unfortunately, the project remains unproduced.

That December he caught the attention of another pop superstar. The December issue of *Fame* magazine carried a cover story about Brando, but it was a black and white picture of the star when he starred in *The Wild One* that impressed Madonna. According to columnist Liz Smith, "She tracked down photographer Phil Stern and paid him $575 for a 16-by-20-inch print." Smith speculated that it was, "A gift, perhaps, for 'the Wild One' in her own life—Sean Penn?"

JERICHO

Brando and Donald Cammell (*Performance, Revolution*) were friends. When Cammell's 1988 film, *White of the Eye,* was threatened with an "X" rating, Brando, who believed the rating had affected *Last Tango in Paris,* personally went to bat for the film with the Motion Picture Association, commending its "originality, artistry, and power." The MPAA eventually gave *White of the Eye* an "AR" rating, with only nominal further cuts from the director.

He then agreed to star in Cammell's next picture, *Jericho,* to be produced by Elliott Kastner and Andre Blay. Filming was to begin in June in Mexico. Brando would play the lead as a CIA agent who comes out of retirement for some tricky free-lance work in *Jericho,* a political thriller based on a screenplay he wrote, and co-produced by Brando and longtime associate Elliot Kastner.

Details remained sketchy, but Kastner had produced four previous Brando films including *The Missouri Breaks*. An associate told the *Los Angeles Times* that the movie would begin shooting in Mexico that November and Brando would be guaranteed at least four million dollars for his work.

Despite Brando's stature, *Jericho* did not have a distribution agreement with any major studio, because Brando, according to a Kastner associate, insisted that it be finished before it was shopped. He wanted to deal from a position of strength, according to an associate.

Did this mean that Brando was serious about acting again? "I think so," said another associate. "Marlon gets inspired periodically to do movies. Fortunately for the industry, he's now in that mode."

In September Brando provided a foreword to Stella Adler's book, *The Technique of Acting,* published by Bantam.

But he also spent a lot of time in front of the television, watching his favorite soap, *One Life to Live.*

And he was warned that he was out of his next scheduled picture, *The Freshman,* unless he lost eighty pounds, because at about 330, he was uninsurable. Producers offered to pay for a weight loss program, but Brando insisted he would shed the weight himself before June.

By now his weight was a genuine encumbrance. He had to be loaded onto an electric cart at London's Heathrow Airport so he would not have to negotiate the long walkway.

Christian continued to concern him. When Brando's No. 1 son wiped out his Harley and injured his knee, he rushed to the hospital and bawled him out for riding in the rain. But he soon calmed down and brought Christian home to nurse him back to health.

He was seen with his new best friend, Michael Jackson, at an L.A. concert that February, looking slimmer.

And Jackson was said to have seized control of Brando's eating habits, personally bringing him fresh organically grown vegetables. Just a year and a half earlier Jackson had helped him lose twenty-two pounds, but Brando had gained that back and more. And now they were talking about heading for Russia to make a movie in which Jackson would play the Russian poet Aleksandr Pushkin, with Brando as his mentor.

BIOGRAPHY

He was also said to be furious about a proposed biography by Peter Manso and even more outraged that his sister Jocelyn had been talking to the author. Brando had refused to speak to her since she gave some unflattering interviews about him six years earlier. But when Jocelyn called to wish him a happy sixty-fifth birthday all was forgiven. Michael Jackson gave him a one million dollar antique pocket watch for the occasion.

Manso put an ad in an Omaha, Nebraska, paper asking for information and Brando exploded when he learned one of his sisters had agreed to chat with the writer. He stopped speaking to her for six months.

"CHEYENNE HAS ALWAYS BEEN THE APPLE OF HER FATHER'S EYE"

Cheyenne had been seriously injured in a jeep accident in March 1989 and a shaken Brando had kept a tense bedside vigil beside her in Los Angeles. Cheyenne, twenty, was vacationing on his island when the jeep she was driving struck a log. She was hurled through the windshield and her pretty face was cut to ribbons. She required 50 stitches.

"Cheyenne has always been the apple of her father's eye, and when he got the news in Los Angeles that she had been injured and disfigured, he put the phone down and sobbed," a source close to the Brando family revealed. "He was saying over and over, 'My baby! Her beauty's ruined. She's going to be scarred for life. I've got to do something.' "

Cheyenne was rushed to a hospital in Tahiti after the accident, but the next day Brando had her flown to Los Angeles.

"Marlon called plastic surgeons and arranged for a private room at UCLA Medical Center, then called his four other grown-up children," said the close source. "He wanted them all to come to UCLA to bolster Cheyenne's spirits. They agreed. When Cheyenne's plane touched down in Los Angeles Marlon was there with a private ambulance to take her to the hospital. Later at the hospital he said, 'I don't care if I have to spend millions, I'm going to make her beautiful again.'

Marlon sat in a private room while surgeons worked stitching up gashes and grafting skin. And he was the first person Cheyenne saw when she came around from the anesthetic. She looked at him from under her bandages and said, "Daddy, don't cry, I'm going to be fine." Then she asked him, "Am I going to be ugly?"

He took her in his arms, tears streaming down his face, and said, "No, baby, Daddy is going to make sure you're beautiful again."

"The night after the operation the nursing staff wanted him to go home and rest, but he wouldn't leave and stayed until morning. He came to the hospital every morning.

Doctors told Brando that in time Cheyenne's scars would heal and because of the very latest surgical techniques, there will be little trace of the damage.

But she underwent two three-hour operations and received about fifty stitches, insiders said.

And she faced more plastic surgery. Brando told doctors he didn't care how much it will cost, or how long it took—all the scars must be gone."

It was said he felt responsible because she had wanted to visit his Canadian movie set around the time of the crash—and he turned her down.

BRANDO A DAD AGAIN—AT 65

Brando had more reason to celebrate that summer: he had become a father again for the sixth time.

He was said to be so excited by the event that he drove his pregnant thirty-one-year-old maid, Christina Ruiz, to the hospital. Christina was admitted to Saint John's Hospital in Santa Monica on May 13, to await the birth of the baby. "Marlon drove me to the hospital. I was in labor for about five hours, and he was very encouraging," she told a reporter. He even donned a hospital gown to be by her side during the delivery. He reportedly had no intention of marrying Christina. But he was paying all her hospital bills, had arranged to buy her a home, and had vowed to support his new daughter, Ninna Priscilla.

He had even given his blessing for the baby to carry the Brando name.

"I'm the happiest dad in the world!" he told a friend. "I can't believe that at my age I could feel all this love and tenderness for such a tiny little person. Christina is a wonderful woman. I'm going to take care of her and my baby Ninna. I'll do the right thing for them."

Christina confirmed that Brando was the father of her baby and that the child was "doing great."

She began working at Mulholland Drive a year and a half earlier. At the time, Brando had recently broken up with Yachio Tsubaki and he was feeling lonely.

"He's always loved exotic women—and he was instantly attracted to dark-haired, olive-skinned Christina. Day by day a relationship developed. Although Marlon is getting older and is overweight, he's still a sexy, powerful and attractive man," said a friend. "They began having an affair—and Christina became pregnant. Marlon was delighted!"

"I wish I'd had a camera as a nurse tried to squeeze Marlon into an extra-large hospital gown. It was funnier than a Jackie Gleason comedy skit! Here was 300-pounds-plus Brando in this blue paper gown, a blue and white hospital hat, and funny shoe covers.

"The gown stretched at the seams, perspiration was dripping through the paper hat, and the paper shoe covers flapped as he walked. Everyone on the floor fought back giggles.

They admired him for not letting any humiliation keep him from witnessing the birth of his child. He was a big, cuddly teddy bear, kind and polite to everyone.

When the baby was born, he said, "Ahh, she's beautiful."

He later turned to one of the staff and said: "See, I didn't faint."

After the birth, Brando spent time with Christina in her hospital room and eagerly held his eight-pound daughter, said an observer. "He was like a twenty-year-old becoming a father for the first time. He was just beaming and told Christina: 'I'm so happy. Thank you!' "

After the birth, Christina's family gathered in her room. "They were all congratulating Marlon on his new daughter. Marlon told them: 'My pet name for Christina is "Ninna," and that's why we named the baby Ninna. I felt that if such a beautiful name could fit Christina, it could also fit our beautiful daughter.

"Ninna will have my name. I want her to know who her father is, and that I love her and was proud to give her my name."

Brando felt strongly for years that a man shouldn't ignore his children when he knows they're his. He had made his feelings about this clear in his deposition in the James Clavell case. He also stated at the time that it was not unusual for him to have sexual relations with his female employees.

Brando left instructions for Christina's medical bills to be sent to his accountant for payment and mother and baby were temporarily staying at his home.

"Christina wanted to live with Marlon and raise their daughter in his home, but Marlon told her: "I have to have my privacy," said a close friend. "He's made arrangements to buy Christina and Ninna a three bedroom home in Sherman Oaks, not far from his. And he plans to visit them frequently."

BRANDO'S SECRET TRIP TO AUSTRALIA

Although Brando publicly dismisses questions about his weight, it does seem to bother him and he cannot help but be aware that at his present size he limits the roles he can take, something his talent never allowed.

That was probably the reason he plunged into his most serious weight-loss program to date, to prepare for *Jericho*. Early in the summer of 1988, his weight up to 320 pounds, he took off for an exclusive Australian fat farm: The $1,000-a-week Camp Eden in Australia's Nerang Valley.

Although Brando's staff insisted that he was in Los Angeles, insiders told journalist Jock Veitch that he was in Australia at a "health adjustment camp."

The camp was carved out of a tropical rain forest in Port Douglas, a small northern Australian town near the Great Barrier Reef. The fat farm was run by Diane Cilento, former wife of Sean Connery, and her husband, playwright Anthony Shaffer, author of *Sleuth*.

Brando reportedly spent about two months there on a Spartan diet of organically grown vegetables and tropical fruit. He was accompanied by Australian trainer Paul Graham, who had helped Arnold Schwarznegger and Mike Tyson get in shape. Graham was said to have Brando on a rigorous exercise schedule.

Brando's one public appearance was at a concert given by Frank Sinatra at the Sanctuary Cove resort.

"Marlon looked great," said a journalist who covered the show.

Just five months later, in August, Cheyenne was a passenger in a car driven by Dag Drollet, her lover for the last three years. He struck and killed a pedestrian. Criminal charges against Drollet were dropped because the victim was drunk. But it was a grim harbinger of the tragedy to come.

COLLAPSE OF *JERICHO*

That August, the *Jericho* project collapsed. Money problems and disagreements had plagued preproduction. Finally, Brando, who had lost seventy pounds for the role, turned to his colleagues and announced: "I don't feel like starving myself for this!"

Jericho was to have been his first starring role in sixteen years, but pressure to lose weight had a negative effect on Brando. He would go on eating binges, then disappear and sleep for days.

Director Donald Cannell was left disgusted over the eighteen months it had taken to prepare the project. "Marlon is full of unholy turmoil," he said. "It makes him destroy whatever he creates.

"Though I had no misgivings about his physical immensity, he has a problem with people constantly nagging him to lose weight."

A spokesman for Emerald Films said that the producers still expected Brando to appear in the movie.

To take his mind off eating, he was reportedly studying

TV repair via correspondence and offering to fix sets of friends and neighbors free of charge.

THE GODFATHER MEETS THE GODFATHER

Brando signed to appear in *The Freshman,* the adventures of a young man, played by Matthew Broderick, whose college career is dramatically altered when he is befriended by a genial father figure, a true gentleman, who happens to be an organized crime leader with an eligible daughter.

He looked forward to a comedy and liked the script: "It was funny and there's no substitute for laughter in this frightened, endlessly twisting world," he said.

One scene required him to ice skate. To prepare, the sixty-five-year-old star took private skating lessons in Westwood, New Jersey.

A CANCER SCARE

In July Marlon had a cancer scare and flew back to Los Angeles for treatment. "Marlon only goes to one doctor—his own," a family friend told journalist Nick Rossi. "He doesn't trust many doctors.

"He's a man who's really afraid. Who knows what the tests will show? He's anxious for the surgery to be done. He's kicking himself for not taking better care of himself. His children and close friends are trying to keep his spirits up with phone calls, visits, and encouraging notes."

Brando feared prostate cancer. He took a room in the celebrity wing of St. John's Hospital in Santa Monica, overlooking the Pacific, checking in under the name Miles Gahan. His surgery was postponed from June 23 because of medical complications.

The door of Brando's room, No. 479, was marked with a warning to visitors: "See the nurse. Contagion caution in effect."

Dr. Douglas Ford, Brando's personal physician, ordered tests that showed few irregularities. Although his weight had soared over 300 pounds, his cholesterol level was below normal. Brando bounced back.

Back on the set of *The Freshman,* Marlon was soon dining with Matthew Broderick and Bruno Kirby in New York's Little Italy. Sitting at another table was John Gotti, the reputed real-life godfather. One of Gotti's aides approached and asked them if they would like to meet him—an offer they could not refuse. Broderick and Brando soon visited Gotti at his nearby hangout, the Ravenite Social Club where observers reported it was hard to tell who was more in awe of whom.

When the *Freshman* company moved to Toronto, Brando was reunited with Maxmillian Schell, his co-star from *The Young Lions.*

In August columnist Liz Smith reported that he had consulted a Tahitian witch doctor who—after chanting and burning leaves, concocted a potion made from seaweed, papaya juice, and fish to help him lose weight. The same month, he was reportedly padding around Mulholland Drive in loose Japanese kimonos, naked underneath, his long hair pulled into a ponytail. Mostly he watched television and ate. "The unholy turmoil in the man—the vanity, cruelty, and arrogance of a prodigiously gifted child—destroys what he's been trying to create," said Donald Cammell. "He begins to destroy what has been built up. Paranoia raises its grinning face at the bottom of his bed."

FALLOUT FROM *DRY WHITE SEASON*

Sadly, the *Dry White Season* project so dear to Brando's heart ended in acrimony.

In October *Daily Variety* columnist Army Archerd reported that Marlon was "mad as hell." Brando was furious that an MGM/UA executive had denied his request to recut *A Dry White Season*. According to Brando, the executive then called the LAPD and reported that Marlon had threatened to kill him and his children.

The executive declined to comment on the matter to Archerd, but Brando assured the columnist that he had received word of the alleged report from three people and he was now planning a "defamation" suit of his own.

"I swear on my children that I did not [threaten him]" Brando assured Archerd. "It's not true. It's not me. I have never done anything physical—except to a couple of paparazzi. (Ron Gallela cost me $40,000.)"

Marlon had, after all, done *Season* for scale. "My price for the other picture [*The Freshman*] was $3.3 million plus eleven percent of the gross." And he claimed that MGM contributed merely $124,000 to anti-apartheid organizations. "I wanted this picture to succeed. I usually don't care that much if a picture is a success, but this picture is such a high silhouette."

According to Marlon, when the *Season* company arrived in England after Africa for his scenes, "They asked me if I would write them. It's not the first time—so I wrote twenty-one pages—my courtroom scenes with Donald [Sutherland]. And I eventually directed myself—as I usually do, anyway (after Kazan cashed in.) Donald and I shared the direction of our scenes. I don't know how I got through the picture. I arrived with jet lag, I had a cold, and I was undergoing a root canal. I finally got it together—and then they pulled the rug out from under me. They cut my scenes out. They cut out the climactic scene where I am confronting the judge and dragged out of the court. The dramaturgy is ruined. There is no climax. Generally I don't give a damn but I do in this picture because of the kind of picture it is."

"Some greeting," Marlon observed, "for an old warhorse coming down from the hills in this role for which I did give a much better performance."

Executives at MGM/UA limited their comments, but one insider claimed that Marlon was so huge that, "they had to cut him out of a scene for his own sake."

It seemed as if no formal complaint had been lodged by either party. "If Marlon Brando had victimized someone, we would have known about it," said a spokesman for the West Los Angeles police where both Brando and the executive lived. The executive had reportedly hired private guards for his family. "He has uniformed security patrolling the grounds of his home in Brentwood," said one observer. "He's convinced Brando wants to harm him."

Marlon vowed he would sue the executive for defamation of character. "I'm not going to sit in my rocking chair and watch the parade go by," he said.

CONNIE CHUNG INTERVIEW

Convinced he had been cheated out of an Oscar-winning performance, Brando decided to put forth his views in an interview on *Saturday Night with Connie Chung* on CBS. The broadcaster had been pursuing an interview with Brando for at least thirteen years, but she did not meet him until the taping in late September. It would be his first TV interview in sixteen years.

Chung flew out to Los Angeles and taped the four-hour interview at Marlon's home. She discovered that he was a fan of her husband, Maury Povich, and watched him regularly on *A Current Affair.*

Chung asked him whether he liked himself heavy. "I don't care," he replied. "I've been heavy, I've been thin, and I'll be thin again." But he acknowledged that it was "too much of a problem." "I simply have to be more active. It's healthier."

A chipper Marlon told Chung that he had lost fifty pounds, but what he really wanted to talk about was *Season*. "I don't give a damn that I hit the cutting room floor," he insisted. "I don't know how many times in how many pictures it's happened. I get up, dust myself off, and go buy a hot dog and watch the pigeons in the park. But pictures that I care about and have some meaning—and I care a great deal about this picture—I hate to see it ruined, run down, shunted off, and presented in a manner when it could be a far more effective drama than it is."

Marlon had contributed his fee to an anti-apartheid organization and he had understood that MGM/UA would do the same, but it never happened. He also claimed that MGM/UA had tried to smear him with false charges that he had threatened an officer of the company, charges he dismissed as "unthinkable."

"I think they made a money decision," he said. "If I know corporate executives, especially in the movie business, I know they were thinking of the money."

"They did not take into consideration the benefits that might befall people in Africa who are suffering as a result of the politics of apartheid," said Brando. "They're hoping I will go away like some evil wind. But they're mistaken because I'm not gonna go away."

BRANDO ANNOUNCES RETIREMENT

After wrapping up the twelve-week Canadian *Freshman* shoot, in an interview with the *Toronto Globe & Mail,* Brando blasted the Tri-Star comedy. The film was "horrible," he said and predicted, "It's going to be a flop." He then announced his retirement. In the article Brando was also quoted as saying that he was fed up with kowtowing to the Hollywood publicity system, detested New York, but adored Canada.

"I'm retiring, I'm so fed up. This picture, except for the Canadian crew, was an extremely unpleasant experience. I wish I hadn't finished with a stinker." Brando's comments came as a surprise to many involved with the comedy. One source said there were "no problems on the set" and that Brando had been "charming, delightful, and wonderful to everyone." Another insider said Brando paid for the wrap party and bought gifts for the cast and crew.

"I didn't realize how utterly pleasant it was to be here," he said of Canada. "I've come from New York, which is a warthog straight from hell. To sing my swan song here is very pleasant."

"This is my last day," he said, concluding the interview, "Two more shots and I'm done with this madness. You can't imagine how happy I am."

The fallout from Brando's announcement probably surprised even him and two weeks later he was forced to backtrack a bit. Saying that "trying personal times" had led him to express a "dim view" of the recently wrapped *Freshman*, he issued a lengthy statement-apology.

Now that filming of *The Freshman* had concluded, Brando said, "I have seen enough of it to be able to say with confidence that it will be a very successful film." He then proceeded in the written press statement to acknowledge just about everyone involved with the film, particularly writer-director Andrew Bergman.

"Clearly I was wrong about the quality of the picture," Brando continued, recalling that years ago when he saw the first cut of *On the Waterfront*, he was "convinced that it was a failure. I left the cutting room unable to look my director, Elia Kazan, in the face," he said. "I was astounded that people thought enough about the picture to have made it a film worthy of remembering.

"Now that I have seen most of *The Freshman,* it is clear to me that the movie contains moments of high comedy that will be remembered for decades to come. . . ." According to Brando, he was even open to appearing in a sequel. "There is no substitute for laughter in this frightened and endlessly twisting world," he said.

Brando concluded with his hope that anyone he might have offended would "accept my sincere apologies for any discomfort I may have caused them."

Brando ended the year on a happy note, uniting all his children for a Thanksgiving dinner he prepared himself. Although, in typical Brando fashion, it was rumored he served a suckling pig, luau-style, instead of traditional turkey.

PROJECTS

It was reported that he had agreed to do David Lean's *Nostromo,* which was scheduled to begin shooting in Mexico in January. In the adaptation of Joseph Conrad's saga of greed and treachery in a mining community, he would play the world-weary Dr. Monygham. George Carafas had the title role and Liam Neeson and Irena Brook (Peter Brook's daughter) would co-star in the Serge Silberman production.

English director David Lean, 81, thought he had persuaded Brando to play a brutish South American general in a film based on Conrad's novel, the story of how the lust for silver corrupts and destroys a host of characters. "I think he's probably the greatest film actor ever. I

wanted him for *Lawrence* [*of Arabia*] and for *Ryan's
Daughter,* Lean said.

AUTO REPAIR

He also took up auto repair. He took lessons from an
expert for three months, and announced that now that he
had quit movies he would repair cars for his friends, and
charge them less than the going rate. He reportedly interrupted one tune-up on a friend's Buick to get himself
a snack. While noshing he heard a loud crash. The car
had rolled down the driveway and smashed into his gate,
because he had forgotten to engage the emergency brake.
The tune-up ended up costing him $1,200 for bodywork.
His size also interfered. He once wedged himself under
the dashboard of his own car while fixing an air condi-
tioner hose. Flailing, he managed to reach the horn and
honked to summon help, but it was fifteen minutes before his Japanese gardener heard the noise and came to
his rescue.

Eleven

The Tragedy

"The messenger of misery has come to my house."
—Marlon Brando, 1990

As the new decade began, Brando was more withdrawn than ever. He lived in seclusion in the Mulholland Drive house overlooking Coldwater Canyon. The other two houses in the sprawling two-acre compound were occupied by Jack Nicholson and actress/restauranteur Helena Kallianiotes, but they hardly saw each other. Brando was protected from the outside world by an electronic gate and an unpublished phone number. He no longer even retained an official agent or a publicist.

BRANDO'S PYRAMID

Thoughts of mortality must have been filling his head early in 1990 when he began building a giant Egyptian pyramid on Tetiaroa. He told friends he wanted the massive structure to house an inner chamber for his own tomb. Some dismissed it as a "$10-million grave marker." Brando had reportedly gotten the idea for this personal mausoleum from his personal witch doctor, Albert Baume Too, who lived on the island. He told one friend that he wanted only to lie there "for all eternity."

The occasional reckless fan who did approach Brando risked public humiliation and a lecture. When asked for an autograph by a woman while waiting for a prescription at Beverly Hills' Thrifty Drugs, he was heard to roar: "It's pathetic that you should do this! It's demeaning to you! Do you realize what America is doing to you? You think because you see someone on TV they're better than you! You think actors are special! I'm just a fat slob!"

But Brando was also a loving father with some troubled children. And early in 1990 none of them was more troubled than his daughter Cheyenne. In January he moved her into Mulholland Drive and reportedly showered her with gifts. Although badly scarred from her accident and suffering other consequences, she still wanted desperately to become a movie star. Cheyenne was petite, 100 pounds and strongly resembled her Tahitian mother. She had reportedly agreed to star in an Italian film, *The Godfather's Favorite Girl,* until her father dismissed it as "outrageous exploitation." She told him she would only turn it down if he would get her a role in his next movie. Cheyenne may have also been jealous of the attention her father paid to her younger sister, Maimiti, Tarita's daughter by another man.

Restless, she returned to Tahiti, to live with her long-time lover, Dag Drollet, and soon informed her father that she was pregnant.

Dag Drollet was a handsome, strapping Tahitian, 6'3" and 225 pounds. He was already the father of a four-year-old daughter, Tieirani, who was being raised by his mother. His father, Jacques Drollet, a high-ranking Tahitian official, claimed to have served during World War II in a Free French naval liaison unit with the United States.

Cheyenne, who had quit her third high school at the age of twenty, had been involved in an intense relationship with Drollet for almost four years, but he was reportedly seeking to end it. "Dag has lived with Cheyenne since she was fourteen," said a friend, "He was the most popular boy on the island. His father was an education minister and Dag was well-educated and handsome."

But Cheyenne was showing more signs of instability. In April, five months pregnant, she went horseback riding with a photographer friend. The friend warned her to keep her horse at a walk, but Cheyenne replied: "No, I want to go for it." The friend reported: "She didn't care." Her behavior became increasingly bizarre. She would blow her nose on her shirt or burst into laughter at odd moments.

That same month, Brando reportedly put Dag in control of his beloved island.

Brando was now doubly concerned, for his daughter and her unborn child. According to Albert Lecaill, Dag's stepfather, Brando had no confidence in French doctors or the clinics of Tahiti. He wanted Cheyenne to come to Los Angeles to get psychiatric care and to have her baby. After Brando failed to convince his daughter to come to

Los Angeles, Dag urged her to go and agreed to accompany her.

According to Lecaill, Dag discussed the trip with his stepfather two or three weeks before the couple left Tahiti. "He said perhaps it's better they separate," Lecaill recalls. "What he did coming to Los Angeles was the last thing to help her, the last act."

And so, in early May, Dag Drollet and Cheyenne Brando came to stay indefinitely at the house on Mulholland Drive. On May 13, Dag telephoned his mother in Tahiti to report that he and Cheyenne were still having problems. Also staying at the house at the time were Marlon himself and Cheyenne's mother, Tarita, still beautiful at fifty-eight.

Soon, they were joined in the sprawling twelve-room house by another Brando offspring: Christian Devi Brando. He was now a hulking six feet, 160 pounds, and was back from Europe when he found his half sister and her lover installed in his home.

Although Christian considered Mulholland Drive his home and still had his own room there, his official residence was the small gray ranch house on Wonderland Avenue high in Laurel Canyon in the Hollywood Hills that his father had bought for him. The house had a run-down look, possibly because of Christian's absence, and the yard was strewn with junk.

He was seen often at the Canyon Country Store where he would buy food for the homeless people and once reportedly gave his pickup truck to the leader of a street gang in return for the gang's promise to stop terrorizing the store's proprietor.

Christian and his girlfriend of several years, Laurene

Landon, were living apart, but still saw each other. He was said to be most comfortable off by himself in the woods, fishing or backpacking. "He was very shy with the name of Brando," said one friend, cable television talk-show host Skip E. Lowe. "He preferred being introduced simply as Christian."

Christian had a dark side, and that February it had already flashed in an eerie preview of tragedy to come.

Ricardo Alvarez, a homeless fifty-six-year-old prop-man, had met Christian three years earlier while hanging out in Laurel Canyon with a bunch of down-and-outers dubbed the "downboys."

"I was living out of my car at the time. Christian and I hit it off at once and we just started partying together," Alvarez recalls.

"On a typical day we'd get together at about 10 A.M. with a bunch of guys and we wouldn't stop drinking beer until we passed out. There were times we smoked joints, snorted coke, and used whatever other mind-blowing drugs we could lay our hands on.

"And when it came to partying, Christian was king. The rest of us usually didn't have a dime, but Christian would fish into that bottomless pocket of his and let the good times roll.

"He was incredibly generous with all of us—but especially me. I was the one who gave him the nickname, 'Padron.' It's Spanish and means head of the ranch. He always loved that name.

"But there was a dark side to Christian—he could turn downright nasty when he got too high.

And that's just what happened one night in February

when Christian stuck a gun at Alvarez's head—and pulled the trigger.

Christian and his pals spent that day partying with beer and drugs, said a source who witnessed the shooting.

"They were doing a strong drug known as angel dust or PCP. Christian had never done it before.

"After a couple of hours of partying the guys took a break and decided to get back together that night.

"And that's when everything began to unravel."

Around 9:00 P.M. Alvarez and two buddies drove to Christian's house in a 1978 Chevy Caprice, bringing along a case of beer—and a bag of cocaine, said Alvarez.

"We pulled up to his house, and as soon as Christian saw us he burst out of the door like a wild man. My heart nearly stopped when I realized he was waving a gun and firing into the air.

"The driver must have frozen in horror. But one of the guys thought he could handle Christian's fury. He got out of the car carrying a twelve-pack of beer.

"Christian was on him in a flash. He held his gun on the guy with one hand while he beat him senseless with the other. The guy fell to the ground without once raising his hand in defense.

"Christian's girlfriend Laurene was there sobbing. She begged us to leave but it was already too late. Then Christian staggered over to the car. He reached through the window and pointed the gun right at the driver's face. He was wild-eyed and rambling incoherently, like a crazy man. A twisted grin crept across his face and he let out a blood-curdling howl. He was like a rabid wolf.

"I don't know where I got the courage," says Alvarez, "but I realized I had to stop him before someone got hurt. 'Padron. This is crazy,' I spit out from the backseat. 'For God's sake, we're your friends.'

"Christian's eyes narrowed. He reached across the car seat—and suddenly I was looking down the barrel of the gun.

"In my heart I uttered a single prayer for forgiveness. I knew the time had come to meet my maker.

"I watched in horror as Christian pulled the trigger." There was a blinding flash as the gun discharged and the next thing Alvarez knew a warm flow of blood was streaming down the side of his face. He put his hand to his head and felt a two-inch burn above his left ear.

"It felt like the side of my head was on fire and I think the smell of burned hair will stay with me for the rest of my days."

The eyewitness recalled, "The bullet was lodged in the back of the seat. The angle Christian had shot at somehow caused the bullet to graze Ricardo's temple but didn't inflict a serious wound.

Christian staggered around the yard "like a zombie," then went into the house. The witness recalls, "The guys took off in the car like a bat out of hell and ended up at one of the guys' mother's house." She cleaned Alvarez's wound and bandaged it up.

"None of them wanted to call the police or an ambulance. The driver didn't have a license and the guys were carrying drugs. And no one wanted to make trouble for Christian.

Alvarez spent the night at his friend's mother's house. And, when Christian saw him the next day, he told Alvarez he had no recollection of firing the gun at him—and even invited him to his house for dinner.

"He begged me to forgive him. We drank beer and his girlfriend cooked steaks on the grill," Alvarez said.

"It turned into another party. It was like the whole thing never happened."

A few days after Christian shot Alvarez, it became chillingly clear how troubled young Brando was when he ran into the friend he'd beaten up outside his house the night of the incident.

The friend told Christian, "Are you crazy? You could've killed someone. I can't believe you pulled the trigger on Alvarez."

"Christian just looked right through us."

When the friend asked him about it and Christian told him, "It was nothing. What's the big deal? No one got hurt.

"Everyone is fine."

But everything was not fine, as events would soon show.

Mulholland Drive was more than Christian's home, it was also the place where he stored his arsenal: a shotgun, a .44-caliber carbine, and two unregistered, fully automatic firearms—an Uzi submachine gun and an M-14 rifle.

According to his friend Bill Cable, Christian's gun collection had a practical purpose. "When we came back from Italy," he said, "Christian started getting threatening phone calls. Someone would say, 'I'm gonna kill your whole f——ing family, and I'm gonna start with you.' I got a lot of those calls when I was at his house. So we both went out and got guns."

TENSIONS GROW ON MULHOLLAND DRIVE

Cheyenne and Dag had been at Mulholland Drive for a little over a week, and Dag expected to leave soon. He was scheduled to return to Tahiti in a few days to face trial on a vehicular manslaughter charge stemming from the December accident in which he killed a pedestrian.

In retrospect, friends of both Dag and Christian believe that the two men developed a deadly rivalry. Manea Pambrun, Dag's best friend in Tahiti, believes that, "Christian grew to hate Dag because he was everything that he was not." According to Pambrun: "I think Christian came to believe his father loved Dag more than him—that Dag had pushed him out of his father's affections. What started out as dislike grew into a festering hatred in Christian's mind."

Perhaps aware of that, Brando had been encouraging Christian to begin assuming his role as patriarch. According to an observer, Brando "encouraged all his children to consider Christian a sort of special big brother, a surrogate father."

But Christian would take his newfound responsibility to horrible lengths on the night of May 16.

"I DID IT FOR YOU, DAD"

Knowing that Christian was upset, friends said, Cheyenne invited him to dinner, to talk about it. On the night of May 16, they dined at Jerry's Deli in Studio City, just a few miles from Mulholland Drive. According to Lieutenant Ron Hall, commander of the LAPD's West L.A.

Division, Cheyenne apparently told her brother at dinner that Dag had been "slapping her around." Christian, who had been drinking heavily, became furious and muttered that he was going to "bust" Dag.

According to Cheyenne, a furious Christian drove her back to Mulholland Drive, stopping first at the home of a girlfriend where he picked up a .45 caliber handgun. "But it was so light I thought it was a toy," she later told police. "The only gun I'd ever seen belonged to Marlon, and that was a heavy Magnum."

By the time they reached the house and went inside Cheyenne was concerned enough about Christian's anger to race to tell Marlon and Tarita that the two men were about get into an argument.

While Cheyenne was talking to her parents, they heard a shot ring out. The three of them raced to the den on the other side of the house. There they found Christian, a smoking gun in his hand, standing over Dag who lay dead on the couch.

"What have you done?" Marlon shouted.

Christian stood there and said, "I did it for you, Dad."

Brando went white in the face. He ran to Christian and took the gun from his hand. Then he leaned over Dag, who, he could see now, had been shot at point-blank range in the left side of the face. "I checked for a pulse and I found one," he later told police.

Christian began crying and told his father he wanted to leave the house. But Brando insisted that he "sit down and wait for the police."

Tarita grabbed Cheyenne and pulled her away from Dag. Brando told Tarita, "Get her out of here."

"I immediately called the paramedics and the police and then I returned to Dag," said Brando.

"I started giving him CPR, but he had stopped breathing." But he soon realized the situation was hopeless. He jumped up, picked up the phone and dialed 911, screaming "Get a doctor!" The fire department was there in minutes. Brando, in his pajamas, went down to the gate to meet them.

The firemen rushed to the den. There they found Dag "lying back on the couch, kind of like he was watching TV." The television was still on, and channels flipped continuously as though he was scanning the dial.

The first LAPD officer to arrive at Mulholland Drive that night was Steve Cunningham who arrived shortly after the firemen. He later testified that Brando himself opened the front door. Cunningham asked where he could find his son. "I don't have any idea where he is," Brando answered, "and I can't believe he shot him."

Brando, according to police, said that his son had "always had a very bad temper and could be explosively violent when angry." The actor also said that he did not believe his daughter had been abused by Drollet. The allegations, Brando said, "were totally false and, in fact, the victim had been extremely nice to his daughter."

Brando further explained to police that his daughter had been suffering "psychological problems" since her car accident. She had made numerous unfounded allegations against family members, and was undergoing psychiatric treatment.

"Christian told me he had been fighting with Dag because of Dag's beating of Cheyenne, but in fact that's not true. Dag had been extremely nice to my daughter.

"Cheyenne may have said that stuff to Christian because of the accident," Brando went on, explaining that his daughter had been having "severe psychological problems" since her near-fatal accident. "She often is not completely rational," he said. "Christian has a bad temper and has always been very protective of his sister," Brando told them.

Cunningham found the body of Dag Drollet lying on a couch in the den with a lighter, rolling papers, and a tobacco pouch in one hand and a television remote control in the other.

Christian was in the living room, seated on the floor with Cheyenne. "He had his arm around her shoulder and they were talking," Cunningham later testified. "I could not hear her crying, but I remember she had tears on her face."

Cunningham handcuffed Christian and informed him that he was under arrest. As they waited for the arrival of detectives, Christian appeared relaxed and aware and started talking voluntarily.

"He stated that it was an accident," Cunningham later testified, "that they were struggling over the gun, wrestling, and that the decedent had grabbed the gun and made it go off.

"He stated that he had the gun under the couch, that he kept it [at Mulholland Drive] for the family's protection . . . that he told the decedent to get off the couch," and that a struggle ensued in which it was unclear who was trying to shoot whom.

In a rambling, often contradictory statement to police, Christian explained:

"We were rolling around on the couch. He was beating

my pregnant sister. It was a [expletive] accident. I told him to let go. He had my hands. Then boom. Jesus, man, it wasn't murder. He was trying to shoot me. I don't know who was trying to shoot who. He grabbed me and the [expletive] thing shot him in the head . . . .

"Please believe me, I wouldn't do it in my father's house."

But police investigators said there was no sign of a struggle and added that "we have additional evidence not enclosed in the police report."

A police report filed with the court said his blood alcohol level was 0.19 percent, more than twice California's legal limit of intoxication for motorists. In statements to police, Christian acknowledged that he was intoxicated at the time of the shooting.

"We were both in a fit of rage, and the [expletive] gun went off," Christian told officers. "It's my fault because I had loaded the gun in the house. I had a few drinks in me. We struggled and blewey—he's dead."

Brando led police to Christian's weapons stashed under his bed.

"I don't want those guns here," Brando told them. "Take these guns out of here."

CHRISTIAN FACES POLICE

"I shot him, man, but not on purpose," he was quoted as saying. "I did it because he hurt my sister. My sister is pregnant."

By now it was the morning of May 18. Christian was

taken away, charged with murder and held without bail
at a West Los Angeles jail.

Later that morning, at six A.M., Christian called a longtime friend from jail and left a message on the friend's
answering machine. "Well, I've really done it this time,"
he said. "I shot somebody."

In the days that followed, more facts of the case
emerged. Investigators concluded that Dag Drollet, 26,
was sitting in front of a television with a remote control
in one hand, a cigarette lighter in the other when he was
shot in the face. They also said there was no evidence
of a struggle in the den.

A coroner's spokesman would say only that the "cause
of death was a gunshot wound to the head and neck,"
but an inside source said that Drollet was shot at close
range, with the bullet entering the left side of his face
and exiting the lower back of his neck.

ENTER: WILLIAM KUNTSLER

That night of the tragedy, the first person Brando
turned to would be famed civil rights advocate William
Kuntsler, an old friend. At two A.M., the star placed a
frantic call to Kuntsler in New York.

"What do I do? What do I do?" he pleaded.

Kuntsler told Brando, "take a sedative—and get some
sleep."

"He was distraught," Kuntsler recalled.

The lawyer warned Brando not to visit his son in jail.
"I said to stay away because of all the media," Kuntsler
said.

It was said that Christian was upset but in control, concerned about his situation, his family, and his sister.

Kuntsler immediately went to work getting the Brando version to the media. "Christian says it was an accident," he said. "He feels terrible about it, as anybody would. It's one of those tragic circumstances that happen in families sometimes." It was, Kuntsler insisted, "a classic case of self defense."

On May 22 a bail hearing was held in West Los Angeles Municipal Court. Christian, clad in a prison jumpsuit, sat hunched over the defense table, flanked by his legal team, Kuntsler and his longtime associate Ron Kuby and Los Angeles attorney Daniel Stormer. Brando sat stoically in the front row.

Christian pleaded innocent to one count of murder, one count of illegal possession of an assault rifle, and one count of illegal possession of a silencer.

His lawyers presented Judge Rosemary Shumsky with eighteen declarations from Christian's friends, relatives, and supporters including Jack Nicholson. "He's had enough," Tom Laughlin, Christian's onetime schoolmaster told *People* magazine. "He's had too much excruciating pain in his early life. He didn't need this." (Dag Drollet, of course, was beyond issues of pain or need at this point.)

Each of Christian's attorneys, in turn, described him as a caring, hard-working, and trustworthy citizen who posed no threat to the public and would not flee if released on bail. They were prepared to seek bail as high as $1.25 million.

"Jack Nicholson says he has always been a hard worker . . . and trusts him implicitly," said Daniel Stormer. A fourteen-year-old senior high school student recalled the time he and Christian found an injured opossum. "We took it home to nurse it back to health, but it died the next day," he said. "Christian was very upset."

Ron Kuby acknowledged that his client had a drinking problem. "He's been to detox programs on at least two occasions in the past," Kuby said. "And he is more than willing to go through any kind of detox program."

But Deputy District Attorney Steven Barshop argued that Brando was indeed a flight risk in what he called a "no bail case."

"The defendant went to a residence and got a murder weapon," Barshop said. "The decedent was seated . . . holding in one hand . . . a Bic lighter, negating any theory whatsoever of a struggle."

"This case is criminal homicide," Barshop added. "This case, for the purposes of the bail motion, is first-degree murder."

After hearing forty-five minutes of arguments, Judge Shumsky dismissed the bail motion, saying, "the court finds there is no basis for setting bail in this case."

Outside the court, Kuntsler held a news conference and railed against what he called the judge's "outrageous decision."

"I think she made up her mind before she got here," Kunstler said. "She misused her power."

Visibly shaken, accompanied by Tarita, Brando also made a brief statement outside the courthouse. He told reporters: "We see on the television and read in newspapers things that are unpronounceably sad," said Brando. "The messenger of misery has come to my house, and has also come to the house of Mr. Jacques Drollet in Tahiti.

"To those people who have known these kinds of

tragic circumstances in the world, no explanation is necessary," he continued. "To those people who do not know the nature of this acute misery that both our families suffer, no explanation is possible. We must just be strong and I think that the family, with love and supporting each other, will prevail."

EXIT: WILLIAM KUNTSLER

The day after Christian's bail was denied, William Kunstler announced he planned to take time off from the case to act in a movie directed by Oliver Stone about the famed rock group, The Doors. "I play a lawyer in the movie," said Kunstler.

He soon left the case completely, and was replaced by distinguished Los Angeles attorney Robert L. Shapiro.

Undiscouraged, Brando hired former New York City chief medical examiner Michael Baden to perform an autopsy on Dag Drollet. On May 25 Baden performed a six-hour post mortem on Drollet before the body was flown home to Tahiti for burial.

"We wanted someone with impeccable credentials to review the way the coroner's autopsy was conducted," said Daniel Stormer.

"MARLON'S ON THE VERGE OF A COMPLETE BREAKDOWN"

But Brando was also a prisoner, of his own searing anguish.

Brando would not even speak with his close friend and next-door neighbor, Jack Nicholson.

"Marlon's on the verge of a complete breakdown," Nicholson told a friend. "He's totally withdrawn into himself. I'm worried sick."

As family and friends tried to convince Brando he was not to blame for his son's bloody outburst, Anna Kashfi declared, "Christian desperately wanted his father's approval. But it never happened. Through all the years, he tried to live up to Marlon's expectations and failed.

"Christian told me, 'One of these days I'm going to do something that will make Dad sit up and take notice of me.' Well that poor boy has certainly done that now."

Christian was ordered to return to court June 11 to schedule a preliminary hearing.

"IT'S MURDER IN CASE YOU DIDN'T KNOW IT"

On June 12 Cheyenne gave a statement to detective Andy Monsue at Mulholland Drive in which she said Christian told her he was going to "bust [Dag's] ass." She told Monsue that after they picked up a gun and returned to their father's home, Christian immediately entered the room where Drollet was watching TV. After a brief exchange, she heard Christian say, "Stop touching her," before a single shot rang out.

She told Monsue that when Christian joined her in another room, the gun still in his hand, he said, "I killed him."

Her final words to Monsue: "It's a murder in case you didn't know it."

According to Prosecutor Barshop, because Brando had assured investigators that Cheyenne would remain in the United States until she gave birth, they did not take any steps to keep her from leaving.

But the day after her statement to Detective Monsue, Cheyenne suddenly left the country and returned to Tahiti.

CHEYENNE FLEES

Prosecutors considered Cheyenne a crucial witness in the case against Christian. Six weeks later she gave birth to a son and named Dag as the father. But Dag's parents were not convinced that was true and retained Los Angeles attorney Marshall Morgan to investigate. Morgan ordered tests run on blood and skin samples taken from Cheyenne's newborn son Tuki and Dag's body to see if the child really belonged to Dag.

Her mental and physical condition were dubious. According to Jacques Drollet, she was "in and out" of a hospital "for detoxification for drugs," living with her mother who cared for the baby.

But the baby had more problems than just its troubled mother and questionable parentage. "Tuki is being weaned off his addiction to drugs," a nurse told reporters. "It's not an easy procedure, but since this is the grandson of Marlon Brando, it's more possible. Gradually, the baby can become almost sober."

Tuki was said to be very thin, with big hands and

big feet, the classic signs of malnutrition caused by drugs.

BRANDO THREATENED WITH
$100 MILLION LAWSUIT

When it seemed things could not get worse, Brando was hit by a staggering new blow: Drollet's father hired lawyers to file a $100 million "wrongful death" lawsuit against him. Dag's furious father, wanted Brando to pay.

"The Drollet family is heartbroken and angry about Dag's death," said Drollet's Los Angeles attorney Marshall Morgan.

"Dag was only twenty-six and Jacques feels he was shot like a dog right in Marlon Brando's home. Jacques has become passionate about making people responsible for the death of his son.

"The Drollets want justice done, but they're also planning to file a wrongful death lawsuit against Marlon and Christian Brando. I'll be traveling to Tahiti to meet with Jacques and his Tahitian attorney, François Quinquis, to decide when the suit will be filed."

Both lawyers refused to confirm they would demand $100 million. But sources close to the Drollets said the figure was correct and it was published in the Tahitian newspaper *La Depeche de Tahiti*.

The lawsuit, coming on the heels of Christian's arrest, had added to the turmoil in Brando's life and left him "totally devastated," confided an insider.

"Marlon is an emotional wreck. He just sits and

broods all day long. He doesn't move, he doesn't talk, and sometimes a tear rolls down his cheek.

"He's so distraught that he's even lost about thirty pounds.

"Marlon told a friend: 'My life suddenly fell into a black hole on the night of May 16th.

'Two of my children are going through a living hell— Christian is facing murder one and Cheyenne has to deal with the tragic loss of the man she loved.

'She also may be facing the loss of her firstborn in a custody battle. The Drollets are out for blood.

'All this madness is driving me crazy!' "

Brando had reason to be concerned about the lawsuit because the Drollets were so prominent and well-connected. Jacques's cousin was a cabinet minister and the leader of a political group in Tahiti.

Adding to Brando's woes was his fear that Dag's mother Lisette would seek custody of little Tuki.

"Dag's mother Lisette blames Cheyenne for his death, and Cheyenne is afraid Lisette will try to take her baby away from her by declaring her an unfit mother," revealed the insider.

"There's already a precedent established along those lines. Lisette already has custody of Dag's other love child, a four-year-old girl named Iairini, and has raised her from birth."

Marlon worried over his son, daughter, and new grandchild—and the specter of a civil lawsuit that could wipe him out financially.

"Even if everything turns out 100 percent in his favor, I'm afraid the stress will have taken its toll," said a friend. "Marlon may never be the same again."

TAPE RULED INADMISSIBLE

On Monday, July 23, Christian's team scored a stunning victory when Superior Court Judge Larry Fidler ruled that the tape-recorded statement he gave hours after the shooting was inadmissable as evidence against him.

Brando sat stonily, occasionally taking notes and ignoring the groupies who packed the courtroom. Judge Fidler ruled that Detective Osti had failed to properly read Christian his Miranda rights before questioning him.

Osti testified that when he advised Christian he had a right to remain silent and to have an attorney present during questioning, he "might have left out the part, 'if you can't afford one,' the section that informs suspects that they have a right to appointed counsel, because he assumed Christian's father was a rich man. The beginning of the tape, played in court, confirmed this omission.

Shapiro and his co-counsel Gerald Uelmen, dean of the Santa Clara University law school, argued that the detective had taken advantage of Brando's state of mind, and hastened to get an account of the events from him before an attorney had an opportunity to advise him not to talk.

"We are very pleased with the way the hearing is proceeding," Shapiro said after court recessed for the day.

But despite the apparent setback, Detective Monsue told reporters outside court that Christian had made numerous other admissions that could still be used against him.

"This is a case where you couldn't get the guy to shut up—he talked for three hours," Monsue said. "Christian is a very talkative individual."

CHRISTIAN'S LADIES

Christian was said to have a "harem" of long-legged beauties keeping vigil at Los Angeles County Jail where he was being held.

A number of female supporters showed up at court and outside the Los Angeles jailhouse in the days after Christian was arrested. "Christian draws girls like flies," said his friend Skip E. Lowe. "His problem is that he can't say no. He has a tender heart and an affection for lovely ladies—a trait he got from his dear old dad. He's got a very sexy charisma. Now all of Christian's girlfriends are vying for his attention. They all want to be his one and only doll."

There was his long-time girlfriend; blonde blue-eyed Laurene Landon; sometimes girlfriends Shirley Cumpanes and Joycelyn Lew, the Oriental exotic dancer; another beautiful blond model, Lisa Cavanaugh, from a support group; his dark-haired ex-wife Mary McKenna, who seemed intent on winning him back; Barbara Orwig, a Hollywood go-go dancer who reportedly sent him lipstick-kissed love messages.

Sometimes spats broke out among the women because Christian was only allowed one ten-minute visit a day at the dirty and overcrowded correctional facility.

CHEYENNE'S VERSION

At the July 23 hearing prosecutors also argued over whether statements by Cheyenne to investigators, suggesting a motive for the shooting, should be admitted as evidence, even though she was unavailable for cross-examination. Monsue acknowledged that Cheyenne's comments were "critical" to prove the shooting was premeditated.

The courtroom was tense. On one side sat the Drollet family: Dag's mother, Lisette Lecaill, openly weeping as her son's fatal facial wound was described. Across the aisle: Brando, who closed his eyes and extended his hands at times as if meditating, surrounded by Christian's past and present loves.

Ballistics expert David Butler testified that Drollet was shot at such close range that human tissue remained on the muzzle of the semiautomatic pistol.

"DEATH IS TOO GOOD FOR THE GUY"

At the hearing, Laurene Landon testified that Christian had come to her apartment shortly before the slaying and appeared to be intoxicated, but she denied a prosecution assertion that Christian picked up the murder weapon at the apartment, which he shared with her. She further testified he said Cheyenne was "having boyfriend problems." She also said Cheyenne was lying down in Christian's pickup truck, seemed groggy, and said, "I want to go home."

Deputy D.A. Steven Barshop, arguing for the murder charge, read to the judge a statement Christian had made to the first police officer on the scene.

"I shot him, man, but not on purpose," Brando had stated. "It was an accident. The gun was under the couch. I kept it there."

Later in the statement, Brando declared, "Man, death is too good for the guy."

"Please believe me—I wouldn't do it in my father's house," he said. "We were both in a rage. The (expletive) gun went off."

Prosecutors argued that there was no evidence of the struggle Christian described.

Defense attorney Shapiro told the court that Brando planned to make a shrine to Drollet's memory out of the room in which he was slain. He said that may have been why he resisted efforts by detectives to return to the estate weeks after the shooting to reconstruct the crime.

"Marlon Brando wanted to turn the room into a memorial for the decedent, light a candle and pay respects and then clean up the blood and get on with his life," Shapiro said.

On July 24 Judge Fidler ordered Christian to stand trial for murder and set bail at ten million dollars, saying he believed that was the lowest amount that would ensure that the defendant would not flee the country and would appear for trial. Brando had already offered the court his house, worth more than five million dollars, to ensure his son's return.

LOST PASSPORT

The catch was that the judge required Christian to give up his passport to help ensure that he would not flee to avoid prosecution. His family had the option to post the bond, believed the highest amount in Los Angeles County history, in either cash, property, or a combination.

But Shapiro, said he and the family had been unable to locate Christian's passport and that he could remain in jail "until we find it."

Christian was next scheduled to appear in Superior Court in Santa Monica on August 7 to enter a plea to the murder charges.

Neither Brando nor Christian showed any emotion when the judge announced his decision; Christian's bevy of supporters broke into sobs.

"It's disgusting how all these other women are pretending to be his girlfriends. I've been with Christian for five years," said Laurene, her blond locks flowing over a tight teal suede suit. "I speak to him every day. We all know this was a tragic accident."

She dismissed the theory that Christian was motivated by envy: "It's unbelievable that the D.A. would say that Christian was jealous of Dag!"

As Christian was led from the courtroom, Landon and others burst into tears again.

DAG'S PARENTS SPEAK OUT

Before Dag Drollet's father, his mother and stepfather, Lisette and Albert Lecaill, returned to Tahiti on July 29, they spoke to the press to defend their late son against claims that he had abused Cheyenne.

By the time they came to stay at Mulholland Drive, according to Dag's family, the youth and Cheyenne were strictly friends. "He was sleeping on a mattress in the den where he was killed, and she was living in her own room."

Drollet said Dag had confided that Cheyenne had become "impossible" to live with and told him, "I've heard her saying that she was the most beautiful girl, the most intelligent girl, and the richest girl by her father's fortune."

According to Drollet, she had "four or five boyfriends" before, "but for the first time it was not her who was throwing someone away," it was Dag's decision. "At that moment all her ego, all her pride was wounded."

Drollet said that the accident had a dramatic effect on Cheyenne. Afterwards, she became "very violent in her words and her manner. She has said very serious things, she has hit people . . . . she hit Dag, when she was in a rage."

Drollet insisted that, "Dag never beat Cheyenne. Perhaps on one or two occasions when Cheyenne was in a rage, she was scratching him, hitting him, throwing things at Dag, perhaps he gave her one or two slaps, but he never beat her and nothing at all since she was pregnant, never. Dag is too well-behaved."

According to Lecaill, Brando had telephoned them six hours after the shooting, saying "It was an accident. We more or less accepted that it was." Now that they were in Los Angeles, however, "We asked him to see us and he refused. It's normal if it's an accident, to visit, to see where Dag lived, gather his things, hear of his last hours." He acknowledged that later Christian's attorney had called but by then, "We knew better how it happened and did not want to see him."

MYSTERY SURROUNDS CHEYENNE

In early August, Cheyenne remained in Hospital de Vaiami in Papeete where all details of her medical condition were kept under wraps. Her son, born June 26, was still in Hospital Mamoa. A hospital spokeswoman would only confirm that the babe was still there, but refused to release details of his condition.

"I understand the child was born addicted to drugs," said attorney Marshall Morgan, who represented Drollet's parents. Morgan called Cheyenne a "confirmed junkie" whose habit started "when she was thirteen."

Still confined to the Vaiami mental hospital, Cheyenne was allowed weekend leaves in order to visit her baby. However, journalist Dana Blanchard reported a friend's claim that "after a quick trip to see him, she's out partying. She stays out all night. She wants to get drunk because it makes her forget how horrible life is." Blanchard reported that Cheyenne was seen regularly drinking at the Piano Bar, a club in downtown Papeete, only a few blocks away from the mental hospital. Another observer reported her "plastered" at the Mahana Bar in the Tahara Hyatt Regency.

CHEYENNE FACES THE GUILLOTINE

While Christian sat in jail, he learned that Cheyenne was confined to a squalid mental ward in Tahiti, where she faced charges of plotting the death of her lover.

Under the French law that governed the island, if found guilty, she faced the guillotine.

Dag's bitter father said: "My son helped her all the way to his tomb."

According to her brother Tehotu, the girl had shorn her hair in protest and feared for her life.

"They put Cheyenne in the crazy ward," her tearful brother said outside the decrepit hospital in Papeete. "She cut off all her hair in a fit of rage, her door is padlocked. She sleeps on a mattress that's covered with soiled linen. There's no door to her bathroom, exposing her toilet.

"Cheyenne must wear a uniform of white shorts and a T-shirt. Her simple meals consisted of pineapples, rice, a few pieces of fish, carrots, and onions. Water is all she was allowed to drink.

"The place stinks," her brother said. "It's very hot inside. Paint is chipping off the walls. Cheyenne has never lived like this in her life. She's used to much better."

Twice a week she was transported across the island to Mamoa Hospital to visit Tuki.

A bitter Drollet asked, "How can you shoot someone who is lying down on the couch watching television? I loathe Christian Brando and his family for what they have done. My beloved son was killed Mafia-style in Marlon Brando's house. He was shot practically in the eye from point-blank range. It was a very nasty death.

"Marlon knew Christian was a bad-tempered kid. He knew the kid was drinking and doing dope. He knew all about his guns. But what did Marlon do to protect my son? He did nothing. In Tahiti, you don't invite someone into your house to let them be killed."

On July 2, Drollet went before a Tahitian magistrate

and accused Cheyenne of conspiracy in the killing
"They both plotted to kill my son," he said.

Judge Max Gatti said on July 19 that he accepted the
charge of conspiracy against Cheyenne.

In Los Angeles prosecutors had obtained a federal subpoena in an effort to compel Cheyenne to testify in Christian's case.

"MY SON WAS JUST KILLED LIKE A DOG"

Before leaving Los Angeles, Dag's father, mother, and
stepfather talked to a reporter. According to them, their
son scarcely knew Christian, having met him a few times
in Los Angeles and Tahiti.

"In Polynesia, the rules of hospitality are very strong,
very important, very serious," said an angry Jacques
Drollet. "When you invite someone into your house you
have duties and obligations. You must protect him mate-
rially, morally, physically, and intellectually."

According to Drollet, Brando "knew that his daughter
was not very well balanced. He knew that Christian
Brando was bad-tempered, that there were arms around
the house belonging to Christian, and he knew there
could be some friction between people in his own house
but he didn't protect my son. On the contrary, my son
was just killed like a dog in his house." That house, according to Drollet, was "a bunker with many weapons."

CHRISTIAN PLEADS INNOCENT

On August 7, Christian pleaded innocent to murder
and illegal weapons charges in a Santa Monica court,

and his lawyer asked a judge to reconsider releasing him on "reasonable bail."

Attorney Robert L. Shapiro made the move after Christian answered "yes" to a number of questions concerning his innocent plea in the shooting death of Dag Drollet.

The courtroom was crowded with spectators, friends of Brando, reporters, and even tourists hoping to get a glimpse of the defendant's famous father. But Brando, who had attended most of the previous hearings, did not attend this one.

Shapiro moved for a lower bail, saying outside court that his client "should be treated no differently than anyone else."

The previous bail, set at ten million dollars, was believed to be the highest in Los Angeles County history. Prosecutors had argued for no bail at all, arguing that Brando might flee the country, as his sister already had.

After pleading not guilty, Christian was returned to jail after he failed to post ten million dollars bail and surrender his passport. Attorney Shapiro asked Judge Perez to consider reducing the bail and attaching conditions to it, "that will satisfy the most skeptical person that Christian will definitely appear" for trial.

Perez scheduled a bail hearing for Thursday and pretrial motions for September 14.

"We are going to ask that Christian not be singled out and treated any differently than anyone else would be in a similar situation," Shapiro told reporters outside court.

"Was he really a flight risk?" Shapiro said, "He's just a thirty-two-year-old welder. And he's so high-profile. Where could he go?"

Shapiro had asked Brando not to attend the court hearing to avoid turning it into another circus.

On August 9, bail for Christian was reduced to two million dollars. Judge Perez ruled that ten million dollars was excessive. Brando, who attending the hearing in Santa Monica with his business manager and Miko, presented Christian's passport, which had been a condition of release.

BRANDO HAUNTED BY DAG'S GHOST

Marlon was so tormented he became convinced that Dag's spirit was attacking him in his own bed. He began telling friends that Dag's spirit was roaming Mulholland Drive crying out for revenge.

"Marlon believes he's being haunted by Dag's ghost," confirmed Anna Kashfi.

What's more, he told friends he was also scared out of his wits several times by hearing an eerie instant replay of the fatal shooting, complete with gunshots and screams.

"I can't sleep nights," he confided.

"When I drop off to sleep, the sheets are whipped off my bed, and I wake up in a cold sweat after cold ghostly lips are pressed to my ear and angry curses are whispered. The words burn themselves into my mind: 'They must be punished. I should not have died.' It's terrifying. I know it's Dag's angry spirit."

In his darkest hour, Brando was so desperate for relief that he was getting help from Michael Jackson, who conducted a special ceremony to drive the ghost out of the house.

Brando felt that the only way he could get rid of the ghost was to get Christian and Cheyenne back into the room where Dag was shot so all three could pray for forgiveness. But that was impossible right now.

Christian had been charged with murder and was being held on ten million dollars bail. Cheyenne was in a mental hospital in Tahiti where she had fled after the slaying. Cheyenne had also been charged in Tahiti with complicity to commit murder and, if convicted, she could be sentenced to life in prison.

And now Christian's attorneys planned to reveal at his trial that Cheyenne was high on the drugs LSD and Ecstasy the night of the shooting and provoked her brother into killing by lieing that she'd been beaten by her lover.

As Brando wrestled with his children's crises, he was also going through hell at home.

"The ghost is driving Marlon nuts," disclosed a close friend. "It's turning his posh home into a house of horrors. On several occasions he's been frightened out of his wits by sudden blasts, like gunshots, followed by distant screams of a boy. Marlon told me he also hears voices at night. And the lights in the house suddenly turn on and off by themselves."

A worried family insider disclosed: "Marlon has almost reached the snapping point in this terrible series of events. He's nearly mad with worry and has been seeing ghostly apparitions in his home—apparitions he believes to be Dag Drollet's spirit!"

A friend revealed that Brando was so frantic to end his torment, he pulled Christian aside during one of his son's courtroom appearances and told him: "You have to come home and help me! Dag's ghost is roaming the house crying out for justice. He will never rest until you and Cheyenne together help me exorcise his spirit."

Brando had turned the study where Dag was slain into a shrine. He kept white candles burning twenty-four hours a day around the edges of the room, and went there each night to pray, "in an attempt to appease Dag's angry spirit," said an insider. He told a friend: "I've tried to talk to Dag's spirit, telling him how sorry I am, how sorry we all are."

Brando confided that sometimes when he was in the study praying, a "cold angry breeze" suddenly whipped through the room, instantly snuffing the burning candles.

Since the hauntings began, Michael Jackson had been a regular visitor at the mansion. Jackson urged Brando to stay strong during the crisis.

"Michael told Marlon that he's going to arrange for a medium he knows—a medium with experience in exorcising ghosts—to visit Marlon's home and try to send Dag's ghost on to the hereafter."

During one visit to Brando's home, Michael even conducted a ceremony of his own by spreading fragrant herbs on the spot where Dag died. Jackson told Brando the herbs would "draw love, healing, and peace" to the home.

But peace would elude Brando for a long, long time.

According to a friend, Marlon said: "My daughter told me she was using LSD and Ecstasy the night Drollet was shot. Every word she told Christian about the beatings was the product of a drug-crazed mind."

A source close to the Brando family said that Cheyenne had confessed to a friend: "Christian shot Dag, but I helped pull the trigger by getting him too mad. I said too much. I wish he had shot me instead."

Confided another source: "Marlon's friends and family members are seriously concerned about his emotional state. He's in a state of depression and looks like he hasn't slept or eaten in weeks.

"He just walks around the house mumbling, 'How can this be happening to us? I just want this nightmare to be over with!' "

BAIL REDUCED TO $2 MILLION

Paperwork stalled while Brando decided whether he should use his five million dollar Bel-Air home for collateral for a property bond, or post a cash surety bond. Bail amount is doubled for a property bond, which meant Brando would have to post four million dollars in property. A certified appraisal of the property would also be required. The cash bond, however, required ten percent of the bail amount, or $200,000.

CHRISTIAN RELEASED ON BAIL

On August 15, Christian was scheduled to be released from jail after a judge agreed to accept Brando's home as bond. In a half-hour hearing, Judge Perez said he would allow Brando to post his Mulholland Drive home as collateral for guaranteeing Christian's return to court. Trial was set for October 9.

Sworn in at the August 15 hearing, Brando told the judge it would be a "privilege" to put up his twelve-room home as security. California law stipulates that when property is posted, it must be worth twice as much as the amount of bail.

"This offers . . . Christian the opportunity to show he is ready, willing, and able to fulfill his civic duty," Brando said. He added that he hoped the prosecutor Deputy D.A. Steve Barshop, whom he termed "intractable," would be "surprised" and "disappointed" to see that Christian met his future court dates.

Perez also ordered that Christian refrain from consuming alcohol, or any non-prescription drugs or narcotics and he was to undergo regular testing to prove he was drug-free. Brando had said that his son was an alcoholic and had used drugs.

Perez cautioned Christian that if he failed to appear at court proceedings, his father's home would be sold.

After the hearing, father and son embraced, Brando patting Christian on the back and kissing him on the head before he was led away by bailiffs.

Next, Brando accused Prosecutor Barshop of having reduced his son's life to zero. Barshop responded that that, precisely, was what Christian Brando had done to Drollet.

Brando started to grab Barshop's arm as the prosecutor walked away, shaking his head.

Outside, playing to an unruly press pack, Brando said he had hoped Barshop had changed his "conception of my son as a slathering mad-dog killer." He said he was "deeply, deeply relieved," that Christian would be leaving jail. "This is an extraordinary moment, one I have long ooked forward to," he said, adding he believed that the "best" verdict he could expect of the trial would be accidental manslaughter.

Christian was released on bail on August 15 after three months behind bars. He was scheduled to stand trial on October 9.

As a steady rain fell, Brando spoke to reporters outside the Men's Central Jail: "It's a very simple moment," he said. "A moment long looked forward to."

He went on: "I'm proud to have my son out of jail. We're just going to go home and relax and do whatever Christian wants to do."

Turning to Christian, he said, "Can you smile?"

Christian managed a faint smile.

When asked if jail time affected his relationship with his father, Christian shook his head "no." His father added: "I got fatter and he got thinner."

"I'm just going to go home and try to straighten this out," Christian said. "I want to thank all the people that supported me writing letters and it's good to be out."

They left in two cars—Brando in a chauffeured black Mercedes with the family dog; and Christian in the family Volkswagon with Miko and Laurene. Miko patted Christian's knee as they pulled away.

Minutes after leaving jail, however, Christian was served with a wrongful death civil suit, filed on behalf of the daughter of Dag Drollet. The Brandos hoped a one million-dollar trust fund set up for Tiairani Drollet would be adequate.

"Christian wanted to set it up and turn over what he had in his trust to it. He thought it was the right thing

to do," explained attorney Shapiro. "Marlon supple
mented [it] so it would . . . adequately support the chi
for life."

As soon as Christian was released, father and so
moved into Michael Jackson's Neverland ranch, to u
wind. The strain had already taken a terrible toll an
friends reported Brando had been diagnosed with hig
blood pressure and hypertensive heart disease.

According to his father, Christian would be doir
"hard time" as a welder until his trial. Brando de
manded that Christian work at a construction job nea
his home.

"Marlon has turned into a jailer and become Chri
tian's worst nightmare," said an observer. "Christia
thought that when his dad sprung him on two millic
dollars bail, he'd let him live it up until the trial.

"Boy, was Christian wrong! He was playing aroun
working on his truck's generator, drinking a beer, whe
Marlon told him, 'You're not going to do easy labor he
in my prison!'

"Marlon asked a friend for a favor—and the next thin
Christian knew, he was on a welding job in the blazin
California sun.

"Christian was being paid eighteen dollars an hou
plus overtime," according to the observer. Brando repor
edly told his son he would need to work over 40,00
hours—or more than fifty-two years—to pay him bac
for the bail.

Christian replied, "at that rate, I'll be working into m
afterlife."

Marlon told him: "Shut up and get to work!"

PROSECUTORS RETALIATE—JUDGE REMOVED

Prosecutors, dismayed at the reduced bail, filed an affidavit of prejudice against Judge Perez on September 4, automatically removing him from presiding at Christian's trial. He was immediately replaced by Superior Court Judge Robert W. Thomas.

"We were upset because of the reduction of bail," Deputy D.A. William Clark acknowledged. "Christian Brando would not think twice about having [his father] lose his house. Marlon Brando could make enough money on one film before the end of the year to buy another house."

The next day, Robert Shapiro filed a motion asking that the murder charge against Christian be reduced to manslaughter. He also filed a motion seeking to bar from evidence Christian's tape-recorded interview with the police. He was scheduled to argue the motions before Judge Thomas on September 14.

WILL CHEYENNE TESTIFY?

Prosecutors went to federal court in Los Angeles on September 14 for help in bringing Cheyenne back from Tahiti to testify at Christian's trial. A district attorney's spokeswoman said U.S. District Court would be requested to ask a French court to order her return. They believed her testimony was critical to prove that the shooting was premeditated.

But the federal judge refused to ask the French government to compel Cheyenne to testify or to answer questions by satellite from Tahiti. U.S. District Judge Terry J. Hatter, Jr. told prosecutors they should either seek to serve her with a subpoena through the state courts or cite legal precedents for his acting in the case.

The next step was "the [state] Supreme Court, I think," said Deputy D.A. Barshop.

They believed Cheyenne's testimony was "crucial" to establishing Christian's state of mind before the shooting. Brando claimed the shooting was accidental. Cheyenne told police that he repeatedly had threatened to kill Drollet, but her statement cannot be used unless she is cross-examined.

WAS CHEYENNE A BATTERED WOMAN?

On September 26, at a pretrial hearing, Judge Thomas refused to reduce the charge against Christian from murder to manslaughter. Thomas did rule that tape-recorded statements made by Christian to the police were inadmissible because the detective conducting the interview failed to properly advise him of his Miranda right to have an attorney appointed for him if he could not afford one. This was good news for Christian. Prosecutors had hoped to prove the shooting was premeditated because Christian had admitted in the statement that he got a gun from his girlfriend's house before the incident.

The judge also ordered that Christian be tried separately on an illegal weapons charge, possessing a machine gun, because it had no connection to the alleged murder.

Defense attorney Robert Shapiro told the judge he

would argue that ballistic evidence supported a scenario of a struggle between Brando and Drollet. Shapiro said if the killing was indeed the result of a struggle over a gun, the most that Christian Brando could be convicted of would be manslaughter.

Deputy D.A. Barshop adamantly disagreed: "Shooting somebody in the face at point-blank range is murder," he told the judge.

Brando began what had become his regular chat with reporters on court days by lashing out at Barshop, for trying to force Cheyenne to return from Tahiti.

Brando told the reporters that he had proof that Cheyenne was beaten, supporting Christian's contention that he shot Dag during a quarrel over the bad treatment.

"Cheyenne suffered enormously. She's been beaten physically," he said. "We have clear proof of that."

But he refused to elaborate, telling reporters that "unfortunately, it bears heavily on issues in the trial which will be brought out. You'll have a field day."

This was the first public suggestion that evidence of abuse existed, and conflicted with Brando's previous statements.

"How much more can she take? She suffered a head injury in an auto accident last year. Her entire face was smashed, she has six pieces of metal in her face, she had to have her face remade. She has suffered a nervous breakdown. She's required to be in a sanitarium under a doctor's care," Brando asked the press pack.

"And for that man [Barshop] to keep chasing my daughter when it's been refused by the courts, when it's been refused on every occasion that he has tried to do that, I think is unspeakable. As a father, I am deeply offended."

Brando only lost his composure when he was asked about Cheyenne's child. "Tuki's doing fine, healthy strong. And Cheyenne's doing her best . . ." Brando stopped as tears filled his eyes. "Excuse me, I'm sorry," he said. Sobbing quietly, he headed for his car.

But L.A. Deputy D.A. William Clark was convinced that Cheyenne was not as crazy as Brando said and would testify that Christian had no reason to shoot Drollet. "When Cheyenne talked to the magistrate in Tahiti, she said that there was some violence, but that it was not extreme or persistent, that it was just normal boyfriend-girlfriend fighting," Clark stated.

"Saying she was beaten and proving it in court are two very different things. If they're just making all this up now to distract the media's attention, and then are not going to go through with it in court, we'll be outraged.

"We are not hounding her, as Marlon puts it. In Tahiti before a judge, when he asked her why she didn't go back, she said she wanted to go testify, and would go if she was asked, and if her doctors allowed her to go.

"Marlon stopped short of saying that he would break the law, but said that he would do what he could as a father to stop it.

"The defense is already preparing for her return by saying that she's insane. But the detective who interviewed her said at the time that she was a believable credible witness."

BRANDO CHANGES HIS STORY

Because Brando puts such value on the truth, it is disturbing to note what looks like a complete reversal of his story.

A few months earlier, Brando had stated that Cheyenne had made up lies to Christian, telling him that Dag was beating her. He said she was just stirring things up and still suffering the consequences of her accident. But now, seeing that Christian faced charges of first-degree murder, he was saying it was all true, that Cheyenne was indeed telling Christian the truth, and that there was a struggle in the house, that it was not an execution.

Now Marlon was saying that he supported Christian's claim that the shooting was an accident that took place during a quarrel about the alleged abuse of Cheyenne.

There was another hearing on October 1. This time the judge, seeking time to review documents, delayed ruling until October 4 on changing the October 9 trial date. Prosecutors wanted another month to have Cheyenne subpoenaed from Tahiti. The defense was ready to go.

Prosecutors were expecting to get a decision on their request from Tahiti's French government to help get her out. Co-prosecutor Bill Clark said Cheyenne told a Tahitian judge that she would return to the United States if allowed to leave.

CHRISTIAN'S WEDDING PLANS

Like his father, Christian remained committed to the future and in late September he revealed that he and Laurene Landon were planning to marry.

"All we know is we want to marry as soon as we can and have a family. I'm happy that Laurene's been here and both of us are praying that everything sorts itself out," said Christian.

"I hope I won't have to go back to jail, but if I have to, then, of course, we'll have to wait. At the moment, we're living from day to day."

Christian appeared anxious to have his day in court. "Nobody has heard my side of the story yet. I always thought the law said 'Innocent until proven guilty'—but everyone's been treating me as if I'm guilty unless I can prove myself innocent," he said. "I'm longing to take that stand and give my story."

"Everyone seems to think I'm some sort of Jack the Ripper. I'm nothing like that. I like anonymity and I want my life to be private. I'm not an actor. My father's the actor, not me."

"I've done nothing wrong," he insisted. "It was an accident. I never want to be anywhere near a gun again."

"Christian is a very altruistic person," Laurene added. "He loves children and animals. He's a good person. He's certainly never lied to me."

AUTOBIOGRAPHY

During this period, the always press-wary Brando often chose to communicate to the world through longtime friend Army Archerd, the venerable columnist for *Daily Variety*. In September he told Archerd that he was planning to write his autobiography and was looking for a publisher.

"I was invaded so deeply by the press I've been forced into this position," he explained. "Fifteen books have been written about me, not with or by me, and not accurately. I'll say it accurately. There isn't anything I won't go into. Whatever doesn't kill you makes you stronger." Archerd also reported that Brando had written three scripts for himself and that Christian had joined Alcoholics Anonymous.

The news that Brando's proposed memoirs were on the auction block set off an international multi-million-dollar bidding war.

His London attorney, Belinda Frixou, was handling the sale and summoned interested parties to London for discussions and a possible "chat" with the author.

Frixou, Brando's general adviser for the last decade, denied that he needed the money for his son's legal fees.

"There've been so many different books about him, unauthorized biographies, that it is about time to set the record right and give everybody the correct version," Frixou said.

"He's doing it totally himself," said Frixou, "he's a very good writer and has done scripts before. . . . He's written passages and poems and is a writer I would say of—who would I compare him to? I simply can't—descriptive, floral style. Very, very poetic."

Almost immediately, one publisher, Warner Books, offered two million dollars which was rebuffed as too low.

MURDER TRIAL DELAYED

On October 4, Judge Thomas gave prosecutors a break and delayed the trial until November 5. The delay was

vehemently opposed by attorney Shapiro, who insisted
the trial should go forward as quickly as possible.

Shapiro told the judge that Cheyenne had given five
conflicting statements to authorities about the slaying. He
said that in one statement Cheyenne even implicated another person in the killing.

"The prosecution knows that Cheyenne Brando is a
mentally and emotionally disturbed young lady and no
one can rely on anything she said," Shapiro told the
judge.

In addition, Dag's parents had charged her under
French law with complicity in the murder of the Tahitian.
She was being held under that charge and could not leave
even if she asked to.

A PLEA BARGAIN LOOKS MORE LIKELY

On October 4, Judge Joel Rudoff, acting supervising
judge of the Santa Monica Superior Court, refused to
sign a letter formally requesting cooperation from
authorities in French Polynesia in getting Cheyenne back.

"When you don't want someone to testify, it appears
that all you have to do is send them out of the country,"
said a frustrated Deputy D.A. Barshop. "There doesn't
seem to be any proccess whereby we can get her to return. We continue to search."

"Her testimony is crucial to establish Christian Brando's
state of mind on the evening of the shooting," said co-
prosecutor Bill Clark, adding, "It looks like she won't
be here."

Without Cheyenne's testimony, a plea bargain agreement on lesser charges or a manslaughter conviction seemed more likely.

THE WITCH DOCTOR

Brando said he could not begin his autobiography until he exorcised the demons who had been lurking in the house since the murder. To that end he flew a Tahitian witch doctor into Los Angeles to drive the evil spirits away. The holy man sprinkled herbs and Tahitian water around while reciting incantations.

As for more earthly evils, Brando now had armed guards patrolling the mansion on Mulholland.

CHEYENNE'S SHOCKING DEPOSITION

Things grew even more grim when Cheyenne attempted suicide with a drug overdose because she was overwhelmed with shame after casting the dark shadow of incestuous love on her family in secret court testimony.

That was the shocking claim of sources close to the troubled beauty.

During a startling court deposition before Magistrate Max Gatti in Tahiti's capital of Papeete on September 14, Cheyenne testified that "several times I was made to feel that Christian loved me more than a sister, without, however, there having been any gesture between he and I."

She added: "When he came to see us at the house he always made himself more handsome."

As for her famous father, Cheyenne told the court: "When I was seventeen years old he had asked me to the Beachcomber Hotel (in Tahiti). And I had refused . . .

"He was jealous of my life and of my happiness, and he always wanted me to take care of him. . . ."

However, later in the same deposition, Cheyenne insisted she had never been forced to "submit to incestuous relationships."

But Jacques Drollet told the court that his son had talked with him about incest in the Brando family "following some confidences from Cheyenne."

Magistrate Gatti, though refusing to discuss the testimony at the secret hearing, confirmed to a reporter in Tahiti: "I can say there are stories of incest involving Cheyenne. I cannot say if they are true—I don't know."

Cheyenne's suicide attempt came on November 1, following a blowup with her mother. "Tarita somehow got hold of the details of Cheyenne's testimony and she hit the roof," confided a source close to Cheyenne. "She screamed at Cheyenne: 'Why in the name of God would you ever say those vile things? Have you no shame?'

"Cheyenne flew out the door and went into hiding at friends' homes on the island. After three days she went back to her mother's house and started the fight all over again. The two women were screaming at each other."

Cheyenne then rushed over to her own home in the Brando family compound and swallowed an overdose of tranquilizers and antidepressants prescribed for her.

A friend found her one and a half hours later in a coma and called her personal physician, Dr. Guy Thirouard.

"It was definitely a life-or-death situation for Cheyenne, a very serious overdose," Dr. Thirouard said. "I called an ambulance and instructed the driver to get her to Mamao Hospital as quickly as possible!"

En route to the hospital, Cheyenne, who was wearing only a simple sarong, remained unconscious, said ambulance attendant Teni Hong.

"Cheyenne's mother had tears in her eyes as she held on to her daughter's hand, trying to give her warmth and comfort."

When Brando learned of the crisis, he made plans to fly to his daughter's bedside.

But she regained consciousness the following day, so he remained in Los Angeles where Christian's trial was due to start in days.

Friends worried that even if she fully recovered she might try to take her life again. "Cheyenne felt rotten after talking to Magistrate Gatti and causing such a terrible scandal," said a source close to her. "She decided it was just too shameful to live. We're all praying she will get over her shame and go on with her life."

BRANDO OFFERS DROLLET FAMILY $1 MILLION FOR THEIR SILENCE

In November journalist Lydia Encinas reported that Marlon had offered a million dollars to the Drollet family to buy their silence. The scathing charge was leveled by Jacques Drollet in an exclusive interview with Encinas. He said Brando was hoping to win public sympathy for Christian, but the family flatly refused to make a deal with Brando.

"We don't want Marlon Brando's money. We want to see justice done!" said Drollet.

Brando's offer came in response to the "wrongful death" suit filed against Christian by Jacques's former wife Lisette and her husband Albert Lecaill, legal guardian's for Dag's four-year-old daughter.

"In September, Marlon's son Tehotu and a woman who works for Brando offered Albert and Lisette a million dollars to drop the civil lawsuit," said Jacques. "But the family is not interested in Marlon's money.

"One of the demands of the suit is a paternity test to determine if Dag really is Tuki's father. Dag's blood samples have been preserved by the Los Angeles coroner and we're asking the court to order the test."

Another reason Brando offered the family money was to stop them from filing any more suits that might make Christian look bad, Jacques said.

"Marlon is very concerned that further claims would influence the outcome of Christian's trial. Also, by Marlon acting in a big-hearted way, he thinks he can sway public opinion."

But Jacques refused to give up his faith in the court system.

"I hate Christian," he said. "I hope American justice will punish him and give him the strongest sentence possible."

DEVASTATING NEW EVIDENCE UNEARTHED

Christian's defense case suffered a serious blow in November when it was revealed that he had shot Ricardo Alvarez in the head just three months earlier.

This piece of history was unearthed by the *National*

Enquirer and the new evidence, news to the police and the district attorney, could be used by prosecutors at Christian's upcoming murder trial.

The incident now seemed an eerie preview of the May 16 murder of Dag Drollet.

A respected criminal attorney believed prosecutors would attempt to use the new evidence to prove that the Drollet shooting was not accidental—that Christian was prone to violent outbursts.

The Enquirer tracked Ricardo Alvarez down in Laurel Canyon where he declared: "I was Christian's best friend—but it didn't stop him from firing a loaded gun right at my head!

"I've relived that nightmare a thousand times. And then I think, 'That poor kid he killed could have been me.' "

"It was all pretty much behind me until the day I learned Christian shot Dag. The same thought ran through my mind again and again: 'It could have been me. I could have ended up where Dag is right now!' "

Alvarez and his friends never breathed a word of the shooting to authorities. But now that the *Enquirer* investigation had exposed the incident, it would provide damaging evidence against Christian—whose attorneys would reportedly claim in court that his gun went off accidentally during a struggle with Dag Drollet.

John Rodriguez, a criminal attorney in Southern California, predicted prosecutors would try to present information about the Alvarez shooting during the trial to "show Christian's inclination for violence and firearms.

"They'll try to use it to show a violent personality—

but lawyers for the defense will object vehemently to admission of the evidence."

CHRISTIAN BRANDO FACES NEW CHARGES

The fallout from the *Enquirer* story soon hit the prosecutor's office. As soon as the story appeared, police began scouring Los Angeles to find Ricardo Alvarez and witnesses to the shooting.

Police tracked down one witness, William E. Smith, on November 5. They arrested him on warrants that had been issued when he failed to appear in court on charges of drunk driving and drug possession, threw him in jail, then began questioning him about Christian. They ordered Smith to appear before a grand jury that would decide whether charges of attempted murder should be brought against Christian for the Alvarez shooting.

Smith's testimony could also be used when Christian came to trial for killing Dag Drollet.

"When the *Enquirer* article appeared, the Los Angeles Police Department and the District Attorneys' office took action," Smith's lawyer, Robert Diamond, told the *Enquirer.*

"They began a search focusing in the Laurel Canyon area for anyone they believed may have been a witness to the shooting of Alvarez. In particular, they wanted to question my client, his friend Corey Kronick and Alvarez."

"My client's two warrants had been in the system for several months, but neither the D.A. nor the police took direct action against him until the story of Christian Brando's previous gunplay appeared in the *Enquirer*," said Diamond.

The new information unearthed by the *Enquirer*, "may prove to be the difference between a conviction of murder in the first degree and that of a less severe charge in the Drollet shooting," said Diamond.

"It can show Christian as a drug and alcohol abuser with a penchant for violence—or a cold, calculating killer. A D. A. Bill Clark told me 'That article in the *Enquirer* is definitely having an impact on the Christian Brando case.' "

"BRANDO'S SON IS GETTING AWAY WITH MURDER!"

Dag Drollet's father was outraged that Christian had been allowed to cop a plea and probably faced just a short prison term . . . or no jail at all.

"Christian Brando is getting away with murder!" Jacques Drollet charged. "I never wanted a plea bargain. I wanted to see the murderer of my son tried, convicted and sentenced to the maximum penalty. I didn't raise my children to have them killed like dogs."

Christian was originally charged with murder and faced a possible life sentence if convicted. But because the prosecution's key witness, Cheyenne Brando, refused to return to the United States to testify, the murder case against Christian had collapsed. That was why the District Attorney allowed Christian to plead guilty to the lesser charge of voluntary manslaughter.

Legal experts said that Christian, with no prior convictions, should get no more than five years and possibly as little as two. And he was hoping to stay free entirely.

"My dad says I can probably get off with probation," he told a friend. "I'm so relieved."

But Jacques Drollet had other ideas and planned to urge the judge to hand down stiff punishment at Christian's February 26 sentencing.

"The police bungled the cast against Christian by letting Cheyenne get away," he charged. "This should never have been allowed to happen. I want to make my voice heard before it's too late.

"And I won't let Marlon forget my son. Every year on the anniversary of Dag's murder I will send him a copy of the murder scene photo that shows the lifeless body of my son!"

Marlon was still deeply troubled by the state of Cheyenne who had left Tahiti to go to a psychiatric hospital near Paris where she was on a round-the-clock suicide watch at a private psychiatric hospital. A nurse was with her at all times, even when she went to the bathroom. Her father paid for her $7,500-a-week treatment at the clinic. "I know that my son will come back to me, but sadly, I cannot be so sure about my daughter," he told a friend. "I'm worried sick about Cheyenne."

CHRISTIAN'S SENTENCING

Christian had no prior convictions, and believed he stood a good chance of getting off with mere probation for the slaying. But then shocking evidence of other violent assaults appeared, giving prosecutors the ammunition they needed to put him behind bars for years.

There was the revelation that in February, three months before the death of Dag Drollet, Christian had shot his best friend Ricardo Alvarez in the head. Now it was revealed that earlier that year, Christian had shot at two other men, attacked a third with a hammer and kicked a woman bloody with steel-toed boots.

Christian's former pals Billy Smith and Cory Kronick gave evidence at the sentencing. And after their damning testimony the judge sentenced Christian to ten years.

Los Angeles Deputy District Attorney learned of Christian's prior record by reading the *National Enquirer*. Said Clark: "When we first read in the *Enquirer* about Christian shooting Alvarez, this was news to us—that Christian had committed another violent act. It caught us by surprise.

"And when we started checking it out we found other witnesses—Smith and Kronick—who also had talked to the *Enquirer*.

"We got very lucky with this extra evidence.

"We appreciate very much that help from the *Enquirer*.

"Looking at Christian Brando, it was important for the judge to know whether there was a pattern of violence."

ANNA KASHFI CHARGES: MARLON RUINED CHRISTIAN'S LIFE

On February 28, 1991, Christian Brando was sentenced to ten years in jail for the killing of his half sister's lover. Brando had testified at the sentencing hearing, hoping for leniency, and accused Anna of wrecking Christian's life. He told the court that his son had suffered emotional abuse at the hands of his mother.

Anna was penniless and eking out a living cleaning houses and living in a trailer park near the Mexican border.

Bitter at her son's fate, unable to reach him because he was unable or unwilling to see her, she lashed out in the press, charging that Brando's gay affairs had turned their son into a killer.

"Marlon Brando had gay affairs," she declared, saying that Christian's anguish over his father's bisexuality helped turn him into a killer.

In an exclusive interview with journalist Tony Brenna, Anna said that Marlon's affairs with men had hurt and confused Christian—and were at the root of the anger and hostility that exploded in violence when Christian gunned down Drollet.

"If anyone should be serving ten years in prison it's Marlon—he ruined Christian's life," Anna charged.

"The truth is he was bisexual. Christian was even named after a French actor with whom Marlon admitted having a homosexual affair.

"Marlon put Christian in the position of spending a lifetime hiding the fact that the father he adored was really bisexual."

By the time Brando gained custody when Christian was thirteen, Christian was already emotionally damaged by his father's strange sex life, she told Brenna.

"When he was ten, Christian said, 'I don't understand

Dad. The house is always full of strange men, and Dad dances with them.'

"I think the knowledge that his father had gay affairs lay heavily on Christian's mind.

"And I know Christian had seen Marlon affectionately hugging and kissing men who came to his mansion. He once told me, 'It makes me sick. There are times when Dad can behave like a sissy.' "

When the actor for whom Christian was named visited Marlon at the house, "Marlon suddenly became mincing, wriggling, giggling—very gay," said Anna. "His voice often took on a lisp.

"I knew for sure Marlon was bisexual when one of his gay friends came to me with a picture of him having sex with a man.

"Christian wanted to believe his father was the soul of masculinity. But he knew there were gay episodes in Marlon's life. It was deeply disturbing, a major cause of Christian's anger and hostility.

"I have no doubt it was one of the factors that led Christian to become violent and volatile—a killer."

At Christian's sentencing hearing, Marlon called Anna "cruel" and said she "came as close to being a negative person as I have ever met."

But Anna said: "When Christian lived with Marlon he was cared for by nannies, maids, and secretaries. With me, he had a mother's love. I adored him—and I gave him all the love it's possible for a mother to give. Marlon took him away from me."

The onetime movie starlet was a pathetic sight. According to a British tabloid, she sat in the dark in her San Diego trailer to save money on her electricity bills and eked out a living as a sometime cleaning woman at a nursing home. She had spent a small fortune fighting for custody of Christian. At fifty-seven she was living on Social Security in a mobile home she shared with her cocker spaniel Kimmie. "I've learned to live on nothing," she told a reporter. Her second marriage, in 1970, to Jim Hannaford, ended with his death from cancer in 1987. The only thing that kept her going was the hope that Christian would one day consent to let her visit him in prison. As for Brando, she said: "He's let himself go, but I can't feel sorry. He ruined my life. I wish I'd never met him."

"CHRISTIAN BRANDO
GOT AWAY WITH MURDER"

The case was closed, and Christian began serving his time. But a bitter LA County Deputy D.A. Clark told the *New York Post:* "Christian Brando got away with murder."

THE END OF A DREAM

The year would see the end of another dream. Early in 1991 Brando secretly sold his island paradise to the Japanese for $120 million. Facing staggering costs for Christian's defense and Cheyenne's round-the-clock suicide watch in Paris, he sadly surrendered his beloved Tetiaroa to developers who planned to turn it into a resort for Japanese tourists.

AUTOBIOGRAPHY

In March 1991 Brando made a deal with Random House to write his autobiography. He would reportedly be paid a six million dollar advance for world rights, and he would get to keep his $750,000 signing payment whether he finished the book or not.

BETS

Yet there were still times when the old Brando emerged: the puckish practical joker who loved outrageous bets. Thus that May he was seen in a fake beard and straw hat, selling tires on a busy corner near his home. He was paying off a bet with a friend.

FRENCH BUST BRANDO'S DAUGHTER

That fall there was some encouraging news from Paris. Cheyenne had been made an outpatient at the clinic where she had been confined since her suicide attempt last November. But her father was still paying $2,000 a week for a bodyguard to protect her from outsiders and from herself.

In November Brando removed Cheyenne from the clinic and went into hiding. After covertly tracking Brando to a secluded estate, French police found them in a chateau outside of Orleans. They arrested Cheyenne and charged her with complicity in the shooting death of her lover.

Brando family attorney Jacques Verges warned strongly against transferring her to Tahiti where the charges were issued.

"It would constitute the crime of failing to render aid to a person in danger," he told French television. "In the case of suicide, it would be murder."

Twelve

Picking Up the Pieces

"He has written some marvelous things."
— Harold Evans, Brando's publisher

If there was any doubt that the Brando was still an icon
it was dispelled by rock star John Mellencamp in an *Esquire* magazine interview that March. "If I had to say
here was anybody I like, no matter what, it would be a
guy like Brando," said Mellencamp, who is, like Brando,
a product of the Midwest. "He gets to be my age, he's
tired of fighting his weight, he's tired of [deleted] havin'
to look like what people want him to look like. So what's
he do? To hell with you! I'm a fat, fucking person and
I'm gonna be a fat, fucking person to see what I really
look like. . . . I don't think my job allows for that."

CHRISTOPHER COLUMBUS

Brando agreed to a cameo role as the brilliant, ruthless
inquisitor Torquemada in *Christopher Columbus: The*

Discovery. He would get five million dollars for five days' work.

Brando's scenes were to be filmed on location in Talamanca and the palace of El Alcazar in Segovia, which had been in fact the principal home of King Ferdinand and Queen Isabella.

But when he reported for filming Brando found himself a virtual prisoner of the press. Spain's paparazzi had worked themselves into a frenzy over his presence.

He was pursued by dozens of cars every time he left the Palace Hotel. Once, when he returned from the set he literally had to fight his way through an army of photographers, hotel security guards, and over-zealous press

This sort of mauling and invasion was exactly why Brando had withdrawn from the hurly-burly of stardom, making fewer and fewer films, retreating from the madding crowd. Only the tragic events of the past two years had forced him back in front of the cameras.

At the end of January, Brando wound up *Columbus* and producer Ilya Salkind told *USA Today* that "It's not like *Superman,* where he was only in the beginning. He's a principal, at the beginning, the middle, and end."

Brando wore the robes and skull cap of a Dominican priest and, according to Salkind, "It went well. He's very professional."

In March, Brando spent the weekend in New York and caught Eartha Kitt's act at the Cafe Carlyle. He was so taken by his old friend's performance that he sent her a groaning bouquet of flowers with a note saying how much he enjoyed her.

He had worked with the producers, the father and son team of Alexander and Ilya Salkind, on *Superman* in

1978. Later, in a written response to questions from *Daily Variety,* Brando would explain his decision to take a role in the new production this way:

"Having an appreciable knowledge of the historical facts that Christopher Columbus was directly responsible for the first wave of genocidal obliteration of the native peoples of North America, I wanted to make certain that the history of the interaction between Christopher Columbus and the indigenous inhabitants would be accurately portrayed."

According to Brando, he was "successful in persuading Ilya Salkind after several hours of taped and witnessed conversation, that he could make more money—which was his primary, if not his only, consideration in making this film—by portraying Columbus not as the insipid, bland, false, and idiotic person as he was portrayed in the original script, but as the true villain he was."

Brando came away from their meetings convinced that Ilya Salkind "agreed to my concept. I communicated with both Tom Selleck and George Corraface [who played Columbus], both of whom had the acumen to recognize the basic fault of the story."

According to Brando, Ilya Salkind "affixed his name to a written approval for changes and I was certain we would be successful in having a true history of this cultural clash presented in the film."

But once Ilya's father Alexander arrived on the set, Brando said, "Evidently he gave his son a tongue-lashing and insisted that the picture be returned to its original version."

While Brando acknowledged that he had not seen the

completed picture and therefore could not comment on the results, he noted "with certainty that the Native Americans were presented with cruel inaccuracies and as my contract specifically states that the producers are under the obligation to adhere to historical accuracy, I have no other recourse than to, at the very least, have my name removed from this picture."

In a phone interview with *Daily Variety* Alexander Salkind said he was surprised to learn of Brando's decision to withdraw his name even though he had been aware that Brando wanted his "role changed."

"I had a conference with [Brando] and he wanted to shoot the picture differently," Salkind said. "he wanted to have long fingernails and look horrible. . . . he wrote some scenes and wanted to have a Jewish girl in a cage burned in boiling oil because at that time the Spaniards were after the Jews," said Salkind.

"I didn't want to be cross with him, but we couldn't go his way at all. We didn't want to make a horror picture. We didn't want to have a girl boiling in oil. We wanted an adventure picture."

But, Salkind contended, "He wanted us to show Columbus was very cruel and we showed him normal like he was . . . very severe, very manly."

Brando had other problems with the production. During the five or six days that he was actively involved in the picture in Spain, he became aware that some crew members were not being paid.

"While I was in Spain I don't think that I met one person associated with the film who did not have a complaint and who did not hold the Salkinds in their way of doing business with some measure of contempt," he said.

"Many people complained they were cheated, lied to, inconvenienced, and embarrassed. It came to my attention through members of the crew that they had not been paid and that their checks were uncashable."

Brando said he signed a letter to the Salkinds and their company, drawn up by the crew, stating, "if they were not paid, they would go on strike, and I would have been happy to join them as my signature attested."

As for his own compensation, Brando said he arranged his payment in advance.

"Having worked with the Salkinds before, I was aware of the tricky business tactics that they were wont to employ," he said. "I insisted that all my salary should be put in escrow that would render it beyond their control.

"I was offered five million dollars for roughly ten days work," he said. And he added that he "personally guaranteed the Salkinds $100,000 to cover Tom Selleck's salary should the rewriting, which I undertook, cause the schedule to be increased by one day."

He said he planned to "not only raise these issues with the Salkinds, but in the courts and with the Screen Actors Guild and it is my hope that the full light of world attention will eliminate these issues."

Would he have gotten involved with this project knowing the issues that had been raised?

"In hindsight, I would have accepted the same challenge for the same reasons."

COOKING UP A NEW ROMANCE

Brando had reportedly fallen for young, pretty Los Angeles pastry chef Avra Douglas and whisked her off to

Spain. Aspiring actress Avra met Brando by delivering food he had prepared to his Mulholland Drive mansion. Now she was baking sweets only for Brando.

Residents of a very exclusive Manhattan apartment house where Brando stayed with Douglas, learned that Brando insisted on riding in the elevator alone, leaving other tenants waiting while the elevator operator whizzed past their floors. An anonymous memo covering "elevator protocol" was soon posted in the lobby.

AUTOBIOGRAPHY

Some doubted that Brando would ever complete his much-awaited autobiography. In June, columnist Richard Johnson reported, "Marlon Brando is either a great writer who is penning a brilliant autobiography, or he desperately needs a ghostwriter. It depends on whom you talk to." Harold Evans, Random House president and publisher, assured Johnson that Brando was making great headway on the memoirs, that his writing was eloquent and elegant, and that the book would be a huge hit when it finally hit store shelves.

But naysayers in the publishing world said the project was moving so slowly that the publisher had begged Brando to accept a ghostwriter. He had so far refused.

Instead, he had rehired Alice Marshak, the secretary he inherited from his father in 1957. Brando reportedly lured her out of retirement to help him organize his memories and all the material he was trying to keep track of. Alice had been installed in the studio next to his house on Mulholland and was said to be typing away.

Brando, who had spent some time in Europe before filming his role in *Christopher Columbus: The Discovery*, denied a report in *The New Republic* that he was using a ghostwriter. He claimed he was writing the book himself and intended to "disclose all my life and the people in it, from my earliest memory of playing in my moonlit bed with the naked body of my sleeping beloved Ermi to the present scribbling in my bed of another day."

There was much speculation about the identification of Ermi, who was finally identified as his nanny.

Evans, who had had tea with Brando during the latter's recent swing through New York, assured Johnson that, "He'd lost weight. He was in great spirits. He gave us the beginning of the book. He has written some marvelous things."

Brando had even persuaded Anna Kashfi, some of his directors and friends to write their own versions of the Brando experience. "He believes that a writer doesn't know his own life as well as others know him," said Evans.

CHEYENNE

Cheyenne was now claiming that Brando himself had a hand in the murder of Dag Drollet. The French daily *Le Figaro* reported on April 15 that barely four months earlier that Cheyenne had given a surprisingly candid interview to a judge in Tahiti, where she was now living.

In addition, the paper hinted at problems her father

might be having with law-enforcement authorities as a result of the crime—difficulties that had caused his personal lawyer to quit in frustration.

Cheyenne had been under constant police watch because of her precarious mental state, since the killing. She had repeatedly refused to cooperate with any investigation of the killing, but in a January interview with Tahitian Judge Max Gatti, she revealed that she hated her famous father.

She had told Gatti that she was "certain that it was [Marlon Brando] who asked Christian to kill Dag," *Le Figaro* reported. At the same time, Cheyenne told Gatti that her father "didn't want Dag to die."

Gatti labeled the girl "disturbed" and indicated he didn't place much credence in her remarks.

Meanwhile, French authorities had been requesting a meeting with Brando, to answer "essentially technical" questions that would finalize their part of the murder investigation, the paper said.

However, Brando had steadfastly refused to meet with the investigators—and as a result, his French lawyer had dropped him as a client.

Cheyenne's story took another tragic turn when she made some shocking accusations during a month-long interrogation in Tahiti. Judge Jean-Bernard Talierco said he was proceeding cautiously because of Cheyenne's troubled mental state, but he now wanted to question Brando himself about his role in the murder.

"We need to question Marlon Brando," Judge Talierco said, adding that if Brando refused to return voluntarily to Tahiti, the next step would be to issue an international arrest warrant.

Hair close cropped and smoking one cigarette after another, Cheyenne claimed that it was her father who ordered the murder of Dag Drollet. "I detest my father," she said. "He's constantly manipulating people. I'm sure he asked Christian to kill Dag."

Holed up in his New York City apartment, Brando insisted he had nothing to say. "The American justice system has sentenced my son Christian to ten years in jail," he said. "It has not made charges of complicity against either Cheyenne or myself, and so the case is closed."

Between Christian's legal bills and Cheyenne's psychiatric treatment, Brando was pressed for cash and, according to columnist Cindy Adams, he had even borrowed one million dollars from Michael Jackson.

According to Adams, he was trying hard to complete his memoir, but his memory was not as sharp as his pain. He was reaching out by phone to friends with whom he had made a film or shared something in the past. With some, he would unburden his current anguish, even inquiring how they had survived the travails of raising their own children.

"No matter how the conversations go," said Adams, "the point is always reached where he says: 'Listen, do you remember when we . . .' "

He pressed forward on the manuscript only to lose forty handwritten pages in a New York City taxi. "I was so upset I couldn't eat a thing for fourteen hours," he told a friend. Luckily, the cabbie returned the goods to the hotel the next morning. A relieved Brando tipped him $500.

ANOTHER CHILD

That spring Christina Ruiz, now thirty-three, presented him with another child, a son they named Myles. For the birth of Ninna he had given her a three-bedroom house, now he gave her a huge house in Sherman Oaks that was said to have set him back one million dollars.

Brando also reportedly had Miko's three-year-old son living with him, following the death of the child's mother a year earlier. "Marlon loves the house filled with children's laughter," said an insider. "With a new baby on the way, Marlon now feels that he has another chance."

CHEYENNE

Cheyenne continued to cause him heartache. She returned to the United States in August and spent much of her time secluded in the $900,000 twelve-room home he had bought for her in Sherman Oaks.

She was still facing a murder conspiracy charge in Tahiti, but when Brando learned that Cheyenne, twenty-two, was sleeping with her forty-one-year-old defense attorney, he demanded she change lawyers. But she refused.

Christian's ex-wife, Mary McKenna, thirty-four, was arrested for prostitution, after being picked up on the streets of Hollywood at 9:45 in the morning.

According to LAPD Officer Arthur Holmes, Mary McKenna was charged in Hollywood with soliciting an undercover policeman.

PROJECTS

Brando's name was also linked to the *Whole Earth Review* that March, when he was identified as the sole Beverly Hills resident among the four dozen "Maniacal Supporters" who have given $1,000 to the nonprofit corporation that publishes the *Whole Earth Review*.

Thirteen

Brando Today

"Did we ever sleep together?"
                    —Marlon Brando's transatlantic telephone
                    question to Ursula Andress

The year 1993 started with the news that Random House had received another installment of Brando's memoirs. The publisher refused to confirm or deny.

In March, the doors to a Santa Monica hospital's emergency room burst open late at night and there stood 300-pound Marlon, cradling his tiny one-year-old son Myles in his arms and frantically begging doctors to treat the crying, wheezing child immediately. After a quick inspection doctors discovered the child was suffering from shortness of breath, bronchitis, asthma, a severe ear infection and a 103 degree fever. Brando was reported to be a nervous wreck, alternately pacing and holding his son's hand, as three doctors worked all night on the child, but at dawn came the happy news his fever had broken and he was breathing normally again.

That spring, he was also pleased that Christian had earned his high school GED diploma in the Los Angeles County Jail.

CONTRADICTIONS

Brando remained a man of baffling contradictions. A story went around that summer that he and three friends showed up at the trendy Melrose Place restaurant late one night and were told the kitchen was closed. But as they turned to leave, the owner recognized Brando and offered to prepare a meal. Instead of thanking him, Brando lectured him. "You don't treat people differently just because they're celebrities," he snapped. "I hate when people do this. It's not right." The owner agreed and showed him the door.

CHRISTMAS

Christmas 1993, Brando was said to have driven 390 miles to deliver six gaily wrapped packages of Christian's favorite peanut brittle to him in prison.

Sometimes his physical condition bothered him. He was seen limping in an elevator in a Beverly Hills medical building, leaning on a cane and complaining about his aching leg when a woman asked for his autograph. It set him off: "Can't you see I'm here to see a doctor? I'm a human being. Show some common decency!" he said. The woman made quick exit on the next floor.

CHEYENNE

Cheyenne's hearing was set for March 8 to determine whether she should face criminal charges for allegedly punching a nurse in the face. The nurse claimed that Cheyenne had knocked her unconscious on December 20 at CPC Westwood Hospital, a Los Angeles psychiatric center, where she was an intensive care patient. She also filed a civil suit, and told police that Cheyenne became impatient while waiting to leave the hospital and struck her.

The nurse claimed that she had been "beaten and knocked out" by Cheyenne. "I remember waking up and my face was hurting and throbbing," the nurse told television's *Current Affair.* The nurse, currently on leave, was also suing the hospital.

According to the nurse, Cheyenne's "anger is so intense it will make your hair stand up and give you the chills."

The Los Angeles district attorney's office said that Cheyenne did not break any laws when she fled the United States and refused to testify at her brother's murder trial.

Christian was now in "protective custody," his girlfriend Laurene Landon told *Affair,* because other inmates had "roughed him up."

In May, Judge Jean-Bernard Taliercao dropped the charges against Cheyenne. Dag's father had brought charges in Tahiti against Cheyenne of murder, conspiracy, and non-assistance to a person in danger. Judge Taliercao said his decision was "motivated essentially by elimination of all aspects of the notion of complicity."

He also said the charge of non-complicity did not exist in California. Drollet's father could still appeal.

CHEYENNE'S DISTURBING CLAIMS

Cheyenne continued to make disturbing claims.

In an explosive interview published in France's *Paris Match* magazine, Cheyenne now claimed that Brando manipulated Christian into slaying her boyfriend. And when she confronted Marlon with the charge, he punched her in the mouth, she said.

The troubled beauty, now twenty-three, also claimed her father sexually abused her from the time she was a little girl.

Cheyenne was now living under the name Susan Ferguson in a psychiatric halfway house in the San Francisco area. She said she was taking "very light medications" and that her father was footing the bill for her care.

Cheyenne moved into the home February 2 after a violent argument with her father in Los Angeles.

"I accused him of being an accomplice in Dag's murder. I told him he let my fiancé be killed," Cheyenne told reporter Peter Manso. Furious with pent-up rage, Cheyenne said she "threw a punch" at Marlon and "he punched me back in the mouth."

Cheyenne told Manso that if she had taken the stand at her brother's murder trial, "I would have said that my father was responsible for my fiancé's death." She cited as proof "the fact that my father asked Christian to bring his gun to the house that evening."

She said her father used "voodoo" to manipulate

Christian into shooting Dag. "My father is a very powerful man, much stronger than anyone thinks," she said.

Marlon did not like Dag because he believed the young
man introduced her to drugs, Cheyenne said. She also
claimed that Marlon began sexually abusing her when
she was just seven years old. "My father behaved
strangely with me, touching my chest and giving me mas-
sages on my bed as if he wanted me to mime for him
the acts of love," she said. "He continued touching my
chest even when I was with Dag."

Despite Cheyenne's shocking accusations against her
father, police did not plan to reopen the investigation into
Dag's murder. "Cheyenne has been taken before courts
and shown to be unable to take care of herself or her
son," said L.A. Deputy District Attorney Bill Clark.
"Having a jury believe her on anything would be a problem."

"It was certainly not an accident," Cheyenne told *Paris
Match.* "They tried to say it was accidental, but the gun
didn't go off by itself."

"My father wants the world to believe I'm crazy. He
wants people to think he's helping me, but it's not true.
He's playing a double game with me. He's attacking me
psychologically and that's why I've decided to speak out.

"I've cut all the bridges to him," she said, adding they
had not exchanged a word in five months.

"My birthday was February 20 and he didn't send me
a card. Sometimes I think he has no conscience. His way
of saying 'I'd give my life for you,' as he often tells me,
isn't credible."

The girl also assured *Paris Match* that the first time

she saw her father in *The Godfather,* she realized he was simply playing himself on screen.

"It was my father in flesh and blood," she said. "Afterwards, I saw him for a long time as a myth. A powerful man, capable of manipulating people as he wished. I still think that even today my father has kept a very strong psychological influence over me and I don't know how to get rid of it. I was always Marlon Brando's 'sacrifice.' His sacrificial lamb destined for his personal happiness.

Brando was reportedly still paying $13,500 a month for Cheyenne's psychiatric care, but she dreamed of returning to Tahiti and her son Tuki, now three.

"I call him my little dolphin," she said. "Right now, he's angry with me because I'm not with him . . . he wants me to come home. Everything I do is for him."

Now that the charges that she had acted as an accomplice in the shooting had been dropped, Cheyenne longed to go home to Tahiti. But she could not go because her father had her passports and "refused to give them back to me when I asked," she said.

"This power he has over me prevents me from leading a normal existence. Sometimes I feel like I need to be exorcised." A spokesman for Brando declined to comment on Cheyenne's claims or the *Paris Match* story.

"THIS IS MARLON BRANDO. DID WE EVER SLEEP TOGETHER?"

Brando was working hard on his autobiography, but was having some problems with his memory. He began calling old friends to fill in the blanks.

One such friend, Ursula Andress, angrily hung up on the man who phoned her at 6 A.M. in Rome, identifying himself as Marlon Brando and asking: "Did we ever sleep together?" Later she discovered through mutual friends that the caller really was Brando. She buzzed him back in Los Angeles and he told her he was trying to recall events that took place when he lived in Rome in the 1960s. They chatted for two hours and he later sent her $300 to cover the phone bill.

So did Brando and Andress sleep together? According to Brando biographer Peter Manso, the answer is a resounding "Yes!" But it was in Hollywood in the 1950s, not Rome in the 1960s.

Nevertheless, his enthusiastic publisher Harold Evans told *Variety,* "We have about 100,000 words so far. I just hope he doesn't sign another movie contract anytime soon."

While the world waited, George Englund, who made Brando's book deal at Random House, told *Daily Variety*'s Army Archerd that he was at work on *Marlon & I—Called Each Other Friend* for Warner Books. According to Englund, he had maintained a "code of honor" by never discussing Brando with anyone, but he believed his book would be interesting. He and Brando had a unique thirty-six-year relationship as friend-producer-confidante. Englund said it was not a biography, but a story of their friendship. Englund believed he had long shielded Brando, but now, with Brando writing his own book, he was free to tell his story. He said he had been unable to contact Brando to discuss it with him.

Englund, who produced *The Ugly American,* had directed and written films and TV but admitted, "I've never written a book before—but neither has Marlon. It's a firs together." Englund said he had not read any of the pages of the book Brando had already turned in to Random House.

When Army Archerd asked Englund whether his own book deal was as good as Brando's, Englund laughed, "Hardly!—I'm a better agent for him than for myself."

Actually, the relationship between Englund and Brando was not as amicable as he made it sound. For one thing, Brando's attorney Brenda Frixou had up to now been credited as the one who put his book deal together.

According to Jeannette Walls in *New York Magazine,* Brando had parted company with Englund, apparently over money. "He's prepared to tell all about Brando," a publishing source was quoted as saying.

"Since the word is that Brando's book may take the rest of this century to finish," the source continued, "Englund will probably get the jump on publication and be able to write things that never would have been revealed had they been working together."

It was also reported that Englund was representing Manuel Noriega in negotiations for his autobiography with Random House. The former Panamanian dictator was now serving a 40-year sentence in a Miami prison on drug-trafficking charges.

Ironically, however, when Brando's autobiography was published in the fall of 1994, Englund's own book was not scheduled to be published by Warner Books until fall 1995.

TREASURE ISLAND, THE MUSICAL

On August 17, Brando sued a film company and producer, alleging that a one million dollar check he received for agreeing to appear in a film bounced at the bank. Brando's suit, which sought the one million dollars plus interest, contended that the producer gave the check to a Brando representative on June 20 after Brando agreed to appear in a film called *Treasure Island, the Musical*. The check, drawn on an account in the name of Cinema International Corp., bounced, the suit stated.

Brando's suit also alleged that the producer promised him the money so he could use Brando's name to attract financing for the film. The suit sought one million dollars plus interest and alleged breach of an oral agreement, negligent misrepresentation and fraud.

PROJECTS

Signaling a new commitment to his career, Brando signed with International Creative Management for worldwide representation on November 11. Sources said that he joined ICM because he wanted to start considering more "motion picture opportunities that have recently come his way." The signing team consisted of Ed Limato, Robert Newman, and Dennis Sellinger of London.

"I am thrilled and honored to represent one of the greatest actors of all time," said Limato, whose clients included Anthony Hopkins, Mel Gibson, Richard Gere, Denzel Washington, Michelle Pfeiffer, and Steve Martin.

"We are very proud that Mr. Brando has chosen ICM as his worldwide representatives in all facets," said ICM president Jim Wiatt.

The sixty-five-year-old Brando had not been represented by a talent agent for more than twenty years.

Although ICM declined to reveal Brando's current projects, insiders said he had "been mulling over several choice roles offered to him recently."

MARLON "DUETS" WITH BARBRA STREISAND

Barbra Streisand fans who gathered in Las Vegas for the star's comeback performance at the MGM Grand were surprised to see her "duet" with Brando. Insiders knew she had been a huge admirer of the actor since she was a girl in Brooklyn, watching him in *Guys and Dolls* on the big screen of the Loew's Paradise. She had called him in advance to get his approval for her to sing along with his screen image to the romantic ballad "I'll Know." Army Archerd reported that "It was a show stopper. I can tell you—the audience of 13,000 screamed when Brando appeared on a big screen and warbled to her."

AUTOBIOGRAPHY

That January a jubilant Harold Evans announced that "We have Brando!" Weighing in at 600 pages and costing a reported $5.75 million, the manuscript the star had titled *Brando: Songs My Mother Taught Me* was finally complete. Columnist George Rush reported that, "I'd heard that Brando had written a preface warning the reader not to expect much about his personal life. But Evans assures me that when the book comes out, possibly in September, you will find Brando speaking candidly about his family, his lovers, and himself."

According to Rush, Peter Manso was "not holding his

breath." Manso and his publishers, Hyperion, were determined to beat Brando to the bookstores.

Brando was probably spurred to complete the biography by rumors of the contents of the book coming from Manso who had announced that, "It's time to take off the gloves." Manso claimed that he'd heard that in the preface to the Brando book the actor announced that he would not be writing about his personal life, but only about his art. Manso told Jeannie Williams of *USA Today* that, "Paranoids are always terrified. You have a gorgeous artist who virtually revolutionized acting in this country, and look at what's happened to him. . . . I can talk about the sex, the manipulations, the careers Marlon has wrecked, the suicides of girlfriends. It's very sad, but the legend dies hard." "There are a half-dozen suicides in Marlon's wake," he told *Variety.* "You cannot count the abortions, manipulations, destroyed careers. There is Marlon's bisexuality, a lifetime of psychoanalysis."

Clearly, Manso intended to portray Brando as a tormented soul filled with turmoil and sexual self-doubt.

According to Rush: "Manso recognizes his subject as 'genius,' but also as a self-deceiving charlatan with a shot memory. He smells hypocrisy in the very fact that Brando, the liberal crusader, has told his story to Robert Lindsey, ghostwriter to Ronald Reagan."

It was true that, at the urging of Random House, Brando had enlisted Lindsey, a *New York Times* reporter and author of *The Falcon and the Snowman,* to assist him.

Manso had studied Brando for six years and emerged convinced that he was "far less than we all believed."

Manso told Rush that his book would include a scene in which "Marlon sat naked in a sweat lodge with five

Indians and reverted to his childhood—speaking as though he were five, then ten, then fifteen years old."

Brando was shocked by the sudden death of comic actor John Candy and Brando vowed to lose weight. His weight had now passed 400 pounds and a doctor who diagnosed him with an eating disorder advised him, "Lose the weight, or lose your life."

The doctor placed Brando on the Pritikin program in Santa Monica, close to his home.

His downfall had been the book: he was so involved, that he was living on peanut-butter-and-jelly sandwiches and his beloved junk food. His favorite snack was said to be two pounds of bacon crammed onto a whole loaf of bread.

His old friend Francis Ford Coppola, who owned a small California winery, sent him a case of his latest vintage. Marlon phoned back to say he loved the wine and would like to do an ad for it. Coppola was thrilled, until Brando's agent called and said he would be happy to do it . . . for $1 million. Coppola passed.

In the spring of 1994 Brando signed with New Line Cinema to star in *Don Juan DeMarco and the Centerfold* his first major screen role since *The Freshman*. He was said to be getting $3.3 million for the role. On his first meeting with the director, Jeremy Leven he solemnly informed him that he did not work past six P.M. and added: "I don't like to start until about two P.M." The director looked horrified, until Brando laughed and admitted he was only joking.

Brando was to begin *Don Juan* in March. He would play Johnny Depp's shrink. Depp's character believes he is the legendary lover Don Juan. The psychiatrist gets so caught up in Depp's case, he postpones his planned retirement to keep treating him. First-time director Jeremy Leven, who also wrote the screenplay, was a Harvard-trained clinical psychologist with a couple of novels and two produced screenplays to his credit (*Creator* with Peter O'Toole and *Playing for Keeps* with Matthew Penn in the mid-80's).

Six weeks before shooting started, columnist George Rush reported that Brando was still baiting Leven with practical jokes. Nevertheless, Leven found him "charming, warm, incredibly smart, and quick witted. I'm still waiting to be intimidated."

He confirmed that Brando had been working "very hard" on his weight. "How much he'll lose, I don't know. It's really his personal goal."

Leven suspected that the role of a burnt-out psychiatrist rejuvenated by a case spoke to Brando because, "he's at a point where he himself wants to go back to work, wants to further his legacy.

"One night he and I were talking with Francis [Ford Coppola, who was producing the movie]. We were discussing different directors. Elia Kazan's name came up. Right there, Marlon did the whole taxicab scene from *On the Waterfront*. To see him, at 69 years old, doing the scene he did as a young man, and hitting it right on— Francis and I looked at each other and shook our heads."

MICHAEL JACKSON

In January Brando found himself touched by another scandal when his friend Michael Jackson was the subject of a Los Angeles County grand jury investigating molestation allegations against Jackson. His No. 2 son Miko, a former Jackson bodyguard, testified for two hours before a Santa Barbara grand jury investigating Jackson.

PROJECTS

Even the roles he was mentioned for, such as Orson Welles or disgraced financier Robert Maxwell indicated that his size had become the most dominant thing about him.

CONCLUSION

As 1994 drew to a close, Brando could take some comfort in the fact that his autobiography would finally be making its way to bookstores. He would have his chance to tell the story his way.

Yet Brando remained Brando to the end, full of puckish personality and protective gestures. Most poignant of all his memories may be the chapter he devotes to the late Russell the raccoon. The feisty little animal had been Brando's constant companion in the early years, and although Russell's behavior was not always "civilized," his very wildness may have been the envy of his human companion.

Columnist George Rush reported that Russell's chapter was merely six pages long. In comparison a chapter devoted to *On the Waterfront* took up seven pages while *Apocalypse Now* numbered three. Even in his memoirs,

Brando seemed to be trying to minimize his great body of work.

Soon readers will be able to judge for themselves.

Bibliography

BOOKS

Adler, Stella, *THE TECHNIQUE OF ACTING,* Bantam Books, 1988

Brando, Anna Kashfi, and E.P. Stein, *BRANDO FOR BREAKFAST,* Crown Publishers, 1979

Capote, Truman, *A CAPOTE READER,* Random House, 1987

Collier, Peter, *THE FONDAS: A Hollywood Dynasty,* G. P. Putnam's Sons, 1991

Fiore, Carlo, *BUD: THE BRANDO I KNEW,* Dell Publishing Co., 1974

Garfield, David, *A PLAYER'S PLACE: The Story of The Actors Studio,* Macmillan, 1980

Geist, Kenneth L., *PICTURES WILL TALK: The Life and Films of Joseph L. Mankiewicz,* Scribners, 1978

Martin, Sara Hines, *HEALING FOR ADULT CHILDREN OF ALCOHOLICS: How to Break From the Past and Grow Emotionally and Spiritually,* Bantam Books, 1989

Higham, Charles, *BRANDO: The Unauthorized Biography,* NAL Books, New American Library, 1987

Hirsch, Foster, *A METHOD TO THEIR MADNESS:*

The History of the Actors Studio, W.W. Norton & Co., 1984

Holden, Anthony, *BEHIND THE OSCAR: The Secret History of the Academy Awards,* Simon & Schuster, 1993

Huston, John, *JOHN HUSTON: An Open Book,* Alfred A. Knopf, 1980

Lewis, Robert, *SLINGS AND ARROWS: Theater in My Life,* Stein and Day, 1984

McNeil, Alex, *TOTAL TELEVISION: A Comprehensive Guide to Programming from 1948 to the Present,* Penguin Books, 1991

Meredith, Burgess, *SO FAR, SO GOOD,* Little, Brown and Company, 1994

Morella, Joe, and Edward Z. Epstein, *BRANDO: The Unauthorized Biography,* Crown Publishers, Inc., 1973

Offen, Ron, *BRANDO,* Henry Regnery Company, 1972

Ryan, Paul, *MARLON BRANDO: A Portrait,* Carroll & Graf, 1992

Summers, Anthony, *GODDESS: The Secret Lives of Marilyn Monroe,* Macmillan, 1985

Thomas, Tony, *THE FILMS OF MARLON BRANDO,* a Citadel Press Book, Carol Publishing Group, 1992

MAGAZINES & NEWSPAPERS

Bacon, James, "Toast on Wry Ham," Associated Press, August 19, 1962

Condon, Bob, "The Search for Marlon Brando," *New York Herald Tribune,* March 27, 1966

Daniels, Mary, "Carmelita Pope: 'Bud' Brando's 'Sweetheart,' *Chicago Tribune,* 9/12/76

Hyams, Joe, "Brando Tells of Mutiny in 'Mutiny,' " *New York Herald Tribune,* October 2, 1961

Maas, Peter, "The Mutiny of Marlon Brando: A $6,000,000 Nightmare, *The Saturday Evening Post,* June 12, 1962

Miron, Charles, "Meet the New Marlon Brando," *Movie Life,* May 1968

Poirier, Normand, "The Secret Wife of Marlon Brando," *New York Post,* June 30, 1961

Semple, Lorenzo, Jr., "Young Man From Everywhere," *Theatre Arts,* 1948

Unsigned, "After Trying Hollywood, Brando, and Suicide, Rita Moreno Has Settled Down," *People,* April 21, 1975

Weaver, John D., Hollywood's Most Outspoken Actress, *Holiday,* November 1961

Newspapers Unsigned. Most notably the following:
"Anna Slaps Brando's Face," *New York Daily News,* December 29, 1961

"Brando, Flat on His Back, Is Hit With Paternity Suit," *New York Daily News,* July 20, 1963

"Brando Has a New Mrs. and a New Jr., His Ex Sez," *New York Daily News,* April 28, 1961

"Brando Says His Ex Shuts the Son Out of His Eyes," *New York Daily News,* January 9, 1960

"Brando Testifies He Married Both Wives in a Family Way," *New York Daily News,* February 18, 1965

"The Secret Wife of Marlon Brando," *New York Post,* June 30, 1961

Chapter Notes

Chapter One: The All American Boy

"I became mother . . ." Higham, p. 16

Henry Fonda: Collier, p. 15

"Of course he was a spoiled brat . . ." confidential source, 3/4/75

"One afternoon Buddy tied me to a tree . . ." confidential source, 3/4/75

"At least you could get your laundry done . . ." Fiore, p. 20

"My father was indifferent . . ." Capote, p. 543

Marine: Fiore, p. 20

"She made it almost impossible . . ." Morella and Epstein, p. 9

"He used to do a lot of farm work . . ." *Chicago Tribune* 9/12/76

Pets and livestock: Capote, p. 542

Curtain Raisers Club: Higham, p. 24

"He arrived, walking . . ." *Chicago Tribune* 9/12/76

"I took a bottle of hair tonic . . ." Confidential source, 5/17/83

"Bud was always horsing around . . ." Ryan, p. 13

Chapter Two: Bright Lights, Big City

"Would you go to bed with my mother?" Fiore p. 19
"He could not function sexually . . ." Kashfi, p. 3
"Are you an alcoholic?" Lewis, p. 176
"I want a complete characterization . . ." Lewis, p. 185
"You stepped in what?" Garfield, p. 55
"I was afraid of analysis at first . . ." Kashfi, p. 38
"We would pass each other . . ." Meredith, p. 182
"I honestly think . . ." Kashfi, p. 39
"like a laser beam . . ." Condon, p. 16

Chapter Three: Brando in Hollywood

"Why it's filled with horseshit . . ." Kashfi, p. 29
". . . two exiles . . ." Weaver
"Marlon has always liked Latin women . . ." *People,*
   4/21/75
"The subject isn't juvenile delinquency . . ." Thomas, p. 70
". . . shirtless, . . ." Kashfi, p. 48
Josanne posed nude: Kashfi, p. 51, Offen, p. 98
"Marlon is too independent . . ." Offen, p. 98
"CAN'T YOU HELP?" Geist, p. 255
"Frank's playing his part all wrong . . ." Fiore, p. 135
"Who is that good-looking broad . . ." Kashfi, p. 54

Chapter Four: The Marriage from Hell

First date with Anna Kashfi: Kashfi, p. 55
"my noble tool" Kashfi, p. 56
Shared memories: Kashfi, p. 71
"I wish my mother were alive . . ." Kashfi, p. 72

"Marlon yearned to share himself . . ." Kashfi, p. 74

Keep the engagement a secret: Kashfi, p. 75

A woman's black wig: Kashfi, p. 89

"With women, I've got a long bamboo pole . . ." Fiore, p. 190

"By the time the lilies arrived . . ." Kashfi, p. 109

The honeymoon: Kashfi, p. 109

O'Callaghan revelations: Kashfi, p. 110

"He attracts women . . ." *People,* 6/4/90

"Anna was completely out of the picture . . ." Higham, p. 197

Domestic life: Kashfi, p. 119

"During one argument . . ." Fiore, p. 212

Mango incident: Kashfi, p. 125; Higham, p. 198

Trapped in her unhappy marriage: Kashfi, p. 126

"No, you son of a bitch! . . ." Kashfi, p. 138

". . . while I was home in bed . . ." Kashfi, p. 155

"She had broken into my house . . ." Court records, *New York Daily News,* 2/18/65

"I came up to Marlon's house . . ." ibid

"I lost count of the false noses . . ." Higham, p. 206

Chapter Five: Sayonara, Etc.

"Marlon's the most exciting person . . ." Capote, p. 520

"Instead of mumbling . . ." Fiore, p. 184

Marie Cui, *New York Post,* 7/21/63

Chapter Six: Brando Directs!

"Some men show . . ." Fiore, p. 226

"It's been trying . . ." Morella and Epstein, p. 81

"No tits . . ." Fiore, p. 227
"She was like an exposed nerve . . ." ibid
"I was afraid . . ." Morella and Epstein, p. 81

Chapter Seven: Brando Enters the Tabloid Inferno

"Secret Wife" *New York Daily News,* 4/28/91; *New York Post,* 6/30/61;
Slap: *New York Daily News,* 12/29/61
"Money in Gossip" *Morning Telegraph,* 5/2/63; *World Telegraph & Sun,* 4/19/63
Flat on His Back: *New York Daily News,* 7/20/63; *New York Times,* 8/7/63
Rita Moreno: Morella and Epstein, p. 89; Charles Higham, p. 220
"Mommy is Sick" *People,* 6/4/90; AP, 12/9/64; *New York World Telegram & Sun,* 12/8/64
The New Brando: *People,* 6/4/90
"I Have Ladies in My Home . . ." *New York Daily News;* 2/18/65; *New York Post,* 10/3/65
Brando Loses: *New York Post,* 10/3/65; *New York Herald Tribune,* 10/1/65; *New York Post,* 4/24/85
Movita: *Movie Life,* May 1968

Chapter Eight: The Turkey Parade

'The Nadir of My Creative Resources . . ." Hyams, 10/2/61
'He Would Put Ear Plugs In . . ." Bacon, 8/19/62
'I've Been in Some Pictures . . ." *New York Herald Tribune,* 10/3/61
'custard pie" Bacon, 8/19/62

Brando picketing: *New York Post,* 7/28/63, 8/23/63; *World Telegram & Sun,* 1/18/64

"A Key Figure . . ." *New York Post,* 2/24/64

Brando Risks Second Arrest: *New York Post,* 3/3/64

Tetiaroa: *New York Post,* 8/19/86

"It's been a while . . ." *Movie Life,* May 1968

Chapter Nine: The Comeback

"I don't think the film is about the Mafia at all . . ." Morella and Epstein, p. 131

"He made me the pig I am . . ." *Star,* 6/13/89

"They were nervous . . ." *New York Post,* 1/26/94

"It's like acting with God . . ." *Star,* 6/13/89

Wedding scene: Morella and Epstein, p. 132

"Know why? . . ." *New York Post,* 9/3/93

Kidnapping: *People* 6/4/90

"I was suddenly considered undesirable . . ." *New York Post,* 1/20/87

Nutrition: *New York Post,* 5/29/86

Midnight food binge: *Miami Herald,* 8/15/89

Chapter Ten: The Roller Coaster 1980's

"I know he sees a lot of projects . . ." *Los Angeles Time.* 9/1/88

". . . an irresponsible parent." *New York Daily News* 1/31/94

Brando's deposition: Confidential source, 8/8/89

"Without Yachio my life would be empty . . ." Confidential source, 1/18/93

"Tetiaroa will rise again!" Confidential source, 9/27/8.

Christian and Tehotu: Confidential source, 2/21/84, 3/27/84, 9/24/84

Michael Jackson: Confidential source, 3/20/84

Winky: Confidential source, 8/21/84, 9/11/84

Yachio: Confidential source, 5/1/84, 9/24/84, 10/6/84, 11/16/84

Christian's Brush with Death: Confidential source, 10/29/85

Cheyenne: Confidential source, 9/17/85; 8/19/86

Christian: 3/12/85; 2/4/86

Mary McKenna: Confidential source, 9/30/86; *New York Post,* 5/18/90

Mandela project: *Variety,* 10/8/86

Eddie Murphy: *New York Post,* 6/17/87, 6/22/87

"We are one planet . . ." *Miami Herald,* 6/24/87

Legend project: confidential source, 7/7/87

Miko: confidential source, 2/3/87

Yachio: confidential source, 12/8/87

Prison arts program: *Palm Beach Post* 9/4/87

Yachio: confidential source, 11/29/88

Christian: *National Star,* 11/8/88

"Why don't you ask them for more money? . . ." *National Star,* 8/25/87

"Christian is so sensitive . . ." *People,* 6/4/90

Sauna: Confidential source, 11/22/88

Yachio: Confidential source, 9/20/88, 11/29/88

Michael Jackson: Confidential source, 1/3/89

The Freshman: Confidential source, 12/27/88

Heathrow: *New York Post,* 1/18/89

Michael Jackson: Confidential source, 3/14/89, 7/4/89

Jocelyn: Confidential source: 2/7/89, 5/30/89, 1/21/92

Michael Jackson: Confidential source, 5/2/89

Cheyenne: Confidential source, 9/5/89

Christina Ruiz: Confidential source, 8/8/89

Australia: *Hollywood Reporter,* 5/24/88

TV repair: Confidential source, 4/11/89

Cancer scare: *National Star,* 7/11/89

"The unholy turmoil in the man . . ." *Miami Herald,* 8/13/89

"They asked me if I would write them . . ." *Daily Variety,* 10/4/89

"Some greeting for an old war-horse . . ." *Houston Chronicle,* 10/29/89

Auto repair: Confidential source, 11/14/89

Chapter Eleven: The Tragedy

Pyramid: *National Star,* 4/17/90

"It's pathetic . . ." ibid, 1/2/90

Cheyenne: *People,* 6/4/90

Jacques Drollet: *Los Angeles Times,* 7/28/90

Dag Drollet: *National Star,* 6/5/90

"He said perhaps it's better . . ." *Los Angeles Times,* 7/18/90

"He was very shy . . ." *People,* 6/4/90

Ricardo Alvarez: Confidential source, 11/6/90

Christian's arsenal: *New York Post,* 5/18/90

Manea Pambrun: *National Star,* 6/5/90

"I started giving him CPR . . ." Confidential source, 6/5/90

"psychological problems" *Los Angeles Times,* 5/23/90

"Cheyenne may have said . . ." *National Star,* 6/4/90

Police investigation: *Los Angeles Times,* 5/23/90, 7/24/90

"I don't want those guns here," *New York Post,* 5/18/90

"Well, I've really done it this time . . ." *People,* 6/4/90

William Kuntsler: *New York Post,* 5/18/90

Tom Laughlin: *People,* 6/4/90

Court proceedings: *Los Angeles Times,* 5/23/94

Kuntsler: *Los Angeles Times,* 5/24/90

Anna Kashfi: Confidential source, 6/5/90

Cheyenne: *USA Today,* 9/19/90

Cheyenne Flees: Confidential source, 11/20/90, *National Star* 9/4/90

Brando Threatened: Confidential source, 7/24/90

Tape Ruled: *Los Angeles Times,* 7/24/90

Christian's Ladies: *National Star,* 7/3/90

"Death is Too Good . . ." *Hollywood Reporter,* 7/25/90; *USA Today,* 7/25/90

Lost Passport: *USA Today,* 7/25/90

Dag's Parents: *Los Angeles Times,* 7/28/90

Mystery Surrounds Cheyenne: *National Star,* 8/14/90

Guillotine: *National Star,* 8/7/90

"My Son Was Killed . . ." *Los Angeles Times,* 7/28/90

Christian Pleads Innocent: *Hollywood Reporter,* 8/8/90; Los Angeles *Times,* 8/8/90; *Newsday,* 8/10/90

Dag's Ghost: Confidential source, 8/14/90

Christian Released on Bail: *Los Angeles Times,* 8/15/90; *USA Today,* 8/16/90, confidential source

Prosecutors Retaliate: *Los Angeles Times,* 9/5/90; *Hollywood Reporter,* 9/7/90

Will Cheyenne Testify: *Los Angeles Times,* 9/15 & 9/18/90

Was Cheyenne a Battered Woman: Confidential source, 11/13/90; *Los Angeles Times,* 9/27/90; *National Star,* 10/16/90

Brando Changes: *National Star,* 10/16/90; *USA Today,* 10/2/90

Christian's Wedding Plans: *National Star,* 10/2/90

Autobiography: *Houston Chronicle,* 9/18/90; *Los Angeles Times,* 9/26/90

Murder Trial Delayed: *Hollywood Reporter,* 10/5/90

Plea Bargain: *Los Angeles Times,* 10/5/90

Witch Doctor: Confidential source, 10/2/90; 10/16/90

Cheyenne's Deposition: Confidential source, 11/20/90

Brando Offers $1 Million: Confidential source, 11/13/90

Devastating New Evidence: Confidential source, 11/6/90

New Charges: Confidential source, 11/27/90

"Brando's Son . . ." Confidential source, 1/29/91; 2/26/91; *National Star,* 5/5/92

Christian's Sentencing: Confidential source, 3/19/91

Anna Kashfi: Confidential source, 7/24/90; 3/19/91; *New York Post,* 10/3/92

"Christian Brando Got Away With Murder," *New York Post,* 3/18/91

The End of a Dream: Confidential source, 3/5/91

Autobiography: *Entertainment Weekly,* 1/8/93

Bets: Confidential source, 5/21/91

French Bust: Confidential source, 10/8/91; *New York Post,* 11/16/91

Chapter Twelve: Picking Up the Pieces

Mellancamp: *New York Post,* 2/24/92

Christopher Columbus: Confidential source, 1/24/92; *New York Daily News,* 1/28/92; *Daily Variety,* 4/21/92

Cooking up a New Romance: *National Star,* 3/31/92 4/7/92

Autobiography: *New York Daily News,* 6/7/92

Cheyenne: *National Star,* 5/5/92; *New York Post,* 8/16/92, 11/13/92; Confidential source, 4/14/92

Another child: Confidential source, 8/4/92; *National Star,* 3/10/92

Cheyenne: Confidential source, 8/18/92

Mary McKenna: *New York Daily News,* 9/3/92; *Newsday,* 9/2/92

Chapter Thirteen: Brando Today

Myles: Confidential source, 3/30/93

Christian: *USA Today,* 4/2/93

Contradictions: Confidential source, 7/27/93

Christmas: Confidential source, 12/28/93; *National Star,* 5/4/93

Cheyenne: *Houston Chronicle,* 2/21/93; *USA Today,* 2/17/93; *Daily Variety,* 5/27/93

Cheyenne's Disturbing Claims: Confidential source, 7/6/93; *National Star,* 7/6/93

"Did We Ever Sleep Together?" Confidential source, 8/10/93; *New York Daily News,* 9/28/93; *Daily Variety,* 9/11/93; *New York Daily News,* 9/19/93; *New York Magazine,* 9/20/93; *Miami Herald,* 8/12/93

Treasure Island: *Hollywood Reporter,* 8/19/93; *Los Angeles Times,* 8/19/93

Projects: *Hollywood Reporter,* 11/12/93

Streisand: *Daily Variety,* 1/6/94

Autobiography: *New York Daily News,* 1/31/94; *USA Today,* 1/21/94; *National Star,* 2/8/94; *New York Post,*

2/15/94; *New York Daily News,* 1/31/94, 3/24/94; Confidential source, 2/22/94, 5/3/94

Michael Jackson: *USA Today,* 3/17 & 18/94

Projects: Confidential source: 9/23/89, 3/17/92

FUN AND LOVE!